The
Civil War and
Reconstruction Eras

DOCUMENTS DECODED

The ABC-CLIO series *Documents Decoded* guides readers on a hunt for new secrets through an expertly curated selection of primary sources. Each book pairs key documents with in-depth analysis, all in an original and visually engaging side-by-side format. But *Documents Decoded* authors do more than just explain each source's context and significance—they give readers a front-row seat to their own investigation and interpretation of each essential document, line by line.

TITLES IN ABC-CLIO'S DOCUMENTS DECODED SERIES

The Civil War and Reconstruction Eras

DOCUMENTS DECODED

John R. Vile

An Imprint of ABC-CLIO, LLC

Santa Barbara, California • Denver, Colorado

Library of Congress Cataloging-in-Publication Data

Names: Vile, John R., author.
Title: The Civil War and Reconstruction eras : documents decoded / John R. Vile.
Description: Santa Barbara, California : ABC-CLIO, 2018. | Series: Documents decoded |
Includes bibliographical references and index.
Identifiers: LCCN 2017013245 (print) | LCCN 2017013674 (ebook) | ISBN 9781440854293 (ebook) |
ISBN 9781440854286 (alk.paper : alk. paper)
Subjects: LCSH: United States—History—Civil War, 1861–1865—Sources. | Reconstruction
(U.S. history, 1865–1877)—Sources. | United States—History—1849–1877—Sources.
Classification: LCC E464 (ebook) | LCC E464 .V55 2018 (print) | DDC 973.7—dc23
LC record available at https://lccn.loc.gov/2017013245

ISBN: 978-1-4408-5428-6 (print)
978-1-4408-5429-3 (ebook)

22 21 20 19 18   1 2 3 4 5

This book is also available as an eBook.

ABC-CLIO
An Imprint of ABC-CLIO, LLC

ABC-CLIO, LLC
130 Cremona Drive, P.O. Box 1911
Santa Barbara, California 93116-1911
www.abc-clio.com

This book is printed on acid-free paper ∞

Manufactured in the United States of America

Contents

SECTION II
DEATH OF LINCOLN TO INAUGURATION OF GRANT

SECTION III
THE REST OF RECONSTRUCTION

Introduction

In 1876 the nation held a grand exposition in Philadelphia marking the nation's one-hundredth birthday of independence (the date that had been "four score and seven years" from Lincoln's Gettysburg Address). The nation obviously had much to celebrate. It had emerged from a bloody conflict that had called into question its continued existence as a single entity. The Thirteenth Amendment had ended slavery, and the Fourteenth Amendment had defined citizenship so that it now included African Americans. At least on paper, the South had been "reconstructed." Just seven years earlier, the first transcontinental railroad line had been completed, and the Exposition featured an exhibition by Alexander Graham Bell of the telephone. The nation was harnessing the power of the steam engine and would soon take its place among the world's greatest powers.

Americans looked back on the previous decade and a half with a sense of wonder. The nation had been tested and had emerged victorious, but it remained deeply divided by issues of race, however much they were (at least for most whites) fading into the background. Although an ad hoc commission had resolved the matter, the election that surrounded the centennial celebrations revealed that there were still flaws in the Electoral College system of selecting the president. As troops were scheduled to leave the South, many African Americans rightfully remained fearful for their lives and property, and in another 20 years the U.S. Supreme Court would officially announce a policy of racial segregation justified by the doctrine of "separate but equal."

The Background

The Civil War and Reconstruction periods did not materialize out of nowhere. African Americans had been imported into North America since 1619. However well the Founders build a trifurcated system of government in 1787, they chose to leave the institution of slavery in place. They permitted the continuing importation of slaves (although they did not use the word) for 20 years, they required the return of fugitive slaves, and they even counted slaves as three-fifths of a person for purposes of representation in the U.S. House of Representatives. Many blithely hoped that slavery would die a fairly natural death as it was already doing in Northern states that did not have large plantations cultivating cotton, rice, and tobacco. In any event, the delegates meeting in Philadelphia in 1787 had more immediate problems to address including the division of powers among the three branches of the national government and the proper mix of state and national powers.

Many of America's most illustrious founders are on record as denouncing slavery as at best a necessary evil. Thomas Jefferson confessed to waking up in the middle of the night in fear of the punishment of a just God on such an institution. Having slaves, he would say, was like holding a wolf by the ears, and so it proved to be. For the most part, however, these framers regarded slavery as a state issue, and the system of federalism that they devised and implemented allowed existing states to set their own policies with regard to it.

Instead of dying out, the invention of the cotton gin assured that the demand for slave labor increased, especially in the Deep South. As the institution continued to disappear in the North, it was easier and easier to view slavery as an unmitigated evil. In the face of such an evil, abolitionists called for immediatism. There could be no compromise. Slavery must end, and it must end now.

Southern opinion was also becoming more adamant. Leading spokesmen argued that slavery was not simply a necessary evil but a positive good. In their view, whites were superior to blacks, who needed their care. Indeed, Southern spokesmen argued that the condition of Southern slaves was better than that of Northern industrial workers whose employers could readily fire them at will and had no legal obligation to care for their families.

Although such diverging opinions were almost impossible to reconcile, American statesmen did their best to do so. In 1820, they decided to balance the admission of another slave state (Missouri) with the admission of a free one (Maine) and to draw a line in the Louisiana Territory north of which slavery would be banned and south of which it would be permitted. Similarly, in 1850, Henry Clay helped navigate an elaborate compromise between North and South that would give the Union another decade of life.

But while the union remained unified on paper, the doctrines of nullification and secession were eating at its foundations. According to the first doctrine, states had the right to nullify federal laws, like the so-called tariff of abominations of 1828, which they believed to be unfair and unconstitutional. According to the second doctrine, states had the same right to leave the union voluntarily as they had in entering it. The doctrine of popular sovereignty further abetted this idea. If new states had the right (as Stephen A. Douglas and the Kansas-Nebraska Act of 1854 asserted that they did) to choose whether they would become slave or free, then it seemed only logical that existing states might choose to ally only with other states that were either slave or free. Southern states were especially annoyed by the continuing condemnation expressed by the doctrine espoused by the new Republican Party that slavery was an evil that should be kept from expanding and that should be put on a path of ultimate extinction. Could the South continue in a Union led by a party leader with such a view? Could he be trusted not to seek to outlaw an institution that he so detested?

The Election of 1860 and the Coming of the Civil War

The election of 1860, which occurred not long after John Brown's famous raid on Harper's Ferry through which he had hoped to catalyze a slave revolt, provided the answer. The election featured a Republican (Abraham Lincoln), a Northern Democrat (Stephen A. Douglas), a Southern Democrat (John Breckenridge), and a candidate from the newly formed Constitutional Union Party (John Bell), none of whom received a majority of the popular vote, but one of whom was able to capture a majority of the Electoral College. Although Lincoln had no plans for immediate emancipation, he believed that his oath of office committed him to preserve the Union. Some Southern leaders, who would soon fire on Fort Sumter off the coast of South Carolina, which Lincoln sought to resupply, were just as adamant that the time had come for them to seek to dissolve this connection.

Even before Lincoln was inaugurated and voiced the sentiments that "we are not enemies, but friends," Southern states beginning with South Carolina were announcing their independence from the Union. A week after Lincoln's speech, seven such states (the number would eventually grow to 11) had drawn up their own constitution. Confidently evoking God's authority, it largely followed that of 1787 but made it clear that it would neither hide behind euphemisms nor apologize for the institution of slavery, which it now mentioned by name. As Alexander Stevens, the vice president of the new confederacy, would proclaim, the American Founders had mistakenly built their Constitution on the doctrine that all men were created equal. By contrast, the Confederacy would firmly rest on the idea that whites were superior to blacks. And so, as Lincoln would say with a resignation that bordered on fatalism, "the war came."

Both sides entered the war with different perspectives. To the North, the war was a civil (meaning domestic rather than well-mannered) war, or a rebellion. Southern statesmen and generals, particularly those who had previously pledged to uphold the Constitution of the United States, were traitors, and the people they led were dupes. To the South, the war was a replay of the American Revolution. One people had become two, and each was now a nation-state. The war was accordingly a war between the states, or even a war of Northern aggression against cherished Southern institutions, most notably slavery.

Although Lincoln later interpreted the resulting loss of life and property as divine judgment that wiped out the benefits that prior slave labor had brought to the nation, neither side anticipated the high cost that the war would bring or the length of time that it would endure. The war also seemed to test whether it was possible to preserve Republican government amid such a fierce conflict. Lincoln issued successive calls for mobilization, and faced with opposition to such measures he soon suspended the writ of habeas corpus to cope with actions by Northerners who were partial to the Southern cause. Initially, however, Lincoln continued to view the war as an attempt to save the Union. As casualties mounted, he eventually recognized that he could mobilize the population if he added the goal of once and for all, ending the system of chattel slavery that had led to the house divided.

Like some prominent American Founders, Lincoln had long toyed with the idea of resettling former slaves in Africa or South America. In April 1862, he left this as a possibility for the slaves whose freedom was purchased in the District of Columbia. Finally, after an earlier preliminary declaration, on January 1, 1863, Lincoln used his power

as commander in chief to issue the Emancipation Proclamation, which sounded the ultimate death knell for slavery and promised "a new birth of freedom." Initially applicable only behind enemy lines, once the slavery genie emerged from its bottle, it would not return, and the crowning achievement of the Civil War was an amendment (the Thirteenth) that once and for all ended chattel slavery throughout the United States.

Other Developments

One of the fascinating aspects of compiling a book like this is to see that no matter how much effort was devoted to the war effort, other aspects of government continued. There was mail to be delivered, and there were roads to be built. The West was still being settled. During much of the war, building continued on the Capitol Dome, which would symbolically link both houses of Congress even as Lincoln was attempting to reiterate the bands that united North and South. In 1862, the nation appropriated lands to link East and West through railways and pledged lands for state construction of colleges and universities that would promote agricultural and mechanic arts, and in 1872 it would set aside lands for the Yellowstone National Park. In 1864, the nation adopted a new immigration law encouraging Europeans to replace American Easterners who continued to migrate westward. By 1875 it was expressing fears of immigrants from Japan and China that would blossom into restrictive quotas in the next century and that would leave a legacy that arguably continued with the internment of Japanese Americans during World War II.

Lincoln's Reelection and Assassination

In addition to such matters, there was the matter of elections, including the 1864 contest for the presidency. One of the most remarkable aspects of the Civil War is that, amid all the charges that

Lincoln was exercising unconstitutional powers, it did not disrupt this quadrennial cycle (and its example has been sufficient to see that none have been disrupted since). It is difficult to know for sure what would have happened had General George McClellan been elected as president in 1864, but Lincoln was among those who thought that it was a distinct possibility, and McClellan was far more willing to compromise than to continue to confront the South, which had shown striking resiliency during the opening years of the war.

Eventually buttressed by battlefield victories, Lincoln was, of course, reelected, and in Ulysses S. Grant he finally found a general who was willing to pay the price in blood to grind down Southern armies until they had little option but surrender (one of the clearest signs of Southern desperation was its decision the previous month to organize slaves into companies to fight on its behalf). Robert E. Lee, the South's greatest general, realized that the end was near and refused to pursue a guerrilla policy of continuing resistance that could have bogged the nation down in years of additional war, while Grant recognized that the best way to assure a restored Union was to treat surrendering troops with respect.

In the Second Inaugural Address, Lincoln had announced that the nation would proceed "With malice toward none, with charity for all," but it is one thing to announce a broad doctrine and quite another to implement it. We know from his veto of the Wade-Davis Bill that Lincoln was willing to accept the reestablishment of loyal Southern governments on a more liberal basis than was Congress, but, like more radical Republican members of Congress, he undoubtedly also felt an increasing obligation to African Americans who had fought valiantly on behalf of the Union and had the same aspirations for freedom as did other men.

Hardly had the nation finished celebrating the news of Lee's surrender than Lincoln was gunned down at Ford's Theatre, not only triggering national grief and fear but further highlighting the continuing animosities that divided North and South. Lincoln belonged to the ages, and whatever compromises he might have been able to strike were soon eclipsed by his successor, Andrew Johnson, who became best known for his own temper and intransigence and for his view that once the issue of slavery had been resolved, it was time to revert to state control over civil rights and liberties.

Reconstruction

Freed from the restraints of slavery, one can only imagine the jubilation that African Americans must have felt. One can equally imagine the fears of Southern whites who had been inculcated with the idea that blacks were their inferiors. In their view, slaves who left their plantations were little better than, and just as threatening as, vagrants. If the Southern economy were to recover from the ravages of war, it would need their labor. Slavery might now be illegal, but the crops still needed to be gathered, and Southern states could hardly accept millions of people as their wards.

Southern restrictions on former freedmen, which sought to return them to a virtual stage of peonage, made it clear that continued to regard them as second-class citizens. Congress responded with a series of civil rights acts, most of which had to be adopted over President Johnson's veto, but what is enacted through law can also be repealed through law. If Congress were to secure the rights of African Americans, it was appropriate to do so through constitutional amendment, a task that succeeded better than attempts to remove President Johnson through impeachment for offenses that were more personal and political than legal.

A year after dividing the South into military districts and requiring Southern states to accept constitutional guarantees as a condition to seating their congressional delegations, the nation adopted the Fourteenth Amendment. Reversing the Dred Scott Decision of 1857, which had denied that blacks could be U.S. citizens, the amendment extended citizenship to all persons born or naturalized in the United States (except "Indians not taxed") and sought to assure each of them appropriate rights. Subsequent sections of the amendment allowed

Congress to reduce the representation of states that disenfranchised African-American men (an option it never exercised), to disqualify individuals who had led the insurrection against the United States from voting, to affirm Union obligations while repudiating Confederate debt, and to vest Congress with special enforcement powers.

Still, most of the rights that Section 1 of the Fourteenth Amendment articulated would lie in near abeyance for almost a century, but at least on paper the amendment guaranteed the privileges and immunities of U.S. citizenship, due process of law, and the equal protection of laws to all. By the end of the century, each of these guarantees had been trimmed. The Slaughterhouse Cases decided that the privileges and immunities of U.S. citizenship (as opposed to whatever rights states might choose to protect) were limited, and *Minor v. Happersett* decided (to the chagrin but hardly to the surprise of most women) that one of these rights and immunities was not the right to woman's suffrage. In the period immediately following that covered in this volume, the Court subsequently invalidated the Civil Rights Act of 1875 in the Civil Rights Cases of 1883 by limiting state control over discrimination in public accommodations to those involving state, rather than private, action. *United States v. Cruikshank* (1876) further extended this state action doctrine in a way that made it difficult to punish those who engaged in physical intimidation of African Americans, and *Plessy v. Ferguson* (1896) further lent its approval to racial segregation.

After Ulysses S. Grant, who would serve two terms, replaced Andrew Johnson as president in the election of 1868, the nation did adopt the Fifteenth Amendment (1870) prohibiting discrimination, at least on paper, on the basis of race or previous condition of servitude. Because the Constitution still did not make voting a positive right, states were able to evade this provision for almost a hundred years before the Voting Rights Act of 1965 finally gave it some teeth. By contrast, although women would have to wait longer than African-American men for formal constitutional protection, when they finally received the vote with the adoption of the Nineteenth Amendment in 1920, they faced almost no obstacles to casting their ballots.

Back to the Centennial

In 1876, the nation's population and size had increased but still bore the deep scars, and the bitter resentments, of war. Native-American Indians, who remained excluded from the guarantees of citizenship recognized in the Fourteenth Amendment, continued their sad retreat across the plains. Their victory over General Custer at Little Big Horn in 1876 was an anomaly, not quite a last stand, hardly a sign that they were about to retake their former lands.

Looking back over the Civil War, the Supreme Court had declared in *Texas v. White* (1869) that the Constitution had created "an indestructible Union . . . of indestructible states." Although the postbellum amendments had hardly resolved all issues of state/national relations, the war had ultimately settled the issue of slavery, which had provided the greatest bone of contention between the nation's two major sections.

Within 30 years, the nation would gain a colonial empire in a war with Spain; within 50 years, the nation would participate in a major world war; and within 80 years, it would become the world's greatest super power. The sense of nationhood had been further forged in the fires of war, but the scars of this conflict, and particularly the divergent racial heritage that had spawned it, would continue to bedevil the nation even as it ascended to heights of world glory.

Notes on This Volume

Although this book was written as a stand-alone volume, I very much view it as a continuation of three previous volumes in this series. The first, dealing with Founding Documents, explains the foundations of America's constitutional legacy. The second, dealing with The Early Republic, discusses how this legacy was put into practice by the nation's first six presidents. The third, dealing with the Antebellum period between the election of Andrew Jackson in 1828 and the inauguration of Lincoln, is particularly important in providing the background for this volume, which takes up the story through the Civil War (1861–1865) and Reconstruction (1865–1877).

This volume contains the edited texts of more than 60 original documents and accompanying introductions and commentary. I have designed each of these books with the needs of high school students, college students, and general citizens in mind. Like previous volumes, this one includes a timeline, suggestions for further reading, and an index.

In compiling these volumes, I have learned that there is a substantial difference between reading histories of a period and actually examining primary documents. It has been said that history is a "trail of symbols," and parchments symbols can be as potent a force as armies and physical monuments. I have attempted judicious editing so that students can read fundamental provisions of laws and speeches without becoming overwhelmed by details.

As in previous volumes, I have introduced each reading and annotated each document not in the expectation that my own interpretations are final but in the hopes that they will guide students through technical terms and provoke their own reflections. As a student of American constitutional law, I am especially interested in U.S. Supreme Court decisions, but I have tried to maintain a judicious balance (the pun is intentional) in

this book among the texts of congressional laws, presidential speeches and proclamations, and judicial decisions. I have also included occasional documents from the states and from popular culture, as, for example, the texts of "Dixie" and "The Battle Hymn of the Republic."

As I have tried to indicate in this essay, history rarely seems to proceed in a straight line. I have had to choose only a sample of the documents available, but I have done so cognizant that there are multiple threads in American history. Although history was long dominated by narratives of the deeds of white males, I have included documents that also illume the lives of women, African Americans, and immigrants, and I would encourage students to look for still other perspectives that will deepen their own understandings.

As with past volumes, I am grateful to editors at ABC-CLIO, especially Kevin Hillstrom and Michelle Scott, and also the editors at production, Gordon Hammy Matchado and Ezhil R. Kuppan of Apex CoVantage. I am the son and husband of public school teachers. Having further witnessed the great dedication of such teachers during my own daughters' years in public schools (as well as heroic efforts by parents to provide education for their children at home), I publish this book in hopes that it will be a valuable resource for those who believe that a knowledge of the past is essential to building a viable future and of enhancing civic participation.

John R. Vile
Middle Tennessee State University

The Civil War and Reconstruction Eras

SECTION I

Civil War

Daniel Decatur Emmett's
"(I Wish I Was In) Dixie's Land"

1859

Americans often express pride in the region where they were born, raised, and live, and Southerners were no exception. The following tune, while loved in both North and South, was at hand even before Southern states sought to secede and became something of a Southern anthem during the Civil War, much as the song "Yankee Doodle Dandy" had served for patriot forces during the Revolutionary War. The tune's implicit acceptance of slavery provides a fascinating comparison with Julia Ward Howe's "The Battle Hymn of the Republic," which was probably the nearest Union equivalent.

I wish I was in de land ob cotton,
Old times dar am not forgotten,
Look away! Look away! Look away! Dixie Land.
In Dixie Land whar' I was born in,[1]
Early on one frosty mornin',
Look away! Look away! Look away! Dixie Land.

CHORUS:

Den I wish I was in Dixie, Hoo-ray! Hoo-ray!
In Dixie land, I'll took my stand to lib and die in Dixie;
Away, away, away down south in Dixie,
Away, away, away down south in Dixie.[2]

Old Missus marry Will-de-weaber,
Willium was a gay deceaber;
Look away! Look away! Look away! Dixie Land.
But when he put his arm around 'er
He smiled as fierce as a forty-pounder,
Look away! Look away! Look away! Dixie Land.

[1]Southerners often romanticized slavery as being good both for the African Americans, who Southerners thought were incapable of taking care of themselves, and for slave owners, and this song is in African-American dialect. Cotton was a major Southern crop largely picked by African Americans in less than idyllic conditions. This heightens the paternalistic quality of the song, with its references to treasured memories of life in the South.

[2]Southerners considered the South to be their homeland, and they viewed the conflict over slavery as a war between two equally sovereign states (North and South), one of which they were defending.

(CHORUS)

His face was sharp as a butcher's cleaver,
But dat did not seem to greab 'er;
Look away! Look away! Look away! Dixie Land.
Old Missus acted the foolish part,
And died for a man dat broke her heart,
Look away! Look away! Look away! Dixie Land.

(CHORUS)

Now here's a health to the next old Missus,
An all the gals dat want to kiss us;[3]
Look away! Look away! Look away! Dixie Land.
But if you want to drive 'way sorrow,
Come and hear dis song to-morrow,
Look away! Look away! Look away! Dixie Land.

(CHORUS)

Dar's buckwheat cakes an' Injun batter,
Makes you fat or a little fatter;[4]
Look away! Look away! Look away! Dixie Land.
Den hoe it down and scratch your grabble,
To Dixie land I'm bound to trabble,
Look away! Look away! Look away! Dixie Land.

(CHORUS)

[3] The song seems to equate the love of slaves for their Missus (the slave owner's wife) with their regard for their girlfriends, which could have been fairly disconcerting if given too much thought. Perhaps this is why this stanza is not as widely remembered or as frequently sung as the first.

[4] The South has a distinctive cuisine, here associated with buckwheat cakes and "Injun batter," that would likely bring fond memories to Confederate soldiers.

Source: Daniel Decatur Emmett, "(I Wish I Was in) Dixie's Land." New York: Firth, Pond & Co., 1860.

South Carolina Ordinance of Secession

December 20, 1860

INTRODUCTION

Just as the U.S. Constitution was preceded by the Declaration of Independence, so too Southern states adopted ordinances of secession from the United States prior to forming their own confederacy. South Carolina, whose militia would begin the Civil War by firing on Fort Sumter, off the coast of Charleston, was the first to adopt such a resolution in December 1860, even before the new Republican president was inaugurated.

AN ORDINANCE to dissolve the union between the State of South Carolina and other States united with her under the compact entitled "The Constitution of the United States of America."

We, the people of the State of South Carolina,[1] in convention assembled, do declare and ordain, and it is hereby declared and ordained, That the ordinance adopted by us in convention on the twenty-third day of May, in the year of our Lord one thousand seven hundred and eighty-eight, whereby the Constitution of the United States of America was ratified, and also all acts and parts of acts of the General Assembly of this State ratifying amendments of the said Constitution, are hereby repealed; and that the union now subsisting between South Carolina and other States, under the name of the "United States of America," is hereby dissolved.[2]

Done at Charleston the twentieth day of December, in the year of our Lord one thousand eight hundred and sixty.

Source: Official Records, Ser. IV, vol. 1, p. 1.

[1]Notice the parallel between the opening words of this paragraph and those of the U.S. Constitution, with "the people of the State of South Carolina" now substituted for the "People of the United States."

[2]The doctrine of secession, which had largely been formulated by South Carolina's John C. Calhoun, was based on the notion that the U.S. Constitution was a compact that individual states could dissolve.

Jefferson Davis's Inaugural Address

February 18, 1861

INTRODUCTION

Even before the inauguration of Abraham Lincoln (1809–1865), a number of Southern states had seceded and selected their own president. Jefferson Davis (1808–1889) was a former Mississippi congressman and one-time secretary of war, who sought both to justify the separation and to stress the manner in which he believed that the new government was more consistent with the original Constitution of 1787. The speech is especially notable for its many invocations of God.

Gentlemen of the Congress of the Confederate States of America, Friends, and Fellow-citizens: Called to the difficult and responsible station of Chief Magistrate of the Provisional Government which you have instituted, I approach the discharge of the duties assigned to me with humble distrust of my abilities, but with a sustaining confidence in the wisdom of those who are to guide and aid me in the administration of public affairs, and an abiding faith in the virtue and patriotism of the people. Looking forward to the speedy establishment of a permanent government to take the place of this,[1] which by its greater moral and physical power will be better able to combat with many difficulties that arise from the conflicting interests of separate nations, I enter upon the duties of the office to which I have been chosen with the hope that the beginning of our career, as a Confederacy, may not be obstructed by hostile opposition to our enjoyment of the separate existence and independence we have asserted,[2] and which, with the blessing of Providence, we intend to maintain.

Our present political position has been achieved in a manner unprecedented in the history of nations. It illustrates the American idea that governments rest on the consent of the governed, and that it is the right of the people to alter or abolish them at will whenever they become destructive of the ends for which they were established. The declared purpose of the compact of the Union from which we have withdrawn was to "establish justice, insure domestic tranquillity, provide for the common defense, promote the general welfare, and

[1] Davis is speaking before all the details of his government have been formulated.

[2] Like members of the Second Continental Congress with respect to Great Britain, the Southern states considered themselves to be an independent nation or people.

6

secure the blessings of liberty to ourselves and our posterity;" and when, in the judgment of the sovereign States composing this Confederacy, it has been perverted from the purposes for which it was ordained, and ceased to answer the ends for which it was established, a peaceful appeal to the ballot box declared that, so far as they are concerned, the Government created by that compact should cease to exist. In this they merely asserted the right which the Declaration of Independence of July 4, 1776, defined to be "inalienable." Of the time and occasion of its exercise they as sovereigns were the final judges, each for itself. The impartial and enlightened verdict of mankind will vindicate the rectitude of our conduct; and He who knows the hearts of men will judge of the sincerity with which we have labored to preserve the Government of our fathers in its spirit.[3]

The right solemnly proclaimed at the birth of the United States, and which has been solemnly affirmed and reaffirmed in the Bills of Rights of the States subsequently admitted into the Union of 1789, undeniably recognizes in the people the power to resume the authority delegated for the purposes of government. Thus the sovereign States here represented have proceeded to form this Confederacy; and it is by abuse of language that their act has been denominated a revolution. They formed a new alliance, but within each State its government has remained; so that the rights of person and property have not been disturbed. The agent through which they communicated with foreign nations is changed, but this does not necessarily interrupt their international relations. Sustained by the consciousness that the transition from the former Union to the present Confederacy has not proceeded from a disregard on our part of just obligations, or any, failure to perform every constitutional duty, moved by no interest or passion to invade the rights of others, anxious to cultivate peace and commerce with all nations, if we may not hope to avoid war, we may at least expect that posterity will acquit us of having needlessly engaged in it. Doubly justified by the absence of wrong on our part, and by wanton aggression on the part of others, there can be no cause to doubt that the courage and patriotism of the people of the Confederate States will be found equal to any measure of defense which their honor and security may require. An agricultural people, whose chief interest is the export of commodities required in every manufacturing country, our true policy is peace, and the freest trade which our necessities will permit. It is alike our interest and that of all those to whom we would sell, and from whom we would buy, that there should be the fewest practicable restrictions

[3]Whereas Northerners generally interpreted the Constitution as laying the foundation for a nation, Southerners tended to interpret the document as a compact among independent states, who had the authority to withdraw when they no longer believed it was accomplishing its purposes.

[4]Davis is arguing that there is no need for war between North and South because they consist of different economies, the North depending chiefly on manufacturing and navigation and the South depending chiefly on agriculture.

upon the interchange of these commodities. There can, however, be but little rivalry between ours and any manufacturing or navigating community, such as the Northeastern States of the American Union.[4] It must follow, therefore, that mutual interest will invite to good will and kind offices on both parts. If, however, passion or lust of dominion should cloud the judgment or inflame the ambition of those States, we must prepare to meet the emergency and maintain, by the final arbitrament of the sword, the position which we have assumed among the nations of the earth.

We have entered upon the career of independence, and it must be inflexibly pursued. Through many years of controversy with our late associates of the Northern States, we have vainly endeavored to secure tranquillity and obtain respect for the rights to which we were entitled. As a necessity, not a choice, we have resorted to the remedy of separation, and henceforth our energies must be directed to the conduct of our own affairs, and the perpetuity of the Confederacy which we have formed. If a just perception of mutual interest shall permit us peaceably to pursue our separate political career, my most earnest desire will have been fulfilled. But if this be denied to us, and the integrity of our territory and jurisdiction be assailed, it will but remain for us with firm resolve to appeal to arms and invoke the blessing of Providence on a just cause.

As a consequence of our new condition and relations, and with a view to meet anticipated wants, it will be necessary to provide for the speedy and efficient organization of branches of the Executive department having special charge of foreign intercourse, finance, military affairs, and the postal service. For purposes of defense, the Confederate States may, under ordinary circumstances, rely mainly upon the militia; but it is deemed advisable, in the present condition of affairs, that there should be a well-instructed and disciplined army, more numerous than would usually be required on a peace establishment.[5] I also suggest that, for the protection of our harbors and commerce on the high seas, a navy adapted to those objects will be required. But this, as well as other subjects appropriate to our necessities, have doubtless engaged the attention of Congress.

With a Constitution differing only from that of our fathers in so far as it is explanatory of their well-known intent, freed from sectional conflicts, which have interfered with the pursuit of the general

[5]Although confederations chiefly depend on component states to raise military forces, Davis recognized that it would be necessary to raise a collective force to deal with the likelihood of war.

welfare, it is not unreasonable to expect that States from which we have recently parted may seek to unite their fortunes to ours under the Government which we have instituted. For this your Constitution makes adequate provision; but beyond this, if I mistake not the judgment and will of the people, a reunion with the States from which we have separated is neither practicable nor desirable. To increase the power, develop the resources, and promote the happiness of the Confederacy, it is requisite that there should be so much of homogeneity that the welfare of every portion shall be the aim of the whole. When this does not exist, antagonisms are engendered which must and should result in separation.

Actuated solely by the desire to preserve our own rights, and promote our own welfare, the separation by the Confederate States has been marked by no aggression upon others, and followed by no domestic convulsion. Our industrial pursuits have received no check, the cultivation of our fields has progressed as heretofore, and, even should we be involved in war, there would be no considerable diminution in the production of the staples which have constituted our exports, and in which the commercial world has an interest scarcely less than our own. This common interest of the producer and consumer can only be interrupted by exterior force which would obstruct the transmission of our staples to foreign markets—a course of conduct which would be as unjust, as it would be detrimental, to manufacturing and commercial interests abroad.

Should reason guide the action of the Government from which we have separated, a policy so detrimental to the civilized world, the Northern States included, could not be dictated by even the strongest desire to inflict injury upon us; but, if the contrary should prove true, a terrible responsibility will rest upon it, and the suffering of millions will bear testimony to the folly and wickedness of our aggressors.[6] In the meantime there will remain to us, besides the ordinary means before suggested, the well-known resources for retaliation upon the commerce of an enemy.

Experience in public stations, of subordinate grade to this care and disappointment are the price of official elevation. You will see many errors to forgive, many deficiencies to tolerate; but you shall not find in me either want of zeal or fidelity to the cause that is to me the highest in hope, and of most enduring affection. Your generosity has

[6]Davis is attempting to shift responsibility for war and the ensuing casualties to the Northern states.

bestowed upon me an undeserved distinction, one which I neither sought nor desired. Upon the continuance of that sentiment, and upon your wisdom and patriotism, I rely to direct and support me in the performance of the duties required at my hands.

We have changed the constituent parts, but not the system of government. The Constitution framed by our fathers is that of these Confederate States. In their exposition of it, and in the judicial construction it has received, we have a light which reveals its true meaning.[7]

[7]Davis regarded the Confederate Constitution as following the intent of the framers of the document of 1787 from which it was constructed.

Thus instructed as to the true meaning and just interpretation of that instrument, and ever remembering that all offices are but trusts held for the people, and that powers delegated are to be strictly construed, I will hope by due diligence in the performance of my duties, though I may disappoint your expectations, yet to retain, when retiring, something of the good will and confidence which welcome my entrance into office.

It is joyous in the midst of perilous times to look around upon a people united in heart, where one purpose of high resolve animates and actuates the whole; where the sacrifices to be made are not weighed in the balance against honor and right and liberty and equality. Obstacles may retard, but they cannot long prevent, the progress of a movement sanctified by its justice and sustained by a virtuous people. Reverently let us invoke the God of our fathers to guide and protect us in our efforts to perpetuate the principles which by his blessing they were able to vindicate, establish, and transmit to their posterity. With the continuance of his favor ever gratefully acknowledged, we may hopefully look forward to success, to peace, and to prosperity.

Source: James D. Richardson, *A Compilation of the Messages and Papers of the Confederacy Including the Diplomatic Correspondence 1861–1865.* Nashville: United States Publishing Company, 1905.

Peace Convention Resolutions

February 27, 1861

INTRODUCTION

In the same month when seven state delegations met in Montgomery, Alabama, to draw up a preliminary Southern government, 132 delegates from 21 states met at a Peace Convention in the Willard Hotel in Washington, DC, presided over by former president John Tyler, to draw up a constitutional amendment that might avert war. Many of the proposals were similar to those that were introduced in Congress and known as the Crittenden Compromise. Congress did not adopt either set of proposals, but the convention is credited with keeping border states in the Union until Lincoln could be inaugurated.

Section 1. In all the present territory of the United States north of the parallel of 36° 30' of north latitude, involuntary servitude, except in punishment of crime, is prohibited. In all the present territory south of that line, the status of persons held to involuntary service or labor, as it now exists, shall not be changed; nor shall any law be passed by Congress or the Territorial Legislature to hinder or prevent the taking of such persons from any of the States of this Union to said territory, nor to impair the rights arising from said relation; but the same shall be subject to judicial cognizance in the Federal courts, according to the course of the common law. When any Territory north or south of said line, within such boundary as Congress may prescribe, shall contain a population equal to that required for a member of Congress, it shall, if its form of government be republican, be admitted into the Union on an equal footing with the original States, with or without involuntary servitude as the Constitution of such States may provide.[1]

[1] This was an attempt to restore the terms of the Missouri Compromise, which the Supreme Court had invalidated in *Dred Scott v. Sandford* (1857).

Section 2: No territory shall be acquired by the United States, except by discovery, and for navel and commercial stations, depots, and transit routes, without the concurrence of a majority of all the Senators from States which allow involuntary servitude, and a majority of all the Senators from States which prohibit that relation; nor shall territory be acquired by treaty, unless the votes of a majority of the

[2] States had often approved or disapproved of the acquisition of new territories, especially in the American Southwest, on the basis of whether they thought that they would add to the strength of existing slave-holding states. This provision would have required consent of a majority of both free and slave states before such future acquisitions.

Senators from each class of states hereinbefore mentioned be cast as part of the two-thirds majority necessary to the ratification of such treaty.[2]

[3]This provision, similar to the proposed Corwin Amendment, would essentially have frozen slavery in the states where it existed as well as the nation's capital (where, however, it prohibited slave sales), while forbidding slave transit through free states or territories.

Section 3. Neither the Constitution nor any amendment thereof shall be construed to give Congress to regulate, abolish, or control, within any State, the relation established or recognized by the laws thereof touching persons held to labor or involuntary service therein, nor to interfere with or abolish involuntary service in the District of Columbia without the consent of Maryland and without the consent of the owners, or making the owners who do not consent just compensation; nor the power to interfere with or prohibit representatives and others from bringing with them to the District of Columbia, retaining and taking away, persons so held to labor or service in any State or Territory of the United States to any other State or Territory thereof, where it is established or recognized by law or usage; and the right during transportation, by sea or river, of touching at ports, shores, and landings, and of landing case of distress, shall exist; but not the right of transit in or through any State or Territory, or of sale or traffic, against the laws thereof. Nor shall Congress have power to authorize any higher rate of taxation on persons held to labor or service than on land. The bringing into the District of Columbia of persons held to labor or service for sale; or placing them in depots to be afterwards transferred to other places for sale as merchandise, is prohibited.[3]

[4]This was designed to provide for the enforcement of the fugitive slave clause.

Section 4. The third paragraph of the second section of the fourth article of the Constitution shall not be construed to prevent any of the States, by appropriate legislation, and through the actions of their judicial and ministerial officers, from enforcing the delivery of fugitives from labor to the persons to whom such service or labor is due.[4]

Section 5. The foreign slave-trade is hereby forever prohibited; and it shall be the duty of Congress to pass laws to prevent the importation of slaves, coolies, or persons held to service or labor, into the United States and the Territories from places beyond the limits thereof.

Section 6. The first, third, and fifth sections, together with this section of these amendments, and the third paragraph of the second section of the first article of the Constitution, and the third paragraph of the second section of the fourth article thereof, shall not be amended or abolished without the consent of all the States.[5]

Section 7. Congress shall provide by law that the United States shall pay to the owner the full value of his fugitive from labor, in all cases where the marshal, or other officer, whose duty it was to arrest such fugitive, was prevented from so doing by violence or intimidation from mobs or riotous assemblages, or when, after arrest, such fugitive was rescued by like violence or intimidation, and the owner thereby deprived of the same; and the acceptance of such payment shall preclude the owner from further claim to such fugitive. Congress shall provide by law for securing to the citizens of each State the privileges and immunities of citizens in the several States.[6]

[5]This is an "entrenchment" clause, designed to require unanimous consent to any changes in the Constitution related to slavery. Southern states were increasingly concerned that two-thirds of both houses of Congress and three-fourths of the states might otherwise work to abolish slavery.

[6]The last provision is a reference to the rights of slave owners to their slave property. A similar provision would later be incorporated into the Fourteenth Amendment with respect to other federal rights.

Source: L. E. Crittenden, *A Report of the Debates and Proceedings in the Secret Sessions of the Conference Convention for Proposing Amendments to the Constitution of the United States held at Washington, D.C. in February, A.D. 1861.* New York: D. Appleton, 1864, 440–452.

The Proposed Corwin Amendment

March 2, 1861

INTRODUCTION

After the failure of a series of amendments known as the Crittenden Compromise, Congress proposed this amendment. Named the Corwin Amendment after Ohio Republican Thomas Corwin, who had chaired a committee of 33 House Republicans, the amendment was supported by New York Republican William Seward, who had the support of Abraham Lincoln. Between May 1861 and February 1862, the states of Ohio, Maryland, and Illinois ratified this amendment, but it was superseded by another amendment in 1865 that ended involuntary servitude.

Joint Resolution to amend the Constitution of the United States.

Resolved by the Senate and House of Representatives of the United States of America in Congress assembled,

That the following article be proposed to the Legislatures of the several States as an amendment to the Constitution of the United States, which, when ratified by three-fourths of said Legislatures, shall be valid, to all intents and purposes, as part of the said Constitution, viz.:

"Article Thirteen.

¹Although Lincoln had opposed the spread of slavery, he believed that the Constitution protected it in states where it already existed so he was able to support this amendment, which did not speak to slavery in the territories.

"No amendment shall be made to the Constitution which will authorize or give to Congress the power to abolish or interfere, within any State, with the domestic institutions thereof, including that of persons held to labor or service by the laws of said State.'₁

APPROVED, March 2, 1861.

Source: 12 U.S. Statutes at Large, 36th Cong., 2d Sess., 1861, 251.

Abraham Lincoln's First Inaugural Address

March 4, 1861

INTRODUCTION

In February 1861, even before newly elected President Abraham Lincoln took office, a group of seven Southern states had joined together in a confederacy with the intention of seceding from the United States. At his inauguration, Lincoln, therefore, faced a disunited nation, which he sought to bind back together through rhetoric.

Fellow-Citizens of the United States

In compliance with a custom as old as the Government itself, I appear before you to address you briefly and to take in your presence the oath prescribed by the Constitution of the United States to be taken by the President before he enters on the execution of this office.

I do not consider it necessary at present for me to discuss those matters of administration about which there is no special anxiety or excitement.

Apprehension seems to exist among the people of the Southern States that by the accession of a Republican Administration their property and their peace and personal security are to be endangered. There has never been any reasonable cause for such apprehension. Indeed, the most ample evidence to the contrary has all the while existed and been open to their inspection. It is found in nearly all the published speeches of him who now addresses you. I do but quote from one of those speeches when I declare that—

I have no purpose, directly or indirectly, to interfere with the institution of slavery in the States where it exists. I believe I have no lawful right to do so, and I have no inclination to do so.[1]

Those who nominated and elected me did so with full knowledge that I had made this and many similar declarations and had never

[1] Lincoln, who had adamantly opposed the expansion of slavery, denied that he intended to interfere with it in states where it was already established. Throughout his early presidency, his central goal was that of preserving the Union.

recanted them; and more than this, they placed in the platform for my acceptance. . . .

I now reiterate these sentiments, and in doing so I only press upon the public attention the most conclusive evidence of which the case is susceptible that the property, peace, and security of no section are to be in any wise endangered by the now incoming Administration. I add, too, that all the protection which, consistently with the Constitution and the laws, can be given will be cheerfully given to all the States when lawfully demanded, for whatever cause—as cheerfully to one section as to another.

There is much controversy about the delivering up of fugitives from service or labor. The clause I now read is as plainly written in the Constitution as any other of its provisions:

No person held to service or labor in one State, under the laws thereof, escaping into another, shall in consequence of any law or regulation therein be discharged from such service or labor, but shall be delivered up on claim of the party to whom such service or labor may be due.

[2]Lincoln likewise pledges to uphold the provisions of the fugitive slave clause in Article IV, Section 2, and the laws adopted to uphold it.

It is scarcely questioned that this provision was intended by those who made it for the reclaiming of what we call fugitive slaves; and the intention of the lawgiver is the law. All members of Congress swear their support to the whole Constitution—to this provision as much as to any other. To the proposition, then, that slaves whose cases come within the terms of this clause "shall be delivered up" their oaths are unanimous. Now, if they would make the effort in good temper, could they not with nearly equal unanimity frame and pass a law by means of which to keep good that unanimous oath?[2]

There is some difference of opinion whether this clause should be enforced by national or by State authority, but surely that difference is not a very material one. If the slave is to be surrendered, it can be of but little consequence to him or to others by which authority it is done. And should anyone in any case be content that his oath shall go unkept on a merely unsubstantial controversy as to how it shall be kept?

Again: In any law upon this subject ought not all the safeguards of liberty known in civilized and humane jurisprudence to be introduced, so that a free man be not in any case surrendered as a slave? And might it not be well at the same time to provide by law for the enforcement of that clause in the Constitution which guarantees that "the citizens of each State shall be entitled to all privileges and immunities of citizens in the several States"?

I take the official oath to-day with no mental reservations and with no purpose to construe the Constitution or laws by any hypercritical rules; and while I do not choose now to specify particular acts of Congress as proper to be enforced, I do suggest that it will be much safer for all, both in official and private stations, to conform to and abide by all those acts which stand unrepealed than to violate any of them trusting to find impunity in having them held to be unconstitutional. . . .

I hold that in contemplation of universal law and of the Constitution the Union of these States is perpetual. Perpetuity is implied, if not expressed, in the fundamental law of all national governments.[3] It is safe to assert that no government proper ever had a provision in its organic law for its own termination. Continue to execute all the express provisions of our National Constitution, and the Union will endure forever, it being impossible to destroy it except by some action not provided for in the instrument itself.

Again: If the United States be not a government proper, but an association of States in the nature of contract merely, can it, as a contract, be peaceably unmade by less than all the parties who made it? One party to a contract may violate it—break it, so to speak—but does it not require all to lawfully rescind it?

Descending from these general principles, we find the proposition that in legal contemplation the Union is perpetual confirmed by the history of the Union itself. The Union is much older than the Constitution. It was formed, in fact, by the Articles of Association in 1774. It was matured and continued by the Declaration of Independence in 1776. It was further matured, and the faith of all the then thirteen States expressly plighted and engaged that it should be perpetual, by the Articles of Confederation in 1778. And finally, in 1787, one of the

[3]Because he believed the Constitution was perpetual, Lincoln believed that his oath obliged him to support its continuation.

declared objects for ordaining and establishing the Constitution was "to form a more perfect Union."

But if destruction of the Union by one or by a part only of the States be lawfully possible, the Union is less perfect than before the Constitution, having lost the vital element of perpetuity. . . .[4]

[4]Although much of his speech relied on implication, Lincoln cited the provision in the Preamble of the Constitution calling for "a more perfect Union" to support his belief that the new Union was designed to be perpetual.

I therefore consider that in view of the Constitution and the laws the Union is unbroken, and to the extent of my ability, I shall take care, as the Constitution itself expressly enjoins upon me, that the laws of the Union be faithfully executed in all the States. Doing this I deem to be only a simple duty on my part, and I shall perform it so far as practicable unless my rightful masters, the American people, shall withhold the requisite means or in some authoritative manner direct the contrary. I trust this will not be regarded as a menace, but only as the declared purpose of the Union that it will constitutionally defend and maintain itself.

[5]Lincoln makes it clear that he will defend federal properties but will not initiate military action against the Confederacy.

In doing this there needs to be no bloodshed or violence, and there shall be none unless it be forced upon the national authority. The power confided to me will be used to hold, occupy, and possess the property and places belonging to the Government and to collect the duties and imposts; but beyond what may be necessary for these objects, there will be no invasion, no using of force against or among the people anywhere.[5] Where hostility to the United States in any interior locality shall be so great and universal as to prevent competent resident citizens from holding the Federal offices, there will be no attempt to force obnoxious strangers among the people for that object. While the strict legal right may exist in the Government to enforce the exercise of these offices, the attempt to do so would be so irritating and so nearly impracticable withal that I deem it better to forego for the time the uses of such offices.

The mails, unless repelled, will continue to be furnished in all parts of the Union. So far as possible the people everywhere shall have that sense of perfect security which is most favorable to calm thought and reflection. The course here indicated will be followed unless current events and experience shall show a modification or change to be proper, and in every case and exigency my best discretion will be exercised, according to circumstances actually existing and with a view and a hope of a peaceful solution of the national troubles and the restoration of fraternal sympathies and affections. . . .

From questions of this class spring all our constitutional controversies, and we divide upon them into majorities and minorities. If the minority will not acquiesce, the majority must, or the Government must cease. There is no other alternative, for continuing the Government is acquiescence on one side or the other. If a minority in such case will secede rather than acquiesce, they make a precedent which in turn will divide and ruin them, for a minority of their own will secede from them whenever a majority refuses to be controlled by such minority.[6] For instance, why may not any portion of a new confederacy a year or two hence arbitrarily secede again, precisely as portions of the present Union now claim to secede from it? All who cherish disunion sentiments are now being educated to the exact temper of doing this.

Is there such perfect identity of interests among the States to compose a new union as to produce harmony only and prevent renewed secession?

Plainly the central idea of secession is the essence of anarchy. A majority held in restraint by constitutional checks and limitations, and always changing easily with deliberate changes of popular opinions and sentiments, is the only true sovereign of a free people. Whoever rejects it does of necessity fly to anarchy or to despotism.[7] Unanimity is impossible. The rule of a minority, as a permanent arrangement, is wholly inadmissible; so that, rejecting the majority principle, anarchy or despotism in some form is all that is left.

I do not forget the position assumed by some that constitutional questions are to be decided by the Supreme Court, nor do I deny that such decisions must be binding in any case upon the parties to a suit as to the object of that suit, while they are also entitled to very high respect and consideration in all parallel cases by all other departments of the Government. And while it is obviously possible that such decision may be erroneous in any given case, still the evil effect following it, being limited to that particular case, with the chance that it may be overruled and never become a precedent for other cases, can better be borne than could the evils of a different practice.

[6]Evoking the doctrine of majority rule through which democracies are governed, Lincoln points out that the same justification that will support secession of the Southern states from the Union on the basis of one grievance will open up the secession of another portion of these states from the others.

[7]Lincoln contrasts majority rule under law with the anarchy that he thinks secession would unleash.

At the same time, the candid citizen must confess that if the policy of the Government upon vital questions affecting the whole people is to be irrevocably fixed by decisions of the Supreme Court, the instant they are made in ordinary litigation between parties in personal actions the people will have ceased to be their own rulers, having to that extent practically resigned their Government into the hands of that eminent tribunal.[8] Nor is there in this view any assault upon the court or the judges. It is a duty from which they may not shrink to decide cases properly brought before them, and it is no fault of theirs if others seek to turn their decisions to political purposes. . . .

Physically speaking, we can not separate. We can not remove our respective sections from each other nor build an impassable wall between them. A husband and wife may be divorced and go out of the presence and beyond the reach of each other, but the different parts of our country can not do this. They can not but remain face to face, and intercourse, either amicable or hostile, must continue between them.[9] Is it possible, then, to make that intercourse more advantageous or more satisfactory after separation than before? Can aliens make treaties easier than friends can make laws? Can treaties be more faithfully enforced between aliens than laws can among friends? Suppose you go to war, you can not fight always; and when, after much loss on both sides and no gain on either, you cease fighting, the identical old questions, as to terms of intercourse, are again upon you.

This country, with its institutions, belongs to the people who inhabit it. Whenever they shall grow weary of the existing Government, they can exercise their constitutional right of amending it or their revolutionary right to dismember or overthrow it.[10] I can not be ignorant of the fact that many worthy and patriotic citizens are desirous of having the National Constitution amended. While I make no recommendation of amendments, I fully recognize the rightful authority of the people over the whole subject, to be exercised in either of the modes prescribed in the instrument itself; and I should, under existing circumstances, favor rather than oppose a fair opportunity being afforded the people to act upon it. I will venture to add that to me the convention mode seems preferable, in that it allows amendments to originate with the people themselves, instead of only permitting them to take or reject propositions originated by others, not especially chosen for the purpose, and which might not be precisely such as they would wish to either accept or refuse.[11]

9 Unlike couples who, when they divorce, can move to different locations, Lincoln points out that Southern states will continue to be geographically close to the rest of the Union, whether they remain in or leave the Union, and that the likelihood of resolving differences is greater if they remain than if they leave.

10 Lincoln distinguishes the natural right of revolution from the constitutional right of amending the Constitution.

11 Lincoln says that he favors allowing a convention to meet to propose amendments.

I understand a proposed amendment to the Constitution—which amendment, however, I have not seen—has passed Congress, to the effect that the Federal Government shall never interfere with the domestic institutions of the States, including that of persons held to service. To avoid misconstruction of what I have said, I depart from my purpose not to speak of particular amendments so far as to say that, holding such a provision to now be implied constitutional law, I have no objection to its being made express and irrevocable.[12]

The Chief Magistrate derives all his authority from the people, and they have referred none upon him to fix terms for the separation of the States. The people themselves can do this if also they choose, but the Executive as such has nothing to do with it. His duty is to administer the present Government as it came to his hands and to transmit it unimpaired by him to his successor. . . .

By the frame of the Government under which we live this same people have wisely given their public servants but little power for mischief, and have with equal wisdom provided for the return of that little to their own hands at very short intervals. While the people retain their virtue and vigilance no Administration by any extreme of wickedness or folly can very seriously injure the Government in the short space of four years.

My countrymen, one and all, think calmly and well upon this whole subject. Nothing valuable can be lost by taking time. If there be an object to hurry any of you in hot haste to a step which you would never take deliberately, that object will be frustrated by taking time; but no good object can be frustrated by it.[13] Such of you as are now dissatisfied still have the old Constitution unimpaired, and, on the sensitive point, the laws of your own framing under it; while the new Administration will have no immediate power, if it would, to change either. If it were admitted that you who are dissatisfied hold the right side in the dispute, there still is no single good reason for precipitate action. Intelligence, patriotism, Christianity, and a firm reliance on Him who has never yet forsaken this favored land are still competent to adjust in the best way all our present difficulty.

In your hands, my dissatisfied fellow-countrymen, and not in mine, is the momentous issue of civil war. The Government will not assail you. You can have no conflict without being yourselves the aggressors.

[12]In the meantime, he indicates his support for the Corwin Amendment, which would affirm the continuation of slavery in the states where it already existed.

[13]Lincoln is advising patience and caution and appealing to a common God.

You have no oath registered in heaven to destroy the Government, while I shall have the most solemn one to "preserve, protect, and defend it."

[14] Having exhausted practical and legal arguments for perpetuation of the Union, Lincoln resorts to emotional rhetoric designed to remind both sections of the country of their common heritage.

I am loath to close. We are not enemies, but friends. We must not be enemies. Though passion may have strained it must not break our bonds of affection. The mystic chords of memory, stretching from every battlefield and patriot grave to every living heart and hearthstone all over this broad land, will yet swell the chorus of the Union, when again touched, as surely they will be, by the better angels of our nature.[14]

Source: *Inaugural Addresses of the Presidents of the United States.* Washington, DC: Government Printing Office, 1989.

Constitution of the Confederate States

March 11, 1861

INTRODUCTION

For years Northern and Southern states had argued about the proper interpretation of the U.S. Constitution. This document, written by a Committee of Twelve and debated by delegates to a convention held in Montgomery, Alabama, in March 1861, replaced a similar provisional document of the previous month, before being ratified by the Confederation Congress and by five Confederate states. The document embodied the doctrines of John C. Calhoun (1782–1850) and other Southern secessionists who viewed slavery as a positive good rather than, as their 1787 forbears, as a necessary evil. Although it included a few unrelated innovations, this document left most provisions in place that did not relate directly or indirectly to slavery.

Preamble

We, the people of the Confederate States, each State acting in its sovereign and independent character,[1] in order to form a permanent federal government, establish justice, insure domestic tranquillity, and secure the blessings of liberty to ourselves and our posterity invoking the favor and guidance of Almighty God[2] do ordain and establish this Constitution for the Confederate States of America.

[1] Like the Articles of Confederation, the Confederate Constitution sought to vest primary power, or sovereignty, within individual states.

[2] The document is also notable for explicitly acknowledging God.

Article I

Section I. All legislative powers herein delegated shall be vested in a Congress of the Confederate States, which shall consist of a Senate and House of Representatives.

Sec. 2. (1) The House of Representatives shall be composed of members chosen every second year by the people of the several States; and the electors in each State shall be citizens of the Confederate States, and have the qualifications requisite for electors of the most numerous branch of the State Legislature; but no person of foreign birth, not a citizen of the Confederate States, shall be allowed to vote for any officer, civil or political, State or Federal.

(2) No person shall be a Representative who shall not have attained the age of twenty-five years, and be a citizen of the Confederate States, and who shall not when elected, be an inhabitant of that State in which he shall be chosen.

(3) Representatives and direct taxes shall be apportioned among the several States, which may be included within this Confederacy, according to their respective numbers, which shall be determined by adding to the whole number of free persons, including those bound to service for a term of years, and excluding Indians not taxed, three-fifths of all slaves.[3] The actual enumeration shall be made within three years after the first meeting of the Congress of the Confederate States, and within every subsequent term of ten years, in such manner as they shall by law direct. The number of Representatives shall not exceed one for every fifty thousand, but each State shall have at least one Representative; and until such enumeration shall be made, the State of South Carolina shall be entitled to choose six; the State of Georgia ten; the State of Alabama nine; the State of Florida two; the State of Mississippi seven; the State of Louisiana six; and the State of Texas six.

(4) When vacancies happen in the representation from any State the executive authority thereof shall issue writs of election to fill such vacancies.

(5) The House of Representatives shall choose their Speaker and other officers; and shall have the sole power of impeachment; except that any judicial or other Federal officer, resident and acting solely within the limits of any State, may be impeached by a vote of two-thirds of both branches of the Legislature thereof.[4]

Sec. 3. (1) The Senate of the Confederate States shall be composed of two Senators from each State, chosen for six years by the Legislature thereof, at the regular session next immediately preceding the commencement of the term of service; and each Senator shall have one vote.

(Paragraphs 2–7 omitted. no differences between this and U.S. Constitution.)

[3]Whereas the U.S. Constitution used circumlocutions (often "such other persons"), the Confederate Constitution referred explicitly to slaves.

[4]The U.S. Constitution did not provide a comparable provision for state impeachment of federal officials.

Sec. 4. (1) The times, places, and manner of holding elections for Senators and Representatives shall be prescribed in each State by the Legislature thereof, subject to the provisions of this Constitution; but the Congress may, at any time, by law, make or alter such regulations, except as to the times and places of choosing Senators.

(2) The Congress shall assemble at least once in every year; and such meeting shall be on the first Monday in December, unless they shall, by law, appoint a different day.

Sec. 5. (1) Each House shall be the judge of the elections, returns, and qualifications of its own members, and a majority of each shall constitute a quorum to do business; but a smaller number may adjourn from day to day, and may be authorized to compel the attendance of absent members, in such manner and under such penalties as each House may provide.

(Paragraphs 2–4 omitted. No differences.)

Sec. 6. (1) The Senators and Representatives shall receive a compensation for their services, to be ascertained by law, and paid out of the Treasury of the Confederate States. They shall, in all cases, except treason, felony, and breach of the peace, be privileged from arrest during their attendance at the session of their respective Houses, and in going to and returning from the same; and for any speech or debate in either House, they shall not be questioned in any other place. 'o Senator or Representative shall, during the time for which he was elected, be appointed to any civil office under the authority of the Confederate States, which shall have been created, or the emoluments whereof shall have been increased during such time; and no person holding any office under the Confederate States shall be a member of either House during his continuance in office. But Congress may, by law, grant to the principal officer in each of the Executive Departments a seat upon the floor of either House, with the privilege of discussing any measures appertaining to his department.[5]

[5]This provision, borrowed from parliamentary democracies, permitted members of the cabinet to appear directly before Congress.

Sec. 7. (1) All bills for raising revenue shall originate in the House of Representatives; but the Senate may propose or concur with amendments, as on other bills.

(2) Every bill which shall have passed both Houses, shall, before it becomes a law, be presented to the President of the Confederate

States; if he approve, he shall sign it; but if not, he shall return it, with his objections, to that House in which it shall have originated, who shall enter the objections at large on their journal, and proceed to reconsider it. If, after such reconsideration, two-thirds of that House shall agree to pass the bill, it shall be sent, together with the objections, to the other House, by which it shall likewise be reconsidered, and if approved by two-thirds of that House, it shall become a law. But in all such cases, the votes of both Houses shall be determined by yeas and nays, and the names of the persons voting for and against the bill shall be entered on the journal of each House respectively. If any bill shall not be returned by the President within ten days (Sundays excepted) after it shall have been presented to him, the same shall be a law, in like manner as if he had signed it, unless the Congress, by their adjournment, prevent its return; in which case it shall not be a law. The President may approve any appropriation and disapprove any other appropriation in the same bill. In such case he shall, in signing the bill, designate the appropriations disapproved; and shall return a copy of such appropriations, with his objections, to the House in which the bill shall have originated; and the same proceedings shall then be had as in case of other bills disapproved by the President.[6]

(3) Every order, resolution, or vote, to which the concurrence of both Houses may be necessary (except on a question of adjournment) shall be presented to the President of the Confederate States; and before the same shall take effect, shall be approved by him; or, being disapproved by him, shall be repassed by two-thirds of both Houses, according to the rules and limitations prescribed in case of a bill.

Sec. 8. The Congress shall have power

(1) To lay and collect taxes, duties, imposts, and excises for revenue, necessary to pay the debts, provide for the common defense, and carry on the Government of the Confederate States; but no bounties shall be granted from the Treasury; nor shall any duties or taxes on importations from foreign nations be laid to promote or foster any branch of industry; and all duties, imposts, and excises shall be uniform throughout the Confederate States.

(2) To borrow money on the credit of the Confederate States.

(3) To regulate commerce with foreign nations, and among the several States, and with the Indian tribes; but neither this, nor any

[6]Like many modern state constitutions, the Confederate Constitution provided for a line-item veto of individual items within appropriation bills. Some modern constitutional reformers believe that such a power would help trim federal budgets.

[7]The commerce clause had been a major source for the expansion of federal powers.

other clause contained in the Constitution, shall ever be construed to delegate the power to Congress to appropriate money for any internal improvement intended to facilitate commerce; except for the purpose of furnishing lights, beacons, and buoys, and other aids to navigation upon the coasts, and the improvement of harbors and the removing of obstructions in river navigation; in all which cases such duties shall be laid on the navigation facilitated thereby as may be necessary to pay the costs and expenses thereof.[7]

(4–17) Omitted; same as U.S. Constitution.

(18) To make all laws which shall be necessary and proper for carrying into execution the foregoing powers, and all other powers vested by this Constitution in the Government of the Confederate States, or in any department or officer thereof.[8]

Sec. 9. (1) The importation of negroes of the African race from any foreign country other than the slaveholding States or Territories of the United States of America, is hereby forbidden; and Congress is required to pass such laws as shall effectually prevent the same.[9]

(2) Congress shall also have power to prohibit the introduction of slaves from any State not a member of, or Territory not belonging to, this Confederacy.[10]

(3) The privilege of the writ of habeas corpus shall not be suspended, unless when in cases of rebellion or invasion the public safety may require it.

(4) No bill of attainder, ex post facto law, or law denying or impairing the right of property in negro slaves shall be passed.

(5) No capitation or other direct tax shall be laid, unless in proportion to the census or enumeration hereinbefore directed to be taken.

(6) No tax or duty shall be laid on articles exported from any State, except by a vote of two-thirds of both Houses.

(7) No preference shall be given by any regulation of commerce or revenue to the ports of one State over those of another.

(8) No money shall be drawn from the Treasury, but in consequence of appropriations made by law; and a regular statement and account

This provision sought to limit congressional powers under the clause by confining related appropriations to a narrow list.

[8]Although this clause had also been a source of expanded national power, the Confederate Constitution did not change it.

[9]This provision maintained the prohibition on the import of slaves from foreign countries but made explicit the right to transport slaves from one Confederate state to another, which some feared might otherwise be constrained under the federal commerce power.

[10]Once again, the document specifically recognized individuals as slaves.

of the receipts and expenditures of all public money shall be published from time to time.

(9) Congress shall appropriate no money from the Treasury except by a vote of two-thirds of both Houses, taken by yeas and nays, unless it be asked and estimated for by some one of the heads of departments and submitted to Congress by the President; or for the purpose of paying its own expenses and contingencies; or for the payment of claims against the Confederate States, the justice of which shall have been judicially declared by a tribunal for the investigation of claims against the Government, which it is hereby made the duty of Congress to establish.

[11]This additional provision was designed to put further restraints on budget overruns.

(10) All bills appropriating money shall specify in Federal currency the exact amount of each appropriation and the purposes for which it is made; and Congress shall grant no extra compensation to any public contractor, officer, agent, or servant, after such contract shall have been made or such service rendered.[11]

(11) No title of nobility shall be granted by the Confederate States; and no person holding any office of profit or trust under them shall, without the consent of the Congress, accept of any present, emolument, office, or title of any kind whatever, from any king, prince, or foreign state.

[12]This and the provisions that followed were the first eight of ten amendments in the Bill of Rights, which the U.S. Constitution had added to the end, rather than incorporating into its text.

(12) Congress shall make no law respecting an establishment of religion, or prohibiting the free exercise thereof; or abridging the freedom of speech, or of the press; or the right of the people peaceably to assemble and petition the Government for a redress of grievances.[12]

(13) A well-regulated militia being necessary to the security of a free State, the right of the people to keep and bear arms shall not be infringed.

(14) No soldier shall, in time of peace, be quartered in any house without the consent of the owner; nor in time of war, but in a manner to be prescribed by law.

(15) The right of the people to be secure in their persons, houses, papers, and effects, against unreasonable searches and seizures, shall not be violated; and no warrants shall issue but upon probable cause,

supported by oath or affirmation, and particularly describing the place to be searched and the persons or things to be seized.

(16) No person shall be held to answer for a capital or otherwise infamous crime, unless on a presentment or indictment of a grand jury, except in cases arising in the land or naval forces, or in the militia, when in actual service in time of war or public danger; nor shall any person be subject for the same offense to be twice put in jeopardy of life or limb; nor be compelled, in any criminal case, to be a witness against himself; nor be deprived of life, liberty, or property without due process of law; nor shall private property be taken for public use, without just compensation.

(17) In all criminal prosecutions the accused shall enjoy the right to a speedy and public trial, by an impartial jury of the State and district wherein the crime shall have been committed, which district shall have been previously ascertained by law, and to be informed of the nature and cause of the accusation; to be confronted with the witnesses against him; to have compulsory process for obtaining witnesses in his favor; and to have the assistance of counsel for his defense.

(18) In suits at common law, where the value in controversy shall exceed twenty dollars, the right of trial by jury shall be preserved; and no fact so tried by a jury shall be otherwise reexamined in any court of the Confederacy, than according to the rules of common law.

(19) Excessive bail shall not be required, nor excessive fines imposed, nor cruel and unusual punishments inflicted.

(20) Every law, or resolution having the force of law, shall relate to but one subject, and that shall be expressed in the title.[13]

Sec. 10. (1) No State shall enter into any treaty, alliance, or confederation; grant letters of marque and reprisal; coin money; make anything but gold and silver coin a tender in payment of debts; pass any bill of attainder, or ex post facto law, or law impairing the obligation of contracts; or grant any title of nobility.

(2) No State shall, without the consent of the Congress, lay any imposts or duties on imports or exports, except what may be absolutely

[13]This is another of the Confederate Constitution's innovations that some modern reformers of the U.S. Constitution have advocated.

necessary for executing its inspection laws; and the net produce of all duties and imposts, laid by any State on imports, or exports, shall be for the use of the Treasury of the Confederate States; and all such laws shall be subject to the revision and control of Congress.

(3) No State shall, without the consent of Congress, lay any duty on tonnage, except on seagoing vessels, for the improvement of its rivers and harbors navigated by the said vessels; but such duties shall not conflict with any treaties of the Confederate States with foreign nations; and any surplus revenue thus derived shall, after making such improvement, be paid into the common treasury. Nor shall any State keep troops or ships of war in time of peace, enter into any agreement or compact with another State, or with a foreign power, or engage in war, unless actually invaded, or in such imminent danger as will not admit of delay. But when any river divides or flows through two or more States they may enter into compacts with each other to improve the navigation thereof.

Article II

[14] In contrast to the U.S. Constitution, this document provided for a single six-year nonrenewable presidential term.

Section I. (1) The executive power shall be vested in a President of the Confederate States of America. He and the Vice President shall hold their offices for the term of six years; but the President shall not be reeligible.[14] The President and Vice President shall be elected as follows:

[15] This paragraph, and those that immediately follow, continues the Electoral College system for selecting the president and vice president rather than devising an alternative such as direct popular election.

(2) Each State shall appoint, in such manner as the Legislature thereof may direct, a number of electors equal to the whole number of Senators and Representatives to which the State may be entitled in the Congress; but no Senator or Representative or person holding an office of trust or profit under the Confederate States shall be appointed an elector.[15]

(3) The electors shall meet in their respective States and vote by ballot for President and Vice President, one of whom, at least, shall not be an inhabitant of the same State with themselves; they shall name in their ballots the person voted for as President, and in distinct ballots the person voted for as Vice President, and they shall make distinct lists of all persons voted for as President, and of all persons voted for as Vice President, and of the number of votes for each, which lists they shall sign and certify, and transmit, sealed, to the seat of the

Government of. the Confederate States, directed to the President of the Senate; the President of the Senate shall, in the presence of the Senate and House of Representatives, open all the certificates, and the votes shall then be counted; the person having the greatest number of votes for President shall be the President, if such number be a majority of the whole number of electors appointed; and if no person have such majority, then from the persons having the highest numbers, not exceeding three, on the list of those voted for as President, the House of Representatives shall choose immediately, by ballot, the President. But in choosing the President the votes shall be taken by States, the representation from each State having one vote; a quorum for this purpose shall consist of a member or members from two-thirds of the States, and a majority of all the States shall be necessary to a choice. And if the House of Representatives shall not choose a President, whenever the right of choice shall devolve upon them, before the 4th day of March next following, then the Vice President shall act as President, as in case of the death, or other constitutional disability of the President.

(4) The person having the greatest number of votes as Vice President shall be the Vice President, if such number be a majority of the whole number of electors appointed; and if no person have a majority, then, from the two highest numbers on the list, the Senate shall choose the Vice President; a quorum for the purpose shall consist of two-thirds of the whole number of Senators, and a majority of the whole number shall be necessary to a choice.

(5) But no person constitutionally ineligible to the office of President shall be eligible to that of Vice President of the Confederate States.

(6) The Congress may determine the time of choosing the electors, and the day on which they shall give their votes; which day shall be the same throughout the Confederate States.

(7) No person except a natural-born citizen of the Confederate; States, or a citizen thereof at the time of the adoption of this Constitution, or a citizen thereof born in the United States prior to the 20th of December, 1860, shall be eligible to the office of President; neither shall any person be eligible to that office who shall not have attained the age of thirty-five years, and been fourteen years a resident within the limits of the Confederate States, as they may exist at the time of his election.[16]

[16]This provision limits the presidential office to individuals born in the Confederate States or citizens at the time of its adoption, thus precluding the election of an immigrant from the Northern states.

(8) In case of the removal of the President from office, or of his death, resignation, or inability to discharge the powers and duties of said office, the same shall devolve on the Vice President; and the Congress may, by law, provide for the case of removal, death, resignation, or inability, both of the President and Vice President, declaring what officer shall then act as President; and such officer shall act accordingly until the disability be removed or a President shall be elected.

(9) The President shall, at stated times, receive for his services a compensation, which shall neither be increased nor diminished during the period for which he shall have been elected; and he shall not receive within that period any other emolument from the Confederate States, or any of them.

(10) Before he enters on the execution of his office he shall take the following oath or affirmation: "I do solemnly swear (or affirm) that I will faithfully execute the office of President of the Confederate States of America, and, will, to the best of my ability, preserve, protect, and defend the Constitution thereof."

Sec. 2. (1) The President shall be Commander-in-Chief of the Army and Navy of the Confederate States, and of the militia of the several States, when called into the actual service of the Confederate States; he may require the opinion, in writing, of the principal officer in each of the Executive Departments, upon any subject relating to the duties of their respective offices; and he shall have power to grant reprieves and pardons for offenses against the Confederate States, except in cases of impeachment.

(2) He shall have power, by and with the advice and consent of the Senate, to make treaties; provided two-thirds of the Senators present concur; and he shall nominate, and by and with the advice and consent of the Senate shall appoint, ambassadors, other public ministers and consuls, judges of the Supreme Court, and all other officers of the Confederate States whose appointments are not herein otherwise provided for, and which shall be established by law; but the Congress may, by law, vest the appointment of such inferior officers, as they think proper, in the President alone, in the courts of law, or in the heads of departments.

(3) The principal officer in each of the Executive Departments, and all persons connected with the diplomatic service, may be removed from office at the pleasure of the President. All other civil officers of the Executive Departments may be removed at any time by the President, or other appointing power, when their services are unnecessary, or for dishonesty, incapacity, inefficiency, misconduct, or neglect of duty; and when so removed, the removal shall be reported to the Senate, together with the reasons therefor.[17]

(4) The President shall have power to fill all vacancies that may happen during the recess of the Senate, by granting commissions which shall expire at the end of their next session; but no person rejected by the Senate shall be reappointed to the same office during their ensuing recess.

Sec. 3. (1) The President shall, from time to time, give to the Congress information of the state of the Confederacy, and recommend to their consideration such measures as he shall judge necessary and expedient; he may, on extraordinary occasions, convene both Houses, or either of them; and in case of disagreement between them, with respect to the time of adjournment, he may adjourn them to such time as he shall think proper; he shall receive ambassadors and other public ministers; he shall take care that the laws be faithfully executed, and shall commission all the officers of the Confederate States.

Sec. 4. (1) The President, Vice President, and all civil officers of the Confederate States, shall be removed from office on impeachment for and conviction of treason, bribery, or other high crimes and misdemeanors.

Article III

Section I. (1) The judicial power of the Confederate States shall be vested in one Supreme Court, and in such inferior courts as the Congress may, from time to time, ordain and establish. The judges, both of the Supreme and inferior courts, shall hold their offices during good behavior, and shall, at stated times, receive for their services a compensation which shall not be diminished during their continuance in office.[18]

[17]This provision is more detailed than its counterpart in the U.S. Constitution, which does not specify whether Senate concurrence is required for presidential removal of cabinet officers.

[18]Wary of central power, the Confederacy never got around to creating a centralized court system like that of its 1787 counterpart.

Sec. 2. (1) The judicial power shall extend to all cases arising under this Constitution, the laws of the Confederate States, and treaties made, or which shall be made, under their authority; to all cases affecting ambassadors, other public ministers and consuls; to all cases of admiralty and maritime jurisdiction; to controversies to which the Confederate States shall be a party; to controversies between two or more States; between a State and citizens of another State, where the State is plaintiff; between citizens claiming lands under grants of different States; and between a State or the citizens thereof, and foreign states, citizens, or subjects; but no State shall be sued by a citizen or subject of any foreign state.

(2) In all cases affecting ambassadors, other public ministers and consuls, and those in which a State shall be a party, the Supreme Court shall have original jurisdiction. In all the other cases before mentioned, the Supreme Court shall have appellate jurisdiction both as to law and fact, with such exceptions and under such regulations as the Congress shall make.

(3) The trial of all crimes, except in cases of impeachment, shall be by jury, and such trial shall be held in the State where the said crimes shall have been committed; but when not committed within any State, the trial shall be at such place or places as the Congress may by law have directed.

Sec. 3. (1) Treason against the Confederate States shall consist only in levying war against them, or in adhering to their enemies, giving them aid and comfort. No person shall be convicted of treason unless on the testimony of two witnesses to the same overt act, or on confession in open court.

(2) The Congress shall have power to declare the punishment of treason; but no attainder of treason shall work corruption of blood, or forfeiture, except during the life of the person attainted.

Article IV

Section I. Full faith and credit shall be given in each State to the public acts, records, and judicial proceedings of every other State;

and the Congress may, by general laws, prescribe the manner in which such acts, records, and proceedings shall be proved, and the effect thereof.

Sec. 2. (1) The citizens of each State shall be entitled to all the privileges and immunities of citizens in the several States; and shall have the right of transit and sojourn in any State of this Confederacy, with their slaves and other property; and the right of property in said slaves shall not be thereby impaired.[19]

(2) A person charged in any State with treason, felony, or other crime against the laws of such State, who shall flee from justice, and be found in another State, shall, on demand of the executive authority of the State from which he fled, be delivered up, to be removed to the State having jurisdiction of the crime.

(3) No slave or other person held to service or labor in any State or Territory of the Confederate States, under the laws thereof, escaping or lawfully carried into another, shall, in consequence of any law or regulation therein, be discharged from such service or labor; but shall be delivered up on claim of the party to whom such slave belongs, or to whom such service or labor may be due.

Sec. 3. (1) Other States may be admitted into this Confederacy by a vote of two-thirds of the whole House of Representatives and two-thirds of the Senate, the Senate voting by States; but no new State shall be formed or erected within the jurisdiction of any other State, nor any State be formed by the junction of two or more States, or parts of States, without the consent of the Legislatures of the States concerned, as well as of the Congress.[20]

(2) The Congress shall have power to dispose of and make all needful rules and regulations concerning the property of the Confederate States, including the lands thereof.

(3) The Confederate States may acquire new territory; and Congress shall have power to legislate and provide governments for the inhabitants of all territory belonging to the Confederate States, lying without the limits of the several Sates; and may permit them, at such times, and in such manner as it may by law provide, to form States

[19]This provision effectively affirmed the decision in *Dred Scott v. Sandford* (1857), which had ruled that the provision in the Missouri Compromise barring slavery from some U.S. territories was an unconstitutional deprivation of the due process rights of slave owners.

[20]By requiring a vote of two-thirds of Congress, this provision would have made it almost impossible for the addition of free states.

to be admitted into the Confederacy. In all such territory the institution of negro slavery, as it now exists in the Confederate States, shall be recognized and protected be Congress and by the Territorial government; and the inhabitants of the several Confederate States and Territories shall have the right to take to such Territory any slaves lawfully held by them in any of the States or Territories of the Confederate States.[21]

(4) The Confederate States shall guarantee to every State that now is, or hereafter may become, a member of this Confederacy, a republican form of government; and shall protect each of them against invasion; and on application of the Legislature or of the Executive when the Legislature is not in session) against domestic violence.

Article V

Section I. (1) Upon the demand of any three States, legally assembled in their several conventions, the Congress shall summon a convention of all the States, to take into consideration such amendments to the Constitution as the said States shall concur in suggesting at the time when the said demand is made;[22] and should any of the proposed amendments to the Constitution be agreed on by the said convention, voting by States, and the same be ratified by the Legislatures of two-thirds of the several States, or by conventions in two-thirds thereof,[23] as the one or the other mode of ratification may be proposed by the general convention, they shall thenceforward form a part of this Constitution. But no State shall, without its consent, be deprived of its equal representation in the Senate.

Article VI

1. The Government established by this Constitution is the successor of the Provisional Government of the Confederate States of America, and all the laws passed by the latter shall continue in force until the same shall be repealed or modified; and all the officers appointed by the same shall remain in office until their successors are appointed and qualified, or the offices abolished.

2. All debts contracted and engagements entered into before the adoption of this Constitution shall be as valid against the Confederate States under this Constitution, as under the Provisional Government.

3. This Constitution, and the laws of the Confederate States made in pursuance thereof, and all treaties made, or which shall be made, under the authority of the Confederate States, shall be the supreme law of the land; and the judges in every State shall be bound thereby, anything in the constitution or laws of any State to the contrary notwithstanding.

4. The Senators and Representatives before mentioned, and the members of the several State Legislatures, and all executive and judicial officers, both of the Confederate States and of the several States, shall be bound by oath or affirmation to support this Constitution; but no religious test shall ever be required as a qualification to any office or public trust under the Confederate States.

5. The enumeration, in the Constitution, of certain rights shall not be construed to deny or disparage others retained by the people of the several States.

6. The powers not delegated to the Confederate States by the Constitution, nor prohibited by it to the States, are reserved to the States, respectively, or to the people thereof.[24]

[24]These provisions, now incorporated into the text, are recognizable as the Ninth and Tenth Amendments to the U.S. Constitution.

Article VII

1. The ratification of the conventions of five States shall be sufficient for the establishment of this Constitution between the States so ratifying the same.

2. When five States shall have ratified this Constitution,[25] in the manner before specified, the Congress under the Provisional Constitution shall prescribe the time for holding the election of President and Vice President; and for the meeting of the Electoral College; and for counting the votes, and inaugurating the President. They shall, also, prescribe the time for holding the first election of members of Congress under this Constitution, and the time for assembling the same. Until the assembling of such Congress, the Congress under the Provisional Constitution shall continue to exercise the legislative powers granted them; not extending beyond the time limited by the Constitution of the Provisional Government.

[25]The U.S. Constitution required the ratification of 9 of the 13 original states before it went into effect.

Adopted unanimously by the Congress of the Confederate States of South Carolina, Georgia, Florida, Alabama, Mississippi, Louisiana, and Texas, sitting in convention at the capitol, the city of Montgomery, Ala., on the eleventh day of March, in the year eighteen hundred and Sixty-one.

HOWELL COBB, President of the Congress.

Source: James D. Richardson, *A Compilation of the Messages and Papers of the Confederacy Including the Diplomatic Correspondence 1861–1865*. Nashville: United States Publishing Company, 1905.

Alexander H. Stevens's "Corner Stone" Speech

March 21, 1861

INTRODUCTION

Just two and a half weeks after Lincoln delivered his first inaugural address, Alexander H. Stephens (1812–1883), a former U.S. representative from Georgia who would serve as the vice president of the Confederate States of America, analyzes the proposed Confederate Constitution and the principles that it embodies. Although he lauds a number of innovations in the Constitution, he focuses on slavery because he believed it was the cornerstone of the new government.

But not to be tedious in enumerating the numerous changes for the better, allow me to allude to one other though last, not least. The new constitution has put at rest, forever, all the agitating questions relating to our peculiar institution African slavery as it exists amongst us the proper status of the negro in our form of civilization.[1] This was the immediate cause of the late rupture and present revolution. Jefferson in his forecast, had anticipated this, as the "rock upon which the old Union would split." He was right. What was conjecture with him, is now a realized fact. But whether he fully comprehended the great truth upon which that rock stood and stands, may be doubted. The prevailing ideas entertained by him and most of the leading statesmen at the time of the formation of the old constitution, were that the enslavement of the African was in violation of the laws of nature; that it was wrong in principle, socially, morally, and politically. It was an evil they knew not well how to deal with, but the general opinion of the men of that day was that, somehow or other in the order of Providence, the institution would be evanescent and pass away. This idea, though not incorporated in the constitution, was the prevailing idea at that time. The constitution, it is true, secured every essential guarantee to the institution while it should last, and hence no argument can be justly urged against the constitutional guarantees thus secured, because of the common sentiment of the day. Those ideas, however, were fundamentally wrong. They rested upon the assumption of the equality of races. This was an error.[2]

[1] Few Southerners were more explicit in acknowledging that the Southern sentiment had changed from believing that slavery was a necessary evil to arguing that it was a positive good.

[2] Stevens was similarly candid in stating his belief that the Founding idea (expressed in the Declaration of Independence) that all men and races were equal was profoundly mistaken.

It was a sandy foundation, and the government built upon it fell when the "storm came and the wind blew."

Our new government is founded upon exactly the opposite idea; its foundations are laid, its cornerstone rests, upon the great truth that the negro is not equal to the white man; that slavery subordination to the superior race is his natural and normal condition.[3] This, our new government, is the first, in the history of the world, based upon this great physical, philosophical, and moral truth. This truth has been slow in the process of its development, like all other truths in the various departments of science. It has been so even amongst us.

[3]While some have argued that slavery was not the central cause of the Civil War, Stevens is explicit in his belief that the split between North and South, and the very cornerstone of the Confederate Constitution, was based on Southern opposition to the view that whites and blacks were equal and that slavery was therefore immoral.

Source: Henry Cleveland, *Alexander H. Stephens, in Public and Private: With Letters and Speeches, before, during, and since the War* (Philadelphia, 1886), 717–729.

The First Confiscation Act

August 6, 1861

INTRODUCTION

The Fifth Amendment of the U.S. Constitution provides that the government can take private property only for "public use" and only if it provides "just compensation." Laws, however, sometimes permit police to confiscate property that is being used for illegal purposes as in transporting drugs or illegal alcohol. Moreover, during times of war, confiscation of property can become a weapon against those who are opposing the government.

This law, which Congress adopted and which President Lincoln signed early during the Civil War on August 6, 1861, authorized the president to confiscate the property used to wage war against the United States. This included the cargos of ships that violated Lincoln's embargo of Southern ports.

An Act to confiscate Property used for Insurrectionary Purposes.

Be it enacted by the Senate and House of Representatives of the United States of America in Congress assembled, That if, during the present or any future insurrection against the Government of the United States, after the President of the United States shall have declared, by proclamation, that the laws of the United States are opposed, and the execution thereof obstructed, by combinations too powerful to be suppressed by the ordinary course of judicial proceedings, or by the power vested in the marshals by law, any person or persons, his, her, or their agent, attorney, or employé, shall purchase or acquire, sell or give, any property of whatsoever kind or description, with intent to use or employ the same, or suffer the same to be used or employed, in aiding, abetting, or promoting such insurrection or resistance to the laws, or any person or persons engaged therein; or if any person or persons, being the owner or owners of any such property, shall knowingly use or employ, or consent to the use or employment of the same as aforesaid, all such property is hereby declared to be lawful subject of prize and capture wherever found; and it shall be the duty of the President of the United States to cause the same to be seized, confiscated, and condemned.

[1] This section of the law was most relevant to the confiscation of the cargoes of ships that violated the president's embargo orders.

SEC. 2. *And be it further enacted*, That such prizes and capture shall be condemned in the district or circuit court of the United States having jurisdiction of the amount, or in admiralty in any district in which the same may be seized, or into which they may be taken and proceedings first instituted.[1]

SEC. 3. *And be it further enacted*, That the Attorney-General, or any district attorney of the United States in which said property may at the time be, may institute the proceedings of condemnation, and in such case they shall be wholly for the benefit of the United States; or any person may file an information with such attorney, in which case the proceedings shall be for the use of such informer and the United States in equal parts.

SEC. 4. And be it further enacted, That whenever hereafter, during the present insurrection against the Government of the United States, any person claimed to be held to labor or service under the law of any State, shall be required or permitted by the person to whom such labor or service is claimed to be due, or by the lawful agent of such person, to take up arms against the United States, or shall be required or permitted by the person to whom such labor or service is claimed to be due, or his lawful agent, to work or to be employed in or upon any fort, navy yard, dock, armory, ship, entrenchment, or in any military or naval service whatsoever, against the Government and lawful authority of the United States, then, and in every such case, the person to whom such labor or service is claimed to be due shall forfeit his claim to such labor, any law of the State or of the United States to the contrary notwithstanding.[2] And whenever thereafter the person claiming such labor or service shall seek to enforce his claim, it shall be a full and sufficient answer to such claim that the person whose service or labor is claimed had been employed in hostile service against the Government of the United States, contrary to the provisions of this act.

[2] This provision was designed to discourage Southern use of slaves for military purposes by declaring that the Union would refuse to enforce the claims of their owners over them.

APPROVED, August 6, 1861.

CONCLUSION

Although the law gave union generals the right to confiscate such individuals, it did not necessarily make them free. In time, of course, Lincoln would declare in the Emancipation Proclamation that the Union would consider all slaves behind southern lines to be free. Later the Thirteenth Amendment abolished chattel slavery throughout the United States.

Source: *U.S. Statutes at Large, Treaties, and Proclamations of the United States of America*, vol. 12 (Boston, 1863), 319.

John C. Fremont's Order Freeing Slaves of Missouri Rebels

August 30, 1861

INTRODUCTION

John C. Freemont (1813–1890), often dubbed the Pathfinder, earned military fame during the Mexican-American War and was the unsuccessful Republican Party nominee for president in 1856. Assigned to command in Missouri, a border state with rival governments committed to the North and South, Freemont imposed military law and declared all slaves held by Southern sympathizers be freed.

Headquarters of the Western Department
St. Louis, August 30, 1861.

Circumstances, in my judgment, of sufficient urgency, render it necessary that the commanding general of this Department should assume the administrative powers of the State. Its disorganized condition, the helplessness of the civil authority, the total insecurity of life, and the devastation of property by bands of murderers and marauders, who infest nearly every county of the State, and avail themselves of the public misfortunes and the vicinity of a hostile force to gratify private and neighborhood vengeance, and who find an enemy wherever they find plunder, finally demand the severest measures to repress the daily increasing crimes and outrages which are driving off the inhabitants and ruining the State.

In this condition, the public safety and the success of our arms require unity of purpose, without let or hindrance, to the prompt administration of affairs.

In order, therefore, to suppress disorder, to maintain as far as now practicable the public peace, and to give security and protection to the persons and property of loyal citizens, I do hereby extend and declare established Martial Law throughout the State of Missouri.

The lines of the Army of Occupation in this State are for the present declared to extend from Leavenworth by way of the posts of Jefferson City, Rolla, and Ironton, to Cape Girardeau, on the Mississippi River.

All persons who shall be taken with arms in their hands within these lines shall be tried by Court-Martial, and if found guilty will be shot.

The property, real and personal, of all persons, in the State of Missouri, who shall take up arms against the United States, or who shall be directly proven to have taken an active part with their enemies in the field, is declared to be confiscated to the public use, and their Slaves, if any they have, are hereby declared Free men.[1]

All persons who shall be proven to have destroyed, after the publication of this order, railroad tracks, bridges, or telegraphs, shall suffer the extreme penalty of the law.

All persons engaged in Treasonable correspondence, in giving or procuring aid to the Enemies of the United States, in fomenting tumults, in disturbing the public tranquility by creating and circulating false reports or incendiary documents, are in their own interests warned that they are exposing themselves to sudden and severe punishment.

All persons who have been led away from their allegiance, are required to return to their homes forthwith; any such absence, without sufficient cause, will be held to be presumptive evidence against them.

The object of this declaration is to place in the hands of the Military authorities the power to give instantaneous effect to existing laws, and to supply such deficiencies as the conditions of War demand. But this is not intended to suspend the ordinary Tribunals of the Country, where the Law will be administered by Civil officers in the usual manner, and with their customary authority, while the same can be exercised.[2]

[1] Although Lincoln would eventually issue a similar order in the Emancipation Proclamation of January 1, 1863, he revoked this order because he believed it threatened the support of border states where slavery continued to be legal.

[2] In *Ex Parte Milligan* (1866), the U.S. Supreme Court would later rule that military courts had no authority to try nonmilitary personnel when civilian courts were still open.

The commanding general will labor vigilantly for the public Welfare, and in his efforts for their safety hopes to obtain not only the acquiescence, but the active support of the Loyal People of the Country.

J.C. FREMONT
Major-General Commanding.

CONCLUSION

Lincoln, who had reputedly said, "I hope to have God on my side, but I must have Kentucky," was quite concerned about the effect of this order, which Freemont had issued without consulting the President. Lincoln accordingly rescinded the command. Lincoln's action was one of the bases for Horace Greeley's later criticism of the President in "The Prayer of Twenty Millions."

Source: *The War of the Rebellion: A Compilation of the Official Records of the Union and Confederate Armies*, vol. 3. Washington, DC: Government Printing Office, 1881.

Julia Ward Howe's "The Battle Hymn of the Republic"

February 1862

INTRODUCTION

Julia Ward Howe (1819–1910), a Boston abolitionist, wrote this song after visiting an army camp outside Washington, DC, where her minister had suggested that she should write new lyrics to "John Brown's Body."

It was first published in the February 1862 issue of *The Atlantic Monthly*. When being sung, the chorus, in the second paragraph, is repeated after each stanza. Howe's hymn (a term that itself evokes ecclesiastical music) highlights the manner in which men and women of faith, from the time of the Pilgrims to the present, have often interpreted key events in American history like the American Founding, the Civil War, and the Cold War as part of a larger panorama that displays God's sovereignty.

Mine eyes have seen the glory of the coming of the Lord
He is trampling out the vintage where the grapes of wrath are stored,[1]
He has loosed the fateful lightening of His terrible swift sword[2]
His truth is marching on.

Glory! Glory! Hallelujah!
Glory! Glory! Hallelujah!
Glory! Glory! Hallelujah!
His truth is marching on.

I have seen Him in the watch-fires of a hundred circling camps
They have builded Him an altar in the evening dews and damps
I can read His righteous sentence by the dim and flaring lamps
His day is marching on.

I have read a fiery gospel writ in burnish'd rows of steel,
"As ye deal with my condemners, So with you my grace shall deal;"
Let the Hero, born of woman, crush the serpent with his heel[3]
Since God is marching on.

[1] Just as grapes yield juice when they are pressed, so too, human bodies bleed when they are wounded. Howe appears to have taken this analogy from the Biblical book of Isaiah, Chapter 63.

[2] Howe interprets the war as God's judgment on the nation for slavery and expects the war to advance the truth of human equality.

[3] In Genesis 3:15, after discovering that Adam and Eve had disobeyed His instructions and eaten fruit from the forbidden tree, God pronounced judgment on the serpent (Satan) who led them into temptation by pronouncing that "I will put enmity between thee and the woman, and between they seed and her seed; it shall bruise thy head, and thou shalt bruise his heel." Christians interpret this as a prophesy that while Satan will injure the Messiah (the one Howe identifies as "the Hero, born of woman"), the Messiah will ultimately crush the serpent.

He has sounded forth the trumpet that shall never call retreat
He is sifting out the hearts of men before His judgment-seat
Oh, be swift, my soul, to answer Him! be jubilant, my feet!
Our God is marching on.

In the beauty of the lilies Christ was born across the sea,
With a glory in His bosom that transfigures you and me:
As He died to make men holy, let us die to make men free,[4]
While God is marching on.

Source: *Atlantic Monthly*, IX, LII, 10, February 1862.

[4]Howe associates the nation's quest for freedom with Jesus's quest for holiness and undoubtedly expects that freedom will convert, or transform, the nation just as she believes that Jesus converts individual hearts.

An Act for the Release of Certain Persons Held to Service or Labor in the District of Columbia

April 16, 1862

INTRODUCTION

The existence of slavery and slave markets in the nation's capital, where foreign embassies were located, had long been an embarrassment. This law, which preceded both the Emancipation Proclamation and the Thirteenth Amendment, provided for compensated emancipation of such individuals.

Be it enacted by the Senate and House of Representatives of the United States of America in Congress assembled, That all persons held to service or labor within the District of Columbia by reason of African descent are hereby discharged and freed of and from all claim to such service or labor; and from and after the passage of this act neither slavery nor involuntary servitude, except for crime, whereof the party shall be duly convicted, shall hereafter exist in said District.

Sec. 2. *And be it further enacted,* That all persons loyal to the United States, holding claims to service or labor against persons discharged therefrom by this act, may, within ninety days from the passage thereof, but not thereafter, present to the commissioners hereinafter mentioned their respective statements or petitions in writing, verified by oath or affirmation, setting forth the names, ages, and personal description of such persons, the manner in which said petitioners acquired such claim, and any facts touching the value thereof, and declaring his allegiance to the Government of the United States, and that he has not borne arms against the United States during the present rebellion, nor in any way given aid or comfort thereto:[1] *Provided,* That the oath of the party to the petition shall not be evidence of the facts therein stated.

[1] Compensation was to be provided only for those within the capital who remained loyal to the Union cause.

Sec. 3. *And be it further enacted,* That the President of the United States, with the advice and consent of the Senate, shall appoint three commissioners, residents of the District of Columbia, any two of

49

whom shall have power to act, who shall receive the petitions above mentioned, and who shall investigate and determine the validity and value of the claims therein presented, as aforesaid, and appraise and apportion, under the proviso hereto annexed, the value in money of the several claims by them found to be valid: *Provided, however,* That the entire sum so appraised and apportioned shall not exceed in the aggregate an amount equal to three hundred dollars for each person shown to have been so held by lawful claim: *And provided, further,* That no claim shall be allowed for any slave or slaves brought into said District after the passage of this act, nor for any slave claimed by any person who has borne arms against the Government of the United States in the present rebellion, or in any way given aid or comfort thereto, or which originates in or by virtue of any transfer heretofore made, or which shall hereafter be made by any person who has in any manner aided or sustained the rebellion against the Government of the United States.[2]

Sec. 4. *And be it further enacted,* That said commissioners shall, within nine months from the passage of this act, make a full and final report of their proceedings, findings, and appraisement, and shall deliver the same to the Secretary of the Treasury, which report shall be deemed and taken to be conclusive in all respects, except as hereinafter provided; and the Secretary of the Treasury shall, with like exception, cause the amounts so apportioned to said claims to be paid from the Treasury of the United States to the parties found by said report to be entitled thereto as aforesaid, and the same shall be received in full and complete compensation: *Provided,* That in cases where petitions may be filed presenting conflicting claims, or setting up liens, said commissioners shall so specify in said report, and payment shall not be made according to the award of said commissioners until a period of sixty days shall have elapsed, during which time any petitioner claiming an interest in the particular amount may file a bill in equity in the Circuit Court of the District of Columbia, making all other claimants defendants thereto, setting forth the proceedings in such case before said commissioners and their actions therein, and praying that the party to whom payment has been awarded may be enjoined from receiving the same; and if said court shall grant such provisional order, a copy thereof may, on motion of said complainant, be served upon the Secretary of the Treasury, who shall thereupon cause the said amount of money to be paid into said court, subject to its orders and final decree, which payment shall be in full and complete compensation, as in other cases.

[2] This provision was designed to discourage individuals (especially Southerners) from bringing their slaves to the district with the expectation that the government would buy them.

Sec. 5. *And be it further enacted*, That said commissioners shall hold their sessions in the city of Washington, at such place and times as the President of the United States may direct, of which they shall give due and public notice. They shall have power to subpoena and compel the attendance of witnesses, and to receive testimony and enforce its production, as in civil cases before courts of justice, without the exclusion of any witness on account of color; and they may summon before them the persons making claim to service or labor, and examine them under oath; and they may also, for purposes of identification and appraisement, call before them the persons so claimed.[3] Said commissioners shall appoint a clerk, who shall keep files and [a] complete record of all proceedings before them, who shall have power to administer oaths and affirmations in said proceedings, and who shall issue all lawful process by them ordered. The Marshal of the District of Columbia shall personally, or by deputy, attend upon the sessions of said commissioners, and shall execute the process issued by said clerk.

Sec. 6. *And be it further enacted*, That said commissioners shall receive in compensation for their services the sum of two thousand dollars each, to be paid upon the filing of their report; that said clerk shall receive for his services the sum of two hundred dollars per month; that said marshal shall receive such fees as are allowed by law for similar services performed by him in the Circuit Court of the District of Columbia; that the Secretary of the Treasury shall cause all other reasonable expenses of said commission to be audited and allowed, and that said compensation, fees, and expenses shall be paid from the Treasury of the United States.

Sec. 7. *And be it further enacted*, That for the purpose of carrying this act into effect there is hereby appropriated, out of any money in the Treasury not otherwise appropriated, a sum not exceeding one million of dollars.

Sec. 8. *And be it further enacted*, That any person or persons who shall kidnap, or in any manner transport or procure to be taken out of said District, any person or persons discharged and freed by the provisions of this act, or any free person or persons with intent to re-enslave or sell such person or person into slavery, or shall re-enslave any of said freed persons, the person of persons so offending shall be deemed guilty of a felony, and on conviction thereof in any court of competent jurisdiction in said District, shall be imprisoned in the penitentiary not less than five nor more than twenty years.

[3]These are powers, typical of a court or congressional committee, that would allow the commissioners to gather information and aid the quest for justice. Notably, they permitted African Americans to testify.

Sec. 9. *And be it further enacted*, That within twenty days, or within such further time as the commissioners herein provided for shall limit, after the passage of this act, a statement in writing or schedule shall be filed with the clerk of the Circuit court for the District of Columbia, by the several owners or claimants to the services of the persons made free or manumitted by this act, setting forth the names, ages, sex, and particular description of such persons, severally; and the said clerk shall receive and record, in a book by him to be provided and kept for that purpose, the said statements or schedules on receiving fifty cents each therefor, and no claim shall be allowed to any claimant or owner who shall neglect this requirement.

Sec. 10. *And be it further enacted*, That the said clerk and his successors in office shall, from time to time, on demand, and on receiving twenty-five cents therefor, prepare, sign, and deliver to each person made free or manumitted by this act, a certificate under the seal of said court, setting out the name, age, and description of such person, and stating that such person was duly manumitted and set free by this act.[4]

[4]These certificates were designed to provide freedmen with evidence of their new status.

Sec. 11. *And be it further enacted*, That the sum of one hundred thousand dollars, out of any money in the Treasury not otherwise appropriated, is hereby appropriated, to be expended under the direction of the President of the United States, to aid in the colonization and settlement of such free persons of African descent now residing in said District, including those to be liberated by this act, as may desire to emigrate to the Republics of Hayti [Haiti] or Liberia, or such other country beyond the limits of the United States as the President may determine:[5] *Provided*, The expenditure for this purpose shall not exceed one hundred dollars for each emigrant.

[5]American whites, including Lincoln, had long adhered to the notion that because of the difficulties of integrating former slaves into a white-dominated society it might be better to provide for their relocation in Africa or other black-dominated societies. Fortunately, this law did not require acceptance of such relocation as a condition of emancipation.

Sec. 12. *And be it further enacted*, That all acts of Congress and all laws of the State of Maryland in force in said District, and all ordinances of the cities of Washington and Georgetown, inconsistent with the provisions of this act, are hereby repealed.

Approved, April 16, 1862.

Source: 37th Cong., 2d Sess., 54, 1862.

The Homestead Act

May 20, 1862

INTRODUCTION

As America pushed Native Americans westward, it negotiated treaties giving it title to the land. The government then sold this land to settlers to encourage western migration and settlement. This law made cheap parcels of land available to individuals who agreed to cultivate it. It applied not only to those who were already citizens but also to those who stated their intention of becoming so.

An Act to secure Homesteads to actual Settlers[1] on the Public Domain.

Be it enacted by the Senate and House of Representatives of the United States of America in Congress assembled, That any person who is the head of a family, or who has arrived at the age of twenty-one years, and is a citizen of the United States, or who shall have filed his declaration of intention to become such,[2] as required by the naturalization laws of the United States, and who has never borne arms against the United States Government or given aid and comfort to its enemies, shall, from and after the first January, eighteen hundred and sixty-three, be entitled to enter one quarter section or a less quantity of unappropriated public lands, upon which said person may have filed a preemption claim, or which may, at the time the application is made, be subject to preemption at one dollar and twenty-five cents, or less, per acre; or eighty acres or less of such unappropriated lands, at two dollars and fifty cents per acre, to be located in a body, in conformity to the legal subdivisions of the public lands, and after the same shall have been surveyed: *Provided,* That any person owning and residing on land may, under the provisions of this act, enter other land lying contiguous to his or her said land, which shall not, with the land so already owned and occupied, exceed in the aggregate one hundred and sixty acres.[3]

[1] This law was clearly designed to promote cultivation of land rather than speculation in land values.

[2] The law applied both to citizens and to newly arrived immigrants who planned to become citizens. Although it seemed to extend to both men and women, it is doubtful that many women of the day would have been considered to be heads of families.

[3] This clause sought to prevent the accumulation of large landholdings.

Sec. 2. *And be it further enacted,* That the person applying for the benefit of this act shall, upon application to the register of the land office in which he or she is about to make such entry, make affidavit before the said register or receiver that he or she is the head of a family, or is twenty-one years or more of age, or shall have performed service in the army or navy of the United States, and that he has never borne arms against the Government of the United States or given aid and comfort to its enemies, and that such application is made for his or her exclusive use and benefit, and that said entry is made for the purpose of actual settlement and cultivation, and not either directly or indirectly for the use of benefit of any other person or persons whomsoever;[4] and upon filing the said affidavit with the register or receiver, and on payment of ten dollars, he or she shall thereupon be permitted to enter the quantity of land specified: *Provided, however,* That no certificate shall be given or patent issued therefore until the expiration of five years from the date of such entry; and if, at the expiration of such time, or at any time within two years thereafter, the person making such entry; or, if he be dead, his widow; or in case of her death, his heirs or devisee; or in case of a widow making such entry, her heirs or devisee, in case of her death; shall prove by two credible witnesses that he, she, or they have resided upon or cultivated the same for the term of five years immediately succeeding the time of filing the affidavit aforesaid, and shall make affidavit that no part of said land has been alienated, and that he has borne true allegiance to the Government of the United States; then, in such case, he, she, or they, if at that time a citizen of the United States, shall be entitled to a patent, as in other cases provided for by law: *And provided, further,* That in case of the death of both father and mother, leaving an infant child, or children, under twenty-one years of age, the right and fee shall ensure to the benefit of said infant child or children; and the executor, administrator, or guardian may, at any time within two years after the death of the surviving parent, and in accordance with the laws of the State in which such children for the time being have their domicile, sell said land for the benefit of said infants, but for no other purpose; and the purchaser shall acquire the absolute title by the purchase, and be entitled to a patent from the United States, on payment of the office fees and sum of money herein specified.

Sec. 3. *And be it further enacted,* That the register of the land office shall note all such applications on the tract books and plats of his

[4] This provision was designed to exclude individuals who were supporting the Confederacy or who were filing claims on behalf of large landowners.

office, and keep a register of all such entries, and make return thereof to the General Land Office, together with the proof upon which they have been founded.

Sec. 4. *And be it further enacted*, That no lands acquired under the provisions of this act shall in any event become liable to the satisfaction of any debt or debts contracted prior to the issuing of the patent therefore.

Sec. 5. *And be if further enacted*, That if, at any time after the filing of the affidavit, as required in the second section of this act, and before the expiration of the five years aforesaid, it shall be proven after due notice to the settler, to the satisfaction of the register of the land office, that the person having filed such affidavit shall have actually changed his or her residence, or abandoned the said land for more than six months at any time, then and in that event the land so entered shall revert to the government.

Sec. 6. *And be it further enacted*, That no individual shall be permitted to acquire title to more than one quarter section under the provisions of this act;[5] and that the Commissioner of the General Land Office is hereby required to prepare and issue such rules and regulations, consistent with this act, as shall be necessary and proper to carry its provisions into effect; and that the registers and receivers of the several land offices shall be entitled to receive the same compensation for any lands entered under the provisions of this act that they are now entitled to receive when the same quantity of land is entered with money, one half to be paid by the person making the application at the time of so doing, and the other half on the issue of the certificate by the person to whom it may be issued; but this shall not be construed to enlarge the maximum of compensation now prescribed by law for any register or receiver: *Provided*, That nothing contained in this act shall be so construed as to impair or interfere in any manner whatever with existing preemption rights; *And provided, further*, That all persons who may have filed their application for a preemption right prior to the passage of this act, shall be entitled to all privileges of this act.

Provided, further, That no person who has served, or may hereafter serve, for a period of not less than fourteen days in the army or navy of the United States, either regular or volunteers under the laws

[5] The law again reiterated its intention to distribute land among multiple landowners rather than allowing some to buy multiple plots.

thereof, during the existence of an actual war, domestic or foreign, shall be deprived of the benefits of this act on account of not having attained the age of twenty-one years.

Sec. 7. *And be it further enacted,* That the fifth section of the act entitled "An act in addition to an act more effectually to provide for the punishment of certain crimes against the United States, and for other purposes," approved the third of March, in the year eighteen hundred and fifty-seven, shall extend to all oaths, affirmations, and affidavits, required or authorized by this act.

Sec. 8. *And be it further enacted,* That nothing in this act shall be so construed as to prevent any person who has availed him or herself of the benefits of the first section of this act, from paying the minimum price, or the price to which the same may have graduated, for the quantity of land so entered at any time before the expiration of the five years, and obtaining a patent therefore from the government, as in other cases provided by law, on making proof of settlement and cultivation as provided by existing laws granting preemption rights.

APPROVED, May 20, 1862.

Source: Act of May 20, 1862 (Homestead Act), Pub. L. No. 37–64 (May 20, 1862), RG 11, General Records of the U.S. Government, National Archives.

The Pacific Railway Act

July 1, 1862

INTRODUCTION

The United States is composed of a vast land whose people are bound together by beliefs, language, and intermarriage as well as by transportation and commerce. The Constitution sought to promote interstate and foreign commerce and also authorized the construction of "post roads" to facilitate the mail. Although privately owned firms have built most channels of transportation, the government has supported the construction of canals and (in the twentieth and twenty-first centuries) interstate highways and airports. Railroads and steamships were the earliest mechanisms of fast and efficient transportation. Even as the Civil War continued, Congress paused to provide support for a railroad that would link the East and West. The first such line was completed at Promontory, Utah, on May 10, 1869. Lincoln, a former member of the Whig Party, had been a vigorous champion of internal improvements before becoming president.

An Act to aid in the Construction of a Railroad and Telegraph Line from the Missouri River to the Pacific Ocean, and to secure to the Government the Use of the same for Postal, Military, and Other Purposes.[1]

[1] The heading of the law, with its references to mail delivery and military preparedness, is designed to point to its constitutional justifications.

Be it enacted by the Senate and House of Representatives of the United States of America in Congress assembled, That Walter S. Burgess, William P. Blodget . . . [the law lists numerous other names] together with commissioners to be appointed by the Secretary of the Interior, and all persons who shall or may be associated with them, and their successors, are hereby created and erected into a body corporate and politic in deed and in law, by the name, style, and title of "The Union Pacific Railroad Company"; and by that name shall have perpetual succession, and shall be able to sue and to be sued, plead and be impleaded, defend and be defended, in all courts of law and equity within the United States, and may make and have a common seal; and the said corporation is hereby authorized and empowered to layout, locate, construct, furnish, maintain, and enjoy a continuous railroad and telegraph, with the appurtenances, from a point on the one hundredth meridian of longitude west from Greenwich, between the south margin of the valley of the Republican River and the north margin of the valley of the Platte River, in the Territory of Nebraska, to the western boundary of Nevada Territory, upon the route and terms hereinafter provided, and is hereby vested with all the powers, privileges, and immunities necessary to carry into effect the purposes of this act as herein set forth. The capital stock of said company shall consist of one hundred thousand shares of one thousand dollars each, which shall be subscribed for and held in not more than two hundred shares by anyone person, and shall be transferable in such manner as the by-laws of said corporation shall provide. The persons hereinbefore named, together with those to be appointed by the Secretary of the Interior, are hereby constituted and appointed commissioners, and such body shall be called the Board of Commissioners of the Union Pacific Railroad and Telegraph Company, and twenty-five shall constitute a quorum for the transaction of business. . . . [This section further details rules relative to meetings of the commission.]

SEC. 2. And be it further enacted, That the right of way through the public lands be, and the same is hereby, granted to said company for the construction of said railroad and telegraph line; and the right, power, and authority is hereby given to said company to take from the public lands adjacent to the line of said road, earth, stone, timber, and other materials for the construction thereof; said right of way is granted to said railroad to the extent of two hundred feet in width on each side of said railroad where it may pass over the public lands, including all necessary grounds for stations, buildings, workshops, and depots, machine shops, switches, side tracks, turntables, and, water stations. The United States shall extinguish as rapidly as may be the Indian titles to all lands falling under the operation of this act and required for the said right of way and; grants hereinafter made.[2]

SEC 3. And be it further enacted, That there be, and is hereby, granted to the said company, for the purpose of aiding in the construction, of said railroad and telegraph line, and to secure the safe and speedy transportation of the mails, troops, munitions of war, and public stores thereon, every alternate section of public land,[3] designated by odd numbers, to the amount of five alternate sections per mile on each side of said railroad, on the line thereof, and within the limits often miles on each side of said road, not sold, reserved, or otherwise disposed of by the United States, and to

[2] Court decisions have entrusted relations with Native-American Indian tribes to the national government rather than to the states.

[3] The national government, continuing to profit from its monopoly of public lands, sought to subsidize private construction by giving generous portions of this land to private companies for construction purposes.

which a preemption or homestead claim may not have attached, at the time the line of said road is definitely fixed: Provided, That all mineral lands shall be excepted from the operation of this act; but where the same shall contain timber, the timber thereon is hereby granted to said company. And all such lands, so granted by this section, which shall not be sold or disposed of by said company within three years after the entire road shall have been completed, shall be subject to settlement and preemption, like other lands, at a price not exceeding one dollar and twenty-five cents per acre, to be paid to said company.

SEC. 4. [Provided for conveyance of property to company upon completion and inspection of each 40 miles of construction.]

SEC. 5. And be it further enacted, That for the purposes herein mentioned the Secretary of the Treasury shall, upon the certificate in writing of said commissioners of the completion and equipment of forty consecutive miles of said railroad and telegraph, in accordance with the provisions of this act, issue to said company bonds of the United States of one thousand dollars each, payable in thirty years after date, bearing six per centum per annum interest (said interest payable semi-annually,) which interest may be paid in United States treasury notes or any other money or currency which the United States have or shall declare lawful money and a legal tender, to the amount of sixteen of said bonds per mile for such section of forty miles; and to secure the repayment to the United States, as hereinafter provided, of the amount of said bonds so issued and delivered to said company. . . .

SEC. 11. And be it further enacted, That for three hundred miles of said road most mountainous and difficult of construction, to wit: one hundred and fifty miles westwardly from the eastern base of the Rocky Mountains, and one hundred and fifty miles eastwardly from the western base of the Sierra Nevada mountains, said points to be fixed by the President of the United States, the bonds to be issued to aid in the construction thereof shall be treble the number per mile hereinbefore provided,[4] and the same shall be issued, and the lands herein granted be set apart, upon the construction of every twenty miles thereof, upon the certificate of the commissioners as aforesaid that twenty consecutive miles of the same are completed and between the sections last named of one hundred and fifty miles

[4]Recognizing that some areas would provide more obstacles to construction than others, the law provided more generous land grants for such terrain.

each, the bonds to be issued to aid in the construction thereof shall be double the number per mile first mentioned, and the same shall be issued, and the lands herein granted be set apart, upon the construction of every twenty miles thereof, upon the certificate of the commissioners as aforesaid that twenty consecutive miles of the same are completed: Provided, That no more than fifty thousand of said bonds shall be issued under this act to aid in constructing the main line of said railroad and telegraph.

SEC. 12. And be it further enacted, That whenever the route of said railroad shall cross the boundary of any State or Territory, or said meridian of longitude, the two companies meeting or uniting there shall agree upon its location at that point, with reference to the most direct and practicable through route, and in case of difference between them as to said location the President of the United States shall determine the said location. . . .

SEC. 13. And be it further enacted, That the Hannibal and Saint Joseph Railroad Company of Missouri may extend its roads from Saint Joseph, via Atchison, to connect and unite with the road through Kansas, upon filing its assent to the provisions of this act, upon the same terms and conditions, in all respects for one hundred miles in length next to the Missouri River, as are provided in this act for the construction of the railroad and telegraph line first mentioned, and may for this purpose use any railroad charter which has been or may be granted by the legislature of Kansas. . . .

SEC. 14. And be it further enacted, That the said Union Pacific Railroad Company is hereby authorized and required to construct a single line of railroad and telegraph from a point on the western boundary of the State of Iowa, to be fixed by the President of the United States, upon the most direct and practicable route, to be subject to his approval, so as to form a connection with the lines of said company at some point on the one hundredth meridian of longitude aforesaid, . . . from the point of commencement on the western boundary of the State of Iowa, upon the same terms and SEC. 15. And be it further enacted, That any other railroad company now incorporated, or hereafter to be incorporated, shall have the right to connect their road with the road and branches provided for by this act, at such places and upon such just and equitable terms as the President of the United States may prescribe. Wherever the word company is used in this act it shall be construed to embrace the words their associates, successors, and assigns, the same as if the words had been properly added thereto.

SEC. 16. And be it further enacted, That at any time after the passage of this act all of the railroad companies named herein, and assenting hereto, or any two or more of them, are authorized to form themselves into one consolidated company; notice of such consolidation, in writing, shall be filed in the Department of the Interior, and such consolidated company shall thereafter proceed to construct said railroad and branches and telegraph line upon the terms and conditions provided in this act.[5]

SEC. 17. And be it further enacted, That in case said company or companies shall fail to comply with the terms and conditions of this act, by not completing said road and telegraph and branches within a reasonable time, or by not keeping the same in repair and use, but shall permit the same, for an unreasonable time, to remain unfinished, or out of repair, and unfit for use, Congress may pass any act to insure the speedy completion of said road and branches, or put the same in repair and use, and may direct the income of said railroad and telegraph line to be thereafter devoted to the use of the United States, to repay all such expenditures caused by the default and neglect of such company or companies. . . .

SEC. 18. And be it further enacted, That whenever it appears that the net earnings of the entire road and telegraph, including the amount allowed for services rendered for the United States, after deducting all, expenditures, including repairs, and the furnishing, running, and managing of said road, shall exceed ten per centum upon its cost, exclusive of the five per centum to be paid to the United States, Congress may reduce the rates of fare thereon, if unreasonable in amount, and may fix and establish the same by law.[6] And the better to accomplish the object of this act, namely, to promote the public interest and welfare by the construction of said railroad and telegraph line, and keeping the same in working order, and to secure to the government at all times (but particularly in time of war) the use and benefits of the same for postal, military and other purposes, Congress may, at any time, having due regard for the rights of said companies named herein, add to, alter, amend, or repeal this act.

[5]Americans have long been concerned about the power of monopolies and small groups of companies that exert such control over the market that they can raise prices.

[6]Federal subsidies often bring federal regulations, in this case designed to limit the profits of companies that received governmental land grants.

SEC. 19. And be it further enacted, That the several railroad companies herein named are authorized to enter into an arrangement with the Pacific Telegraph Company, the Overland Telegraph Company, and the California State Telegraph Company, so that the present line of telegraph between the Missouri River and San Francisco may be moved upon or along the line of said railroad and branches as fast as said roads and branches are built; and if said arrangement be entered into and the transfer of said telegraph line be made in accordance therewith to the line of said railroad and branches, such transfer shall, for all purposes of this act, be held and considered a fulfillment on the part of said railroad companies of the provisions of this act in regard to the construction of said line of telegraph. And, in case of disagreement, said telegraph companies are authorized to remove their line of telegraph along and upon the line of railroad herein contemplated without prejudice to the rights of said railroad companies named herein.

APPROVED, July 1, 1862.

Source: Pacific Railway Act (July 1, 1862), Enrolled Acts and Resolutions of Congress, 1789–1996, RG 11, General Records of the U.S. Government, National Archives.

The Morrill Act

July 2, 1862

INTRODUCTION

The existence of the Civil War did not mean that all other matters ceased. In the Northwest Ordinance of 1787, Congress had designated land for the support of education, but the Morrill Act (originally introduced in the administration of President James Buchanan who vetoed it) addressed itself specifically to higher education. The bill had strong Northern support but weak support among Southerners who thought that it exceeded national powers.

An Act Donating Public Lands to the several States and Territories which may provide Colleges for the Benefit of Agriculture and Mechanic Arts.[1]

Be it enacted by the Senate and House of Representatives of the United States of America in Congress assembled, That there be granted to the several States, for the purposes hereinafter mentioned, an amount of public land, to be apportioned to each State a quantity equal to thirty thousand acres for each senator and representative in Congress to which the States are respectively entitled[2] by the apportionment under the census of eighteen hundred and sixty: *Provided*, That no mineral lands shall be selected or purchased under the provisions of this Act.

SEC. 2. *And be it further enacted*, That the land aforesaid, after being surveyed, shall be apportioned to the several States[3] in sections or subdivisions of sections, not less than one quarter of a section; and whenever there are public lands in a State subject to sale at private entry at one dollar and twenty-five cents per acre, the quantity to which said State shall be entitled shall be selected from such lands within the limits of such State, and the Secretary of the Interior is hereby directed to issue to each of the States in which there is not the quantity of public lands subject to sale at private entry at one dollar and twenty-five cents per acre, to which said State may be

[1] Prior to the adoption of this law, most colleges within the university were chiefly open to elites and tended to emphasize liberal arts and sciences. This law was aimed at more practical skills. Its sponsor, Vermont Congressman Justin S. Morrill, who had favored tariffs, which had largely benefited Northern states, saw this as a way to benefit states that depended more heavily on agriculture than on trade.

[2] One of America's greatest early assets was the large land area that it encompassed. Much like taxes on modern oil and gas extraction, such lands provided funding for public projects.

[3] The law was designed to provide public lands in loyal states throughout the nation.

entitled under the provisions of this act, land scrip to the amount in acres for the deficiency of its distributive share: said scrip to be sold by said States and the proceeds thereof applied to the uses and purposes prescribed in this act, and for no other use or purpose whatsoever: *Provided,* That in no case shall any State to which land scrip may thus be issued be allowed to locate the same within the limits of any other State, or of any Territory of the United States, but their assignees may thus locate said land scrip upon any of the unappropriated lands of the United States subject to sale at private entry at one dollar and twenty-five cents, or less, per acre: *And provided, further,* That not more than one million acres shall be located by such assignees in any one of the States: *And provided, further,* That no such location shall be made before one year from the passage of this Act.

SEC. 3. *And be it further enacted,* That all the expenses of management, superintendence, and taxes from date of selection of said lands, previous to their sales, and all expenses incurred in the management and disbursement of the moneys which may be received therefrom, shall be paid by the States to which they may belong, out of the Treasury of said States, so that the entire proceeds of the sale of said lands shall be applied without any diminution whatever to the purposes hereinafter mentioned.

SEC. 4. And be it further enacted, That all moneys derived from the sale of the lands aforesaid by the States to which the lands are apportioned, and from the sales of land scrip hereinbefore provided for, shall be invested in stocks of the United States, or of the States, or some other safe stocks, yielding not less than five per centum upon the par value of said stocks; and that the moneys so invested shall constitute a perpetual fund, the capital of which shall remain forever undiminished, (except so far as may be provided in section fifth of this act,) and the interest of which shall be inviolably appropriated, by each State which may take and claim the benefit of this act, to the endowment, support, and maintenance of at least one college where the leading object shall be, without excluding other scientific and classical studies, and including military tactics, to teach such branches of learning as are related to agriculture and the mechanic arts, in such manner as the legislatures of the States may respectively prescribe, in order to promote the liberal and practical education of the industrial classes in the several pursuits and professions in life.[4]

[4]Whereas most existing institutions were devoted chiefly to the study of the liberal arts, these land-grant institutions were to be chiefly dedicated to practical subjects like agriculture and mechanical arts.

SEC. 5. *And be it further enacted*, That the grant of land and land scrip hereby authorized shall be made on the following conditions, to which, as well as to the provisions hereinbefore contained, the previous assent of the several States shall be signified by legislative acts:

First. If any portion of the fund invested, as provided by the foregoing section, or any portion of the interest thereon, shall, by any action or contingency, be diminished or lost, it shall be replaced by the State to which it belongs, so that the capital of the fund shall remain forever undiminished; and the annual interest shall be regularly applied without diminution to the purposes mentioned in the fourth section of this act, except that a sum, not exceeding ten per centum upon the amount received by any State under the provisions of this act may be expended for the purchase of lands for sites or experimental farms, whenever authorized by the respective legislatures of said States.

Second. No portion of said fund, nor the interest thereon, shall be applied, directly or indirectly, under any pretence whatever, to the purchase, erection, preservation, or repair of any building or buildings.

Third. Any State which may take and claim the benefit of the provisions of this act shall provide, within five years from the time of its acceptance as provided in subdivision seven of this section, at least not less than one college, as described in the fourth section of this act, or the grant to such State shall cease; and said State shall be bound to pay the United States the amount received of any lands previously sold; and that the title to purchasers under the State shall be valid.

Fourth. An annual report shall be made regarding the progress of each college, recording any improvements and experiments made, with their cost and results, and such other matters, including State industrial and economical statistics, as may be supposed useful; one copy of which shall be transmitted by mail [free] by each, to all the other colleges which may be endowed under the provisions of this act, and also one copy to the Secretary of the Interior.

Fifth. When lands shall be selected from those which have been raised to double the minimum price, in consequence of railroad grants, they shall be computed to the States at the maximum price, and the number of acres proportionally diminished.

Sixth. No State while in a condition of rebellion or insurrection against the government of the United States shall be entitled to the benefit of this act.[5]

Seventh. No State shall be entitled to the benefits of this act unless it shall express its acceptance thereof by its legislature within three years from July 23, 1866:

Provided, That when any Territory shall become a State and be admitted into the Union, such new State shall be entitled to the benefits of the said act of July two, eighteen hundred and sixty-two, by expressing the acceptance therein required within three years from the date of its admission into the Union, and providing the college or colleges within five years after such acceptance, as prescribed in this act.

SEC. 6. And be it further enacted, That land scrip issued under the provisions of this act shall not be subject to location until after the first day of January, one thousand eight hundred and sixty-three.

SEC. 7. *And be it further enacted*, That the land officers shall receive the same fees for locating land scrip issued under the provisions of this act as is now allowed for the location of military bounty land warrants under existing laws: *Provided*, their maximum compensation shall not be thereby increased.

SEC. 8. *And be it further enacted*, That the Governors of the several States to which scrip shall be issued under this act shall be required to report annually to Congress all sales made of such scrip until the whole shall be disposed of, the amount received for the same, and what appropriation has been made of the proceeds.

CONCLUSION

Although many initially floundered, in time the land-grant universities became beacons of learning, especially relative to agricultural and mechanical disciplines, throughout the nation.

Source: Pub. L. No. 37–108, which established land-grant colleges (July 2, 1862), Enrolled Acts and Resolutions of Congress, 1789–1996, RG 11, General Records of the U.S. Government, National Archives.

The Second Confiscation Act

July 17, 1862

INTRODUCTION

In the eyes of Northerners, those who took up arms against the United States were committing treason, which the Constitution defines as giving aid and comfort to the enemies of the United States. This is the second of two laws (the first was adopted in 1861) in which Congress provided for the confiscation of the property of those who served in the confederate government or led confederate armies. As later criticisms by Horace Greeley would soon show, President Lincoln was tepid toward the first of these laws because he feared that it might result in the loss of border states that still adhered to the Union but still allowed slavery. The law was not enforceable in areas not controlled by federal forces. This law was an obvious precursor to the Emancipation Proclamation and to the Thirteenth Amendment, which abolished slavery. Only rarely did the North actually confiscate homes and plantations, although Northern soldiers did take enemy crops and free the slaves of those who worked for them.

An Act to suppress Insurrection, to punish Treason and Rebellion, to seize and confiscate the Property of Rebels, and for other Purposes.

Be it enacted by the Senate and House of Representatives of the United States of America in Congress assembled, That every person who shall hereafter commit the crime of treason against the United States, and shall be adjudged guilty thereof, shall suffer death, and all his slaves, if any, shall be declared and made free; or, at the discretion of the court, he shall be imprisoned for not less than five years and fined not less than ten thousand dollars, and all his slaves, if any, shall be declared and made free; said fine shall be levied and collected on any or all of the property, real and personal, excluding slaves, of which the said person so convicted was the owner at the time of committing the said crime, any sale or conveyance to the contrary notwithstanding.

SEC. 2. *And be it further enacted,* That if any person shall hereafter incite, set on foot, assist, or engage in any rebellion or insurrection against the authority of the United States, or the laws thereof, or shall give aid or comfort thereto, or shall engage in, or give aid and comfort to, any such existing rebellion or insurrection, and be convicted thereof, such person shall be punished by imprisonment for a period not exceeding ten years, or by a fine not exceeding ten thousand dollars, and by the liberation of all his slaves, if any he have; or by both of said punishments, at the discretion of the court.

SEC. 3. *And be it further enacted*, That every person guilty of either of the offences described in this act shall be forever incapable and disqualified to hold any office under the United States.[1]

SEC. 4. *And be it further enacted*, That this act shall not be construed in any way to affect or alter the prosecution, conviction, or punishment of any person or persons guilty of treason against the United States before the passage of this act, unless such person is convicted under this act.

SEC. 5. *And be it further enacted*, That, to insure the speedy termination of the present rebellion, it shall be the duty of the President of the United States to cause the seizure of all the estate and property, money, stocks, credits, and effects of the persons hereinafter named in this section, and to apply and use the same and the proceeds thereof for the support of the army of the United States, that is to say:[2]

First. Of any person hereafter acting as an officer of the army or navy of the rebels in arms against the government of the United States.

Secondly. Of any person hereafter acting as President, Vice-President, member of Congress, judge of any court, cabinet officer, foreign minister, commissioner or consul of the so-called confederate states of America.

Thirdly. Of any person acting as governor of a state, member of a convention or legislature, or judge of any court of any of the so-called confederate states of America.

Fourthly. Of any person who, having held an office of honor, trust, or profit in the United States, shall hereafter hold an office in the so-called confederate states of America.

[1] This is a precursor to Section 3 of the Fourteenth Amendment, which prohibited those who had so served from assuming federal office, without a two-thirds vote of both houses of Congress, removing such a disability.

[2] Although there may have been some satisfaction in penalizing rebels, this law was clearly designed to shorten the war.

Fifthly. Of any person hereafter holding any office or agency under the government of the so-called confederate states of America, or under any of the several states of the said confederacy, or the laws thereof, whether such office or agency be national, state, or municipal in its name or character: *Provided*, That the persons, thirdly, fourthly, and fifthly above described shall have accepted their appointment or election since the date of the pretended ordinance of secession of the state, or shall have taken an oath of allegiance to, or to support the constitution of the so-called confederate states.

Sixthly. Of any person who, owning property in any loyal State or Territory of the United States, or in the District of Columbia, shall hereafter assist and give aid and comfort to such rebellion; and all sales, transfers, or conveyances of any such property shall be null and void; and it shall be a sufficient bar to any suit brought by such person for the possession or the use of such property, or any of it, to allege and prove that he is one of the persons described in this section.

SEC. 6. *And be it further enacted*, That if any person within any State or Territory of the United States, other than those named as aforesaid, after the passage of this act, being engaged in armed rebellion against the government of the United States, or aiding or abetting such rebellion, shall not, within sixty days after public warning and proclamation duly given and made by the President of the United States, cease to aid, countenance, and abet such rebellion, and return to his allegiance to the United States, all the estate and property, moneys, stocks, and credits of such person shall be liable to seizure as aforesaid, and it shall be the duty of the President to seize and use them as aforesaid or the proceeds thereof. And all sales, transfers, or conveyances, of any such property after the expiration of the said sixty days from the date of such warning and proclamation shall be null and void; and it shall be a sufficient bar to any suit brought by such person for the possession or the use of such property, or any of it, to allege and prove that he is one of the persons described in this section.

SEC. 7. *And be it further enacted*, That to secure the condemnation and sale of any of such property, after the same shall have been seized, so that it may be made available for the purpose aforesaid, proceedings in rem shall be instituted in the name of the United States in any district court thereof, or in any territorial court, or in the United States district court for the District of Columbia, within which the property above described, or any part thereof, may be found, or into which the same, if movable, may first be brought, which proceedings shall conform as nearly as may be to proceedings in admiralty or revenue cases, and if said property, whether real or personal, shall be found to have belonged to a person engaged in rebellion, or who has given aid or comfort thereto, the same shall be condemned as enemies' property and become the property of the United States, and may be disposed of as the court shall decree and the proceeds thereof paid into the treasury of the United States for the purposes aforesaid.

SEC. 8. *And be it further enacted*, That the several courts aforesaid shall have power to make such orders, establish such forms of decree and sale, and direct such deeds and conveyances to be executed and delivered by the marshals thereof where real estate shall be the subject of sale, as shall fitly and efficiently effect the purposes of this act, and vest in the purchasers of such property good and valid titles thereto. And the said courts shall have power to allow such fees and charges of their officers as shall be reasonable and proper in the premises.

SEC. 9. *And be it further enacted*, That all slaves of persons who shall hereafter be engaged in rebellion against the government of the United States, or who shall in any way give aid or comfort thereto, escaping from such persons and taking refuge within the lines of the army; and all slaves captured from such persons or deserted by them and coming under the control of the government of the United States; and all slaves of such person found on [*or*] being within any place occupied by rebel forces and afterwards occupied by the forces of the United States, shall be deemed captives of war, and shall be forever free of their servitude, and not again held as slaves.

SEC. 10. *And be it further enacted*, That no slave escaping into any State, Territory, or the District of Columbia, from any other State, shall be delivered up, or in any way impeded or hindered of his liberty, except for crime, or some offence against the laws, unless the person claiming said fugitive shall first make oath that the person to whom the labor or service of such fugitive is alleged to be due is his lawful owner, and has not borne arms against the United States in the present rebellion, nor in any way given aid and comfort thereto;

and no person engaged in the military or naval service of the United States shall, under any pretence whatever, assume to decide on the validity of the claim of any person to the service or labor of any other person, or surrender up any such person to the claimant, on pain of being dismissed from the service.

SEC. 11. *And be it further enacted*, That the President of the United States is authorized to employ as many persons of African descent as he may deem necessary and proper for the suppression of this rebellion, and for this purpose he may organize and use them in such manner as he may judge best for the public welfare.[3]

SEC. 12. *And be it further enacted*, That the President of the United States is hereby authorized to make provision for the transportation, colonization, and settlement, in some tropical country beyond the limits of the United States, of such persons of the African race, made free by the provisions of this act, as may be willing to emigrate, having first obtained the consent of the government of said country to their protection and settlement within the same, with all the rights and privileges of freemen.

SEC. 13. *And be it further enacted*, That the President is hereby authorized, at any time hereafter, by proclamation, to extend to persons who may have participated in the existing rebellion in any State or part thereof, pardon and amnesty, with such exceptions and at such time and on such conditions as he may deem expedient for the public welfare.

SEC. 14. *And be it further enacted*, That the courts of the United States shall have full power to institute proceedings, make orders and decrees, issue process, and do all other things necessary to carry this act into effect.

APPROVED, July 17, 1862.

Source: *U.S. Statutes at Large, Treaties, and Proclamations of the United States of America*, vol. 12 (Boston, 1863), 589–592.

[3] It is ironic that in a war that resulted in the emancipation of the slaves, there was an initial reluctance to employ African-American soldiers and it extended even to the side that would offer them eventual freedom. It is especially ironic in light of the fact that substantial numbers of African-American soldiers had participated in the Revolutionary War against Great Britain. Regiments were segregated, and black soldiers initially did not receive the same pay as their white counterparts.

Horace Greeley's "The Prayer of Twenty Millions"

August 19, 1862

INTRODUCTION

Horace Greeley (1811–1872), the founding editor of the *New York Tribune*, a one-time congressman, and later an unsuccessful presidential candidate against Ulysses S. Grant in 1872, published this letter almost midway through Lincoln's first term, expressing dissatisfaction with Lincoln's failure to move on the slave issue by aggressively enforcing the Confiscation Act, to deprive rebels of their slaves. Greeley undoubtedly reflected the views of many Northerners for whom the abolition of slavery had become the war's central purpose. Greeley's rhetoric toward the rebels is far less charitable and understanding than Lincoln's and far more characteristic of the radical Republicans who would later craft Reconstruction policies in the South.

To ABRAHAM LINCOLN,
President of the United States

DEAR SIR: I do not intrude to tell you—for you must know already—that a great proportion of those who triumphed in your election, and of all who desire the unqualified suppression of the Rebellion now desolating our country, are sorely disappointed and deeply pained by the policy you seem to be pursuing with regard to the slaves of the Rebels. I write only to set succinctly and unmistakably before you what we require, what we think we have a right to expect, and of what we complain.

[1] Although presidents have the power to enforce the laws, they sometimes exercise discretion as to how vigorously to pursue them.

[2] Greeley thought that the president was too hesitant to use laws to deprive slaveholders of their slaves.

I. We require of you, as the first servant of the Republic, charged especially and preeminently with this duty, that you EXECUTE THE LAWS.[1] Most emphatically do we demand that such laws as have been recently enacted, which therefore may fairly be presumed to embody the present will and to be dictated by the present needs of the Republic, and which, after due consideration have received your personal sanction, shall by you be carried into full effect, and that you publicly and decisively instruct your subordinates that such laws exist, that they are binding on all functionaries and citizens, and that they are to be obeyed to the letter.[2]

II. We think you are strangely and disastrously remiss in the discharge of your official and imperative duty with regard to the emancipating provisions of the new Confiscation Act. Those provisions were designed to fight Slavery with Liberty. They prescribe that men loyal to the Union, and willing to shed their blood in her behalf, shall no longer be held, with the Nations consent, in bondage to persistent, malignant traitors, who for twenty years have been plotting and for sixteen months have been fighting to divide and destroy our country. Why these traitors should be treated with tenderness by you, to the prejudice of the dearest rights of loyal men, We cannot conceive.

III. We think you are unduly influenced by the counsels, the representations, the menaces, of certain fossil politicians hailing from the Border Slave States. Knowing well that the heartily, unconditionally loyal portion of the White citizens of those States do not expect nor desire that Slavery shall be upheld to the prejudice of the Union—(for the truth of which we appeal not only to every Republican residing in those States, but to such eminent loyalists as H. Winter Davis, Parson Brownlow, the Union Central Committee of Baltimore, and to *The Nashville Union*)—we ask you to consider that Slavery is everywhere the inciting cause and sustaining base of treason: the most slaveholding sections of Maryland and Delaware being this day, though under the Union flag, in full sympathy with the Rebellion, while the Free-Labor portions of Tennessee and of Texas, though writhing under the bloody heel of Treason, are unconquerably loyal to the Union. So emphatically is this the case, that a most intelligent Union banker of Baltimore recently avowed his confident belief that a majority of the present Legislature of Maryland, though elected as and still professing to be Unionists, are at heart desirous of the triumph of the Jeff. Davis conspiracy; and when asked how they could be won back to loyalty, replied "only by the complete Abolition of Slavery." It seems to us the most obvious truth, that whatever strengthens or fortifies Slavery in the Border States strengthens also Treason, and drives home the wedge intended to divide the Union. Had you from the first refused to recognize in those States, as here, any other than unconditional loyalty—that which stands for the Union, whatever may become of Slavery, those States would have been, and would be, far more helpful and less troublesome to the defenders of the Union than they have been, or now are.[3]

IV. We think timid counsels in such a crisis calculated to prove perilous, and probably disastrous. It is the duty of a Government so

[3]Especially in the early years of the war, Lincoln was very concerned about keeping border states, some of which still had slavery, in the Union. Greeley believes this is having an adverse effect on his policies.

wantonly, wickedly assailed by Rebellion as ours has been to oppose force to force in a defiant, dauntless spirit. It cannot afford to temporize with traitors nor with semi-traitors. It must not bribe them to behave themselves, nor make . . . fair promises in the hope of disarming their causeless hostility. Representing a brave and high-spirited people, it can afford to forfeit anything else better than its own self-respect, or their admiring confidence. For our Government even to seek, after war has been made on it, to dispel the affected apprehensions of armed traitors that their cherished privileges may be assailed by it, is to invite insult and encourage hopes of its own downfall.[4] The rush to arms of Ohio, Indiana, Illinois, is the true answer at once to the Rebel raids of John Morgan and the traitorous sophistries of Beriah Magoffin.

V. We complain that the Union cause has suffered, and is now suffering immensely, from mistaken deference to Rebel Slavery. Had you, Sir, in your Inaugural Address, unmistakably given notice that, in case the Rebellion already commenced were persisted in, and your efforts to preserve the Union and enforce the laws should be resisted by armed force, you would recognize no loyal person as rightfully held in Slavery by a traitor, we believe the Rebellion would therein have received a staggering if not fatal blow. At that moment, according to the returns of the most recent elections, the Unionists were a large majority of the voters of the Slave States. But they were composed in good part of the aged, the feeble, the wealthy, the timid—the young, the reckless, the aspiring, the adventurous, had already been largely lured by the gamblers and negro-traders, the politicians by trade and the conspirators by instinct, into the toils of Treason. Had you then proclaimed that Rebellion would strike the shackles from the slaves of every traitor, the wealthy and the cautious would have been supplied with a powerful inducement to remain loyal. As it was, every coward in the South soon became a traitor from fear; for Loyalty was perilous, while Treason seemed comparatively safe. Hence the boasted unanimity of the South—a unanimity based on Rebel terrorism and the fact that immunity and safety were found on that side, danger and probable death on ours. The Rebels from the first have been eager to confiscate, imprison, scourge and kill: we have fought wolves with the devices of sheep. The result is just what might have been expected. Tens of thousands are fighting in the Rebel ranks to-day whose, original bias and natural leanings would have led them into ours.

VI. We complain that the Confiscation Act which you approved is habitually disregarded by your Generals, and that no word of rebuke for them from you has yet reached the public ear. Fremont's Proclamation and Hunter's Order favoring Emancipation were promptly annulled by you; while Halleck's No. 3, forbidding fugitives from Slavery to Rebels to come within his lines—an order as unmilitary as inhuman, and which received the hearty approbation of every traitor in America—with scores of like tendency, have never provoked even your own remonstrance.[5] We complain that the officers of your Armies have habitually repelled rather than invited approach of slaves who would have gladly taken the risks of escaping from their Rebel masters to our camps, bringing intelligence often of inestimable value to the Union cause. We complain that those who have thus escaped to us, avowing a willingness to do for us whatever might be required, have been brutally and madly repulsed, and often surrendered to be scourged, maimed and tortured by the ruffian traitors, who pretend to own them. We complain that a large proportion of our regular Army Officers, with many of the Volunteers, evince far more solicitude to uphold Slavery than to put down the Rebellion. And finally, we complain that you, Mr. President, elected as a Republican, knowing well what an abomination Slavery is, and how emphatically it is the core and essence of this atrocious Rebellion, seem never to interfere with these atrocities, and never give a direction to your Military subordinates, which does not appear to have been conceived in the interest of Slavery rather than of Freedom.

VII. [Greeley cites an example in Louisiana.] . . .

VIII. On the face of this wide earth, Mr. President, there is not one disinterested, determined, intelligent champion of the Union cause who does not feel that all attempts to put down the Rebellion and at the same time uphold its inciting cause are preposterous and futile— that the Rebellion, if crushed out tomorrow, would be renewed within a year if Slavery were left in full vigor—that Army officers who remain to this day devoted to Slavery can at best be but halfway loyal to the Union—and that every hour of deference to Slavery is an hour of added and deepened peril to the Union, I appeal to the testimony of your Ambassadors in Europe. It is freely at your service, not at mine. Ask them to tell you candidly whether the seeming subserviency of your policy to the slaveholding, slavery-upholding interest, is not the perplexity, the despair of statesmen of all parties, and be admonished by the general answer.

[5] Greeley criticizes the president for not seizing Southern property more aggressively.

IX. I close as I began with the statement that what an immense majority of the Loyal Millions of your countrymen require of you is a frank, declared, unqualified, ungrudging execution of the laws of the land, more especially of the Confiscation Act. That Act gives freedom to the slaves of Rebels coming within our lines, or whom those lines may at any time inclose—we ask you to render it due obedience by publicly requiring all your subordinates to recognize and obey it. The rebels are everywhere using the late anti-negro riots in the North, as they have long used your officers' treatment of negroes in the South, to convince the slaves that they have nothing to hope from a Union success—that we mean in that case to sell them into a bitter bondage to defray the cost of war. Let them impress this as a truth on the great mass of their ignorant and credulous bondsmen, and the Union will never be restored—never. We cannot conquer Ten Millions of People united in solid phalanx against us, powerfully aided by the Northern sympathizers and European allies. We must have scouts, guides, spies, cooks, teamsters, diggers and choppers from the Blacks of the South, whether we allow them to fight for us or not, or we shall be baffled and repelled.[6] As one of the millions who would gladly have avoided this struggle at any sacrifice but that Principle and Honor, but who now feel that the triumph of the Union is dispensable not only to the existence of our country to the well being of mankind, I entreat you to render a hearty and unequivocal obedience to the law of the land.

Yours,
Horace Greeley
New York, August 19, 1862

Source: L.P. Brockett, *The Life and Times of Abraham Lincoln*. Philadelphia: Bradley, 1865, 308–315.

[6]Greeley believes that a clear articulation of the intention to abolish slavery would unify the North, dispirit the South, and bring black recruits who could turn the tide of war in the Union's favor.

Abraham Lincoln's Response to Greeley

August 22, 1862

INTRODUCTION

Although he was already making plans to issue his Emancipation Proclamation, Lincoln had entered the war with the intention of preserving the Union, and he remained intent on continuing to secure the support of border states with slaves that had sided with the Union. In his response to Horace Greeley's article "The Prayer of Twenty Millions," Lincoln reiterated his position that preservation of the Union was paramount.

Executive Mansion,
Washington, August 22, 1862
Hon. Horace Greeley:

Dear Sir. I have just read yours of the 19th addressed to myself through the *New York Tribune*. If there be in it any statements, or assumptions of fact, which I may know to be erroneous, I do not now and here controvert them. . . . If there be perceptible in it an impatient and dictatorial tone, I waive it in deference to an old friend, whose heart I have always supposed to be right.

As to the policy I "seem to be pursuing" as you say, I have not meant to leave any one in doubt.

I would save the Union. I would save it the shortest way under the Constitution. The sooner the National authority can be restored; the nearer the Union will be "the Union as it was."[1] If there be those who would not save the Union, unless they could at the same time *save* Slavery, I do not agree with them. If there be those who would not save the Union unless they could at the same time *destroy* Slavery, I do not agree with them. My paramount object in this struggle is to save the Union, and is *not* either to save or to destroy slavery. If I could save the Union without freeing *any* slave I would do it, and if I could save it by freeing *all* the slaves I would do it; and if I could save it by freeing some and leaving others alone I would also do that.

[1] Lincoln had pledged to uphold the Constitution, which he thought intended for the Union to be perpetual. He also thought the Constitution left the continuing existence of slavery to the states.

[2]Probably with border states in mind, Lincoln did not think that immediate emancipation would advance the cause of Union.

[3]He may well have been preparing the nation for the Emancipation Proclamation, however, by indicating that he would do whatever it took (including freeing the slaves) to save the Union.

[4]Although Lincoln was not committed to immediate emancipation, he had frequently indicated his detestation of slavery and his commitment to the principle of the Declaration of Independence that "all men are created equal."

What I do about slavery, and the colored race, I do because I believe it helps to save the Union; and what I forbear, I forbear because I do not believe it would help to save the Union.[2] I shall do *less* whenever I shall believe what I am doing hurts the cause, and I shall do *more* whenever I shall believe doing more will help the cause. I shall try to correct errors when shown to be errors; and I shall adopt new views so fast as they shall appear to be true views.[3]

I have here stated my purpose according to my view of *official* duty: and I intend no modification of my oft-expressed *personal* wish that all men everywhere could be free.[4]

Yours,
A. Lincoln

Source: Frank Crosby, *Life of Abraham Lincoln*. Philadelphia: John E. Potter, 1865, 190–191.

Abraham Lincoln's Preliminary Emancipation Proclamation

September 22, 1862

INTRODUCTION

One of the most dramatic actions of the Lincoln administration was his Emancipation Proclamation, which freed slaves behind enemy lines. Although Lincoln issued the proclamation on January 1, 1863, he announced his intention to do so on September 22, 1862.

I, Abraham Lincoln, President of the United States of America, and Commander-in-Chief of the Army and Navy thereof, do hereby proclaim and declare that hereafter, as heretofore, the war will be prosecuted for the object of practically restoring the constitutional relation between the United States, and each of the States, and the people thereof, in which States that relation is, or may be, suspended or disturbed.[1]

That it is my purpose, upon the next meeting of Congress to again recommend the adoption of a practical measure tendering pecuniary aid to the free acceptance or rejection of all slave States, so called, the people whereof may not then be in rebellion against the United States[2] and which States may then have voluntarily adopted, or thereafter may voluntarily adopt, immediate or gradual abolishment of slavery within their respective limits; and that the effort to colonize persons of African descent, with their consent, upon this continent, or elsewhere, with the previously obtained consent of the Governments existing there, will be continued.[3]

That on the first day of January in the year of our Lord, one thousand eight hundred and sixty-three, all persons held as slaves within any State, or designated part of a State, the people whereof shall then be in rebellion against the United States shall be then, thenceforward, and forever free; and the executive government of the United States, including the military and naval authority thereof, will recognize and maintain the freedom of such persons, and will do no act or acts

[1] Lincoln's invocation of his power as commander in chief indicates that he considers this act to be a war measure.

[2] For states within the Union, Lincoln hoped for a plan for compensating slave owners.

[3] Lincoln clung to the idea, supported by earlier statesmen, that many of those who were freed could be deported to Africa.

[4] Although he was willing to consider compensating slaves in the Union, Lincoln planned to emancipate those behind enemy lines without compensation to their owners and pledged military help in securing the freedom of those who fled to their protection.

to repress such persons, or any of them, in any efforts they may make for their actual freedom.[4]

That the executive will, on the first day of January aforesaid, by proclamation, designate the States, and part of States, if any, in which the people thereof respectively, shall then be in rebellion against the United States; and the fact that any State, or the people thereof shall, on that day be, in good faith represented in the Congress of the United States, by members chosen thereto, at elections wherein a majority of the qualified voters of such State shall have participated, shall, in the absence of strong countervailing testimony, be deemed conclusive evidence that such State and the people thereof, are not then in rebellion against the United States.[5]

That attention is hereby called to an Act of Congress entitled "An Act to make an additional Article of War" approved March 13, 1862, and which act is in the words and figure following:

"Be it enacted by the Senate and House of Representatives of the United States of America in Congress assembled, That hereafter the following shall be promulgated as an additional article of war for the government of the army of the United States, and shall be obeyed and observed as such:

"Article—All officers or persons in the military or naval service of the United States are prohibited from employing any of the forces under their respective commands for the purpose of returning fugitives from service or labor, who may have escaped from any persons to whom such service or labor is claimed to be due, and any officer who shall be found guilty by a court martial of violating this article shall be dismissed from the service.

"Sec.2. And be it further enacted, That this act shall take effect from and after its passage."

Also to the ninth and tenth sections of an act entitled "An Act to suppress Insurrection, to punish Treason and Rebellion, to seize and confiscate property of rebels, and for other purposes," approved July 17, 1862, and which sections are in the words and figures following:

[5]Consistent with the fact that he considers this a war measure, Lincoln is trying to offer slave owners in rebel states an inducement to rejoin the Union or risk confiscation of their slaves.

"Sec.9. And be it further enacted, That all slaves of persons who shall hereafter be engaged in rebellion against the government of the United States, or who shall in any way give aid or comfort thereto, escaping from such persons and taking refuge within the lines of the army; and all slaves captured from such persons or deserted by them and coming under the control of the government of the United States; and all slaves of such persons found on (or) being within any place occupied by rebel forces and afterwards occupied by the forces of the United States, shall be deemed captives of war, and shall be forever free of their servitude and not again held as slaves.

"Sec.10. And be it further enacted, That no slave escaping into any State, Territory, or the District of Columbia, from any other State, shall be delivered up, or in any way impeded or hindered of his liberty, except for crime, or some offence against the laws, unless the person claiming said fugitive shall first make oath that the person to whom the labor or service of such fugitive is alleged to be due is his lawful owner, and has not borne arms against the United States in the present rebellion, nor in any way given aid and comfort thereto; and no person engaged in the military or naval service of the United States shall, under any pretence whatever, assume to decide on the validity of the claim of any person to the service or labor of any other person, or surrender up any such person to the claimant, on pain of being dismissed from the service."

And I do hereby enjoin upon and order all persons engaged in the military and naval service of the United States to observe, obey, and enforce, within their respective spheres of service, the act, and sections above recited.

And the executive will in due time recommend that all citizens of the United States who shall have remained loyal thereto throughout the rebellion, shall (upon the restoration of the constitutional relation between the United States, and their respective States, and people, if that relation shall have been suspended or disturbed) be compensated for all losses by acts of the United States, including the loss of slaves.[6]

[6]As chief executive, Lincoln had the power to recommend, but not to mandate, that Congress reimburse Unionists for the emancipation of their slaves.

In witness whereof, I have hereunto set my hand, and caused the seal of the United States to be affixed.

Done at the City of Washington this twenty-second day of September, in the year of our Lord, one thousand, eight hundred and sixty-two, and of the Independence of the United States the eighty seventh.

[Signed:] By the President, Abraham Lincoln,
[Signed:] William H. Seward, Secretary of State

Source: Presidential Proclamation 93 (Preliminary Emancipation Proclamation), Presidential Proclamation 93 (vault), Box 2, RG 11, General Records of the U.S. Government, National Archives.

Abraham Lincoln's Proclamation Suspending the Writ of Habeas Corpus

September 24, 1862

INTRODUCTION

One of Lincoln's most controversial actions as commander in chief of U.S. armed forces was his decision to suspend the writ of habeas corpus, which would enable officials to incarcerate individuals suspected of aiding the rebel cause without stating formal charges. Although the U.S. Constitution provided in Article I, Section 9, that "The Privilege of the Writ of Habeas Corpus shall not be suspended, unless when in Cases of Rebellion or Invasion the public Safety may require it," it listed this provision in a section of the Constitution generally understood to apply to Congress rather than the president. Chief Justice Roger Taney, while on circuit duty, issued an opinion in *Ex Parte Merryman*, 17 Fed. Cas. 9487 (1861), seeking to invalidate such a suspension, but Lincoln had evaded it.

By the President of the United States of America:

A Proclamation

Whereas, it has become necessary to call into service not only volunteers but also portions of the militia of the States by draft in order to suppress the insurrection existing in the United States, and disloyal persons are not adequately restrained by the ordinary processes of law from hindering this measure and from giving aid and comfort in various ways to the insurrection;[1]

Now, therefore, be it ordered, first, that during the existing insurrection and as a necessary measure for suppressing the same, all Rebels and Insurgents, their aiders and abettors within the United States, and all persons discouraging volunteer enlistments, resisting militia drafts, or guilty of any disloyal practice, affording aid and comfort to Rebels against the authority of the United States, shall be subject to

[1] This proclamation was specifically directed against those attempting to interfere with recruitment for federal forces.

martial law and liable to trial and punishment by Courts Martial or Military Commission:

Second. That the Writ of Habeas Corpus is suspended in respect to all persons arrested, or who are now, or hereafter during the rebellion shall be, imprisoned in any fort, camp, arsenal, military prison, or other place of confinement by any military authority of by the sentence or any Court Martial or Military Commission.

In witness whereof, I have hereunto set my hand, and caused the seal of the United States to be affixed.

Done at the City of Washington this twenty fourth day of September, in the year of our Lord one thousand eight hundred and sixty-two, and of the Independence of the United States the 87th.

By the President: ABRAHAM LINCOLN

WILLIAM H. SEWARD, Secretary of State.

Source: Presidential Proclamation Number 94, RG 11, General Records of the U.S. Government, National Archives.

Abraham Lincoln's Emancipation Proclamation

January 1, 1863

INTRODUCTION

Abraham Lincoln accepted the presidency, believing that his primary constitutional duty was to preserve the Union. As the war progressed, however, and the number of casualties increased, he looked for a greater cause to justify the suffering. He also realized that emancipation could reap military dividends by depriving the rebelling states of a key source of wealth and labor. After issuing a preliminary proclamation on September 22, 1862, Lincoln finalized this on January 1, 1863, which is still celebrated as Emancipation Day in some African-American communities.

By the President of the United States of America:

A Proclamation.

Whereas, on the twenty-second day of September, in the year of our Lord one thousand eight hundred and sixty-two, a proclamation was issued by the President of the United States, containing, among other things, the following, to wit:

"That on the first day of January, in the year of our Lord one thousand eight hundred and sixty-three, all persons held as slaves within any State or designated part of a State, the people whereof shall then be in rebellion against the United States, shall be then, thenceforward, and forever free; and the Executive Government of the United States, including the military and naval authority thereof, will recognize and maintain the freedom of such persons, and will do no act or acts to repress such persons, or any of them, in any efforts they may make for their actual freedom.

"That the Executive will, on the first day of January aforesaid, by proclamation, designate the States and parts of States, if any, in which the people thereof, respectively, shall then be in rebellion against the United States; and the fact that any State, or the people thereof, shall on that day be, in good faith, represented in the Congress of the United States by members chosen thereto at elections wherein a majority of the qualified voters of such State shall have participated, shall, in the absence of strong countervailing testimony, be deemed conclusive evidence that such State, and the people thereof, are not then in rebellion against the United States."

Now, therefore I, Abraham Lincoln, President of the United States, by virtue of the power in me vested as Commander-in-Chief, of the Army and Navy of the United States in time of actual armed rebellion against the authority and government of the United States, and as a fit and necessary war measure for suppressing said rebellion,[1] do, on this first day of January, in the year of our Lord one thousand eight hundred and sixty-three, and in accordance with my purpose so to do publicly proclaimed for the full period of one hundred days, from the day first above mentioned, order and designate as the States and parts of States wherein the people thereof respectively, are this day in rebellion against the United States,[2] the following, to wit:

Arkansas, Texas, Louisiana, (except the Parishes of St. Bernard, Plaquemines, Jefferson, St. John, St. Charles, St. James Ascension, Assumption, Terrebonne, Lafourche, St. Mary, St. Martin, and Orleans, including the City of New Orleans) Mississippi, Alabama, Florida, Georgia, South Carolina, North Carolina, and Virginia (except the forty-eight counties designated as West Virginia, and also the counties of Berkley, Accomac, Northampton, Elizabeth City, York, Princess Ann, and Norfolk, including the cities of Norfolk and Portsmouth[)], and which excepted parts, are for the present, left precisely as if this proclamation were not issued.

And by virtue of the power, and for the purpose aforesaid, I do order and declare that all persons held as slaves within said designated States, and parts of States, are, and henceforward shall be free; and that the Executive government of the United States, including the military and naval authorities thereof, will recognize and maintain the freedom of said persons.

And I hereby enjoin upon the people so declared to be free to abstain from all violence, unless in necessary self-defence; and I recommend to them that, in all cases when allowed, they labor faithfully for reasonable wages.[3]

[1]This paragraph highlights the fact that the president was carrying out this action in connection with his powers as commander in chief.

[2]This proclamation applied only to parts of the United States that were still in rebellion. The term is significant. Lincoln never recognized the conflict, as did Southerners, as a war between the states (two independent national entities), but as a civil war, that he was duty-bound to quell.

[3]Lincoln knew of Southern fears of slave revolts and the reaction that his proclamation would bring if it were interpreted as such a call.

And I further declare and make known, that such persons of suitable condition, will be received into the armed service of the United States to garrison forts, positions, stations, and other places, and to man vessels of all sorts in said service.

And upon this act, sincerely believed to be an act of justice, warranted by the Constitution, upon military necessity, I invoke the considerate judgment of mankind, and the gracious favor of Almighty God.

In witness whereof, I have hereunto set my hand and caused the seal of the United States to be affixed.

Done at the City of Washington, this first day of January, in the year of our Lord one thousand eight hundred and sixty three, and of the Independence of the United States of America the eighty-seventh.

By the President: ABRAHAM LINCOLN

WILLIAM H. SEWARD, Secretary of State.

CONCLUSION

Because the proclamation was issued as a war measure consistent with the president's powers as commander-in-chief, it applied only behind enemy lines. The Proclamation was later extended by the Thirteenth Amendment, which applied throughout the United States, and provided greater security to former slaves because it was actually incorporated into the US Constitution.

Source: Presidential Proclamations, 1791–1991, RG 11, General Records of the U.S. Government, National Archives.

The Conscription and Enrollment Act

March 3, 1863

INTRODUCTION

It may seem ironic that wars designed to secure human freedom sometimes demand the involuntary service of those who are needed to wage them. This law, instituted in the middle of the Civil War, provided for a military draft in those states that were unable to raise a sufficient number of volunteers. The law resulted in rioting in New York City.

An Act for enrolling and calling out the national Forces, and for other Purposes.

Whereas there now exist in the United States an insurrection and rebellion against the authority thereof, and it is, under the Constitution of the United States, the duty of the government to suppress insurrection and rebellion, to guarantee to each State a republican form of government, and to preserve the public tranquility;[1] and whereas, for these high purposes, a military force is indispensable, to raise and support which all persons ought willingly to contribute; and whereas no service can be more praiseworthy and honorable than that which is rendered for the maintenance of the Constitution and Union, and the consequent preservation of free government:

Therefore—

Be it enacted by the Senate and House of Representatives of the United States of America in Congress assembled, That all able-bodies male citizens of the United States,[2] and persons of foreign birth who shall have declared on oath their intention to become citizens[3] under and in pursuance of the laws thereof, between the ages of twenty and forty-five years,[4] except as hereinafter excepted, are hereby declared to constitute the national forces, and shall be liable to perform military duty in the service of the United States when called out by the President for that purpose.

[1] Congress fairly consistently accepted Lincoln's view that the war was not a war between two separate nation-states, which would have qualified the South under international law to secure foreign assistance, but a rebellion, which the national government had the duty to suppress.

[2] The United States has never drafted women into the armed services.

[3] It is interesting that this law, like the Homestead Act of the previous year, applied not only to citizens but also to resident aliens who had declared their intention to become U.S. citizens. The law led to rioting by Irish-American immigrants in New York City.

[4] Most drafts have focused on young men both because they are thought to be the most physically fit to fight and because they are less likely to have dependent families.

SEC 2. And be it further enacted, That the following persons be, and they are hereby, excepted and exempt from the provisions of this act, and shall not be liable to military duty under the same, to wit: Such as are rejected as physically or mentally unfit for the service; also, First the Vice-President of the United States, the judges of the various courts of the United States, the heads of the various executive departments of the government, and the governors of the several States. Second, the only son liable to military duty of a widow dependent upon his labor for support. Third, the only son of aged or infirm parent or parents dependent upon his labor for support. Fourth, where there are two or more sons of aged or infirm parents subject to draft, the father, or, if he be dead, the mother, may elect which son shall be exempt. Fifth, the only brother of children not twelve years old, having neither father nor mother dependent upon his labor for support. Sixth, the father of motherless children under twelve years of age dependent upon his labor for support. Seventh, where there are a father and sons in the same family and household, and two of them are in the military service of the United States as non-commissioned officers, musicians, or privates, the residue of such family and household, not exceeding two, shall be exempt. And no persons but such as are herein excepted shall be exempt: Provided, however, That no person who has been convicted of any felony shall be enrolled or permitted to serve in said forces.

SEC. 3. And be it further enacted, That the national forces of the United States not now in the military service, enrolled under this act, shall be divided into two classes: the first of which shall comprise all persons subject to do military duty between the ages of twenty and thirty-five years, and all unmarried persons subject to do military duty above the age of thirty-five and under the age of forty-five; the second class shall comprise all other persons subject to do military duty, and they shall not, in any district, be called into the service of the United States until those of the first class hall have been called.

SEC. 4. And be it further enacted, That, for greater convenience in enrolling, calling out, and organizing the national forces, and for the arrest of deserters and spies of the enemy, the United States shall constitute one or more, as the President shall direct, and each congressional district of the respective states, as fixed by a law of the state next preceding the enrolment, shall constitute one: Provided, That in states which have not by their laws been divided into two or more congressional districts, the President of the United States shall divide the same into so many enrolment districts as he may deem fit and convenient.

5The requirement for a practicing physician or surgeon was probably included with a view toward ascertaining whether those being drafted were physically fit.

SEC 8. And be it further enacted, That in each of said districts there shall be a board of enrolment, to be composed of the provost-marshal, as president, and two other persons, to be appointed by the President of the United States, one of whom shall be a licensed and practising physician and surgeon.[5]

SEC. 10. And be it further enacted, That the enrolment of each class shall be made separately, and shall only embrace those whose ages shall be on the first day of July thereafter between twenty and forty-five years.

SEC. 11. And be it further enacted, That all persons thus enrolled shall be subject, for two years after the first day of July succeeding the enrolment, to be called into the military service of the United States, and to continue in service during the present rebellion, not, however, exceeding the term of three years; and when called into service shall be placed on the same footing, in all respects, as volunteers for three years, or during the war, including advance pay and bounty as now provided by law.

SEC. 12. And be it further enacted, That whenever it may be necessary to call out the national forces for military service, the President is hereby authorized to assign to each district the number of men to be furnished by said district; and thereupon the enrolling board shall, under the direction of the President, make a draft of the required number, and fifty per cent, in addition, and shall make an exact and complete roll of the names of the person so drawn, and of the order in which they drawn, so that the first drawn may stand first upon the said roll and the second second may stand second, and so on; and the persons so drawn shall be notified of the same within ten days thereafter, by a written or printed notice, to be served personally or by leaving a copy at the last place of residence, requiring them to appear at a designated rendezvous to report for duty. In assigning to the districts the number of men to be furnished there from, the President shall take into consideration the number of volunteers and militia furnished by and from the several states in which said districts are situated, and the period of their service since the commencement of the present rebellion, and shall so make said assignment as to equalize the numbers among the districts of the several states, considering and allowing for the numbers already furnished as aforesaid and the time of their service.

SEC. 13. And be it further enacted, That any person drafted and notified to appear as aforesaid, may, on or before the day fixed for his appearance, furnish an acceptable substitute to take his place in the draft; or he may pay to such person as the Secretary of War may authorize to receive it, such sum, not exceeding three hundred dollars,[6] as the Secretary may determine, for the procuration of such substitute; which sum shall be fixed at a uniform rate by a general order made at the time of ordering a draft for any state or territory; and thereupon such person so furnishing the substitute, or paying the money, shall be discharged from further liability under that draft. And any person failing to report after due service of notice, as herein prescribed, without furnishing a substitute, or paying the required sum therefor, shall be deemed a deserter, and shall be arrested by the provost-marshal and sent to the nearest military post for trial by court-martial, unless, upon proper showing that he is not liable to do military duty, the board of enrolment shall relive him from the draft.

SEC. 16. And be it further enacted, That as soon as the required number of able-bodied men liable to do military duty shall be obtained from the list of those drafted, the remainder shall be discharged; . . .

SEC. 17. And be it further enacted, That any person enrolled and drafted according to the provisions of this act who shall furnish an acceptable substitute, shall thereupon receive from the board of enrolment a certificate of discharge from such draft, which shall exempt him from military duty during the time for which he was drafted; and such substitute shall be entitled to the same pay and allowances provided by law as if he had been originally drafted into the service of the United States.

SEC. 18. And be it further enacted, That such of the volunteers and militia now in the service of the United States as may reenlist to serve one year, unless sooner discharged, after the expiration of their present term of service, shall be entitled to a bounty of fifty dollars, one half of which to be paid upon such reenlistment, and the balance at the expiration of the term of reenlistment; and such as may reenlist to serve for two years, unless sooner discharged, after the expiration of their present term of enlistment, shall receive, upon such

[6]One of the more controversial sections of this law, this provision allowed individuals to hire substitutes in their place, thus privileging those who were wealthier over those of lesser means.

reenlistment, twenty-five dollars of the one hundred dollars bounty for enlistment provided by the fifth section of the act approved twenty-second of July, eighteen hundred and sixty-one, entitled "An act to authorize the employment of volunteers to aid in enforcing the laws and protecting public property."

SEC. 25. And be it further enacted, That if any person shall resist any draft of men enrolled under this act into the service of the United States, or shall counsel or aid any person to resist any such draft; or shall counsel or aid any person to resist any such draft; or shall assault or obstruct any officer in making such draft, or in the performance of any service in relation thereto; or shall counsel any person to assault or obstruct any such officer, or shall counsel any drafted men not to appear at the place of rendezvous, or willfully dissuade them from the performance of military duty as required by law, such person shall be subject to summary arrest by the provost-marshal, and shall be forthwith delivered to the civil authorities, and upon conviction thereof, be punished by a fine not exceeding five hundred dollars, or by imprisonment not exceeding two years, or by both of said punishments.[7]

[7]Interference with the draft was considered to be a serious crime that could jeopardize the war effort.

SEC. 33. And be it further enacted, That the President of the United States is hereby authorized and empowered, during the present rebellion, to call forth the national forces, by draft, in the manner provided for in this act.

CONCLUSION

The United States would rely on similar drafts during World War I, World War II, and the Korean and Viet Nam conflicts. The nation currently has an all-volunteer force, although there are periodic calls for universal service.

Source: "An Act for Enrolling and Calling Out the National Forces, and for Other Purposes," Congressional Record, 37th Cong., 3d Sess., 74 and 75 (March 3, 1863).

The Prize Cases

March 10, 1863

INTRODUCTION

In April 1861, after fighting had begun but before Congress was in session, President Lincoln declared a blockade of Southern ports, which resulted in the confiscation of a number of ships. After owners sued for their return, the Supreme Court had to decide whether Lincoln had the authority to issue the blockade, and which ships had been legally confiscated and which ones had not. The issue was complicated by the fact that Lincoln called the Civil War a rebellion rather than a war between the states.

Mr. Justice GRIER.

There are certain propositions of law which must necessarily affect the ultimate decision of these cases, and many others which it will be proper to discuss and decide before we notice the special facts peculiar to each.

They are, 1st. Had the President a right to institute a blockade of ports in possession of persons in armed rebellion against the Government, on the principles of international law, as known and acknowledged among civilized States?

2d. Was the property of persons domiciled or residing within those States a proper subject of capture on the sea as "enemies' property?"

I. Neutrals have a right to challenge the existence of a blockade *de facto*, and also the authority of the party exercising the right to institute it. They have a right to enter the ports of a friendly nation for the purposes of trade and commerce, but are bound to recognize the rights of a belligerent engaged in actual war, to use this mode of coercion, for the purpose of subduing the enemy.[1]

That a blockade *de facto* actually existed, and was formally declared and notified by the President on the 27th and 30th of April, 1861, is an admitted fact in these cases.

[1] Justice Grier is indicating that neutrals have what the Court calls "standing," which means they are able to show that they have a right to appear in a court with an ability to vindicate their interests.

93

That the President, as the Executive Chief of the Government and Commander-in-chief of the Army and Navy, was the proper person to make such notification has not been, and cannot be disputed.

The right of prize and capture has its origin in the "*jus belli*," [law of war] and is governed and adjudged under the law of nations. To legitimate the capture of a neutral vessel or property on the high seas, a war must exist *de facto,* and the neutral must have knowledge or notice of the intention of one of the parties belligerent to use this mode of coercion against a port, city, or territory, in possession of the other.

Let us enquire whether, at the time this blockade was instituted, a state of war existed which would justify a resort to these means of subduing the hostile force.

War has been well defined to be, "That state in which a nation prosecutes its right by force."

The parties belligerent in a public war are independent nations. But it is not necessary, to constitute war, that both parties should be acknowledged as independent nations or sovereign States. A war may exist where one of the belligerents claims sovereign rights as against the other.

Insurrection against a government may or may not culminate in an organized rebellion, but a civil war always begins by insurrection against the lawful authority of the Government.[2] A civil war is never solemnly declared; it becomes such by its accidents—the number, power, and organization of the persons who originate and carry it on. When the party in rebellion occupy and hold in a hostile manner a certain portion of territory, have declared their independence, have cast off their allegiance, have organized armies, have commenced hostilities against their former sovereign, the world acknowledges them as belligerents, and the contest a war. They claim to be in arms to establish their liberty and independence, in order to become a sovereign State, while the sovereign party treats them as insurgents and rebels who owe allegiance, and who should be punished with death for their treason.

The laws of war, as established among nations, have their foundation in reason, and all tend to mitigate the cruelties and misery produced by the scourge of war. Hence the parties to a civil war usually concede to each other belligerent rights. They exchange prisoners, and adopt the other courtesies and rules common to public or national wars.[3]

"A civil war," says Vattel, "breaks the bands of society and government, or at least suspends their force and effect; it produces in the nation two independent parties, who consider each other as enemies and acknowledge no common judge. Those two parties, therefore, must necessarily be considered as constituting, at least for a time, two separate bodies, two distinct societies. Having no common superior to judge between them, they stand in precisely the same predicament as two nations who engage in a contest and have recourse to arms." . . .

As a civil war is never publicly proclaimed, *eo nomine,* against insurgents, its actual existence is a fact in our domestic history which the Court is bound to notice and to know.

The true test of its existence, as found in the writings of the sages of the common law, may be thus summarily stated: "When the regular course of justice is interrupted by revolt, rebellion, or insurrection, so that the Courts of Justice cannot be kept open, *civil war exists,* and hostilities may be prosecuted on the same footing as if those opposing the Government were foreign enemies invading the land."

By the Constitution, Congress alone has the power to declare a national or foreign war. It cannot declare war against a State, or any number of States, by virtue of any clause in the Constitution. The Constitution confers on the President the whole Executive power. He is bound to take care that the laws be faithfully executed. He is Commander-in-chief of the Army and Navy of the United States, and of the militia of the several States when called into the actual service of the United States. He has no power to initiate or declare a war either against a foreign nation or a domestic State. But, by the Acts of Congress of February 28th, 1795, and 3d of March, 1807, he is authorized to called out the militia and use the military and naval forces of the United States in case of invasion by foreign nations and to suppress insurrection against the government of a State or of the United States.[4]

If a war be made by invasion of a foreign nation, the President is not only authorized but bound to resist force by force. He does not initiate the war, but is bound to accept the challenge without waiting

[4]Grier believes that the president's authority to suppress insurrection granted him the authority that he needed to declare an embargo in this case.

⁵Again, Grier is indicating that a de facto war may exist even when it is not officially declared.

for any special legislative authority. And whether the hostile party be a foreign invader or States organized in rebellion, it is nonetheless a war although the declaration of it be "unilateral." Lord Stowell (1 Dodson 247) observes, "It is not the less a war on that account, for war may exist without a declaration on either side. It is so laid down by the best writers on the law of nations. A declaration of war by one country only is not a mere challenge to be accepted or refused at pleasure by the other." . . .⁵

As soon as the news of the attack on Fort Sumter, and the organization of a government by the seceding States, assuming to act as belligerents, could become known in Europe, to-wit, on the 13th of May, 1861, the Queen of England issued her proclamation of neutrality, "recognizing hostilities as existing between the Government of the United States of American and certain States styling themselves the Confederate States of America."

This was immediately followed by similar declarations or silent acquiescence by other nations.

After such an official recognition by the sovereign, a citizen of a foreign State is estopped to deny the existence of a war with all its consequences as regards neutrals. They cannot ask a Court to affect a technical ignorance of the existence of a war, which all the world acknowledges to be the greatest civil war known in the history of the human race, and thus cripple the arm of the Government and paralyze its power by subtle definitions and ingenious sophisms.

The law of nations is also called the law of nature; it is founded on the common consent, as well as the common sense, of the world. It contains no such anomalous doctrine as that which this Court are now for the first time desired to pronounce, to-wit, that insurgents who have risen in rebellion against their sovereign, expelled her Courts, established a revolutionary government, organized armies, and commenced hostilities are not enemies because they are traitors, and a war levied on the Government by traitors, in order to dismember and destroy it, is not a war because it is an "insurrection."

Whether the President, in fulfilling his duties as Commander-in-chief in suppressing an insurrection, has met with such armed hostile resistance and a civil war of such alarming proportions as will compel him to accord to them the character of belligerents is a question to be decided by him, and this Court must be governed by the decisions and acts of the political department of the Government to which this power was entrusted. "He must determine what degree of force the crisis demands." The proclamation of blockade is itself official and conclusive evidence to the Court that a state of war existed which demanded and authorized a recourse to such a measure under the circumstances peculiar to the case.

The correspondence of Lord Lyons with the Secretary of State admits the fact and concludes the question.

If it were necessary to the technical existence of a war that it should have a legislative sanction, we find it in almost every act passed at the extraordinary session of the Legislature of 1861, which was wholly employed in enacting laws to enable the Government to prosecute the war with vigor and efficiency. And finally, in 1861, we find Congress "*ex majore cautela*" and in anticipation of such astute objections, passing an act "approving, legalizing, and making valid all the acts, proclamations, and orders of the President, &c., as if they had been *issued and done under the previous express authority* and direction of the Congress of the United States."[6]

[6]Grier observes that when Congress reconvened, it had retroactively approved Lincoln's actions.

Without admitting that such an act was necessary under the circumstances, it is plain that, if the President had in any manner assumed powers which it was necessary should have the authority or sanction of Congress, that, on the well known principle of law, "*omnis rati-habitio retrotrahitur et mandato equiparatur [Every ratification relates back and is equivalent to a prior authority, Black's Law Dictionary, Revised Fourth Ed.]*," this ratification has operated to perfectly cure the defect. . . .

On this first question, therefore, we are of the opinion that the President had a right, *jure belli*, to institute a blockade of ports in possession of the States in rebellion which neutrals are bound to regard.

II. We come now to the consideration of the second question. What is included in the term "enemies' property?" *[This part of the decision omitted.]*

. . .

Mr. Justice NELSON, dissenting.[7] . . .

[7]Nelson, and three other dissenting justices, took a more formal view of war-making and concluded that it required a prior declaration of war that only Congress could make.

Source: 67 U.S. (2 Black) 635.

Abraham Lincoln's Letter to Erastus Corning and Others

June 12, 1863

INTRODUCTION

During the Civil War, many questioned whether Lincoln was exceeding his constitutional powers. In this case, Erastus Corning (1794–1872), a former congressman and New York businessman, had questioned Lincoln's suspension of the writ of habeas corpus and especially the arrest of former congressman Clement Vallandigham, whom Lincoln had arrested and banished to the Confederacy after his continuing support for its policies. Lincoln intended for his letter to be published, and it was widely read, complete with his own distinctive spellings.

Hon. Erastus Corning and Others.

Gentlemen:

Your letter of May 19, inclosing the resolutions of a public meeting held at Albany, New York, on the 16th of the same month, was received several days ago.

The resolutions, as I understand them, are resolvable into two propositions—first, the expression of a purpose to sustain the cause of the Union, to secure peace through victory, and to support the administration in every constitutional and lawful measure to suppress the rebellion; and, secondly, a declaration of censure upon the administration for supposed unconstitutional action, such as the making of military arrests. And from the two propositions a third is deduced, which is that the gentlemen composing the meeting are resolved on doing their part to maintain our common government and country, despite the folly or wickedness, as they may conceive, of any administration. This position is eminently patriotic, and as such I thank the meeting, and congratulate the nation for it. My own purpose is the same; so that the meeting and myself have a common object, and can have no difference, except in the choice of means or measures for effecting that object.

And here I ought to close this paper, and would close it, if there were no apprehension that more injurious consequences than any merely personal to myself might follow the censures systematically cast upon me for doing what, in my view of duty, I could not forbear. The resolutions promise to support me in every constitutional and lawful measure to suppress the rebellion; and I have not knowingly employed, nor shall knowingly employ, any other. But the meeting, by their resolutions, assert and argue that certain military arrests, and proceedings following them, for which I am ultimately responsible, are unconstitutional. I think they are not. The resolutions quote from the Constitution the definition of treason, and also the limiting safeguards and guarantees therein provided for the citizen on trials for treason, and on his being held to answer for capital or otherwise infamous crimes, and in criminal prosecutions his right to a speedy and public trial by an impartial jury. They proceed to resolve "that these safeguards of the rights of the citizen against the pretentions of arbitrary power were intended more especially for his protection in times of civil commotion." And, apparently to demonstrate the proposition, the resolutions proceed: "They were secured substantially to the English people after years of protracted civil war, and were adopted into our Constitution at the close of the revolution."[1] Would not the demonstration have been better if it could have been truly said that these safeguards had been adopted and applied during the civil wars and during our revolution, instead of after the one and at the close of the other? I, too, am devotedly for them after civil war, and before civil war, and at all times, "except when, in cases of rebellion or invasion, the public safety may require" their suspension.[2] The resolutions proceed to tell us that these safeguards "have stood the test of seventy-six years of trial under our republican system, under circumstances which show that while they constitute the foundation of all free government, they are the elements of the enduring stability of the republic."

No one denies that they have so stood the test up to the beginning of the present rebellion, if we except a certain matter at New Orleans hereafter to be mentioned; nor does any one question that they will stand the same test much longer after the rebellion closes.

[1]Lincoln is essentially summarizing Corning's concern.

[2]Lincoln shares his respect for civil liberties, including the writ of habeas corpus.

[3]Despite Lincoln's respect for civil liberties, he believed that the situation he encountered during the Civil War was unique and thus limited the value of past precedents.

But these provisions of the Constitution have no application to the case we have in hand, because the arrests complained of were not made for treason—that is, not for the treason defined in the Constitution, and upon the conviction of which the punishment is death—nor yet were they made to hold persons to answer for any capital or otherwise infamous crimes; nor were the proceedings following, in any constitutional or legal sense, "criminal prosecutions." The arrests were made on totally different grounds, and the proceedings following accorded with the grounds of the arrests.[3] Let us consider the real case with which we are dealing, and apply to it the parts of the Constitution plainly made for such cases.

Prior to my installation here it had been inculcated that any State had a lawful right to secede from the national Union, and that it would be expedient to exercise the right whenever the devotees of the doctrine should fail to elect a president to their own liking. I was elected contrary to their liking; and, accordingly, so far as it was legally possible, they had taken seven States out of the Union, had seized many of the United States forts, and had fired upon the United States Flag, all before I was inaugurated, and, of course, before I had done any official act whatever. The rebellion thus began soon ran into the present civil war; and, in certain respects, it began on very unequal terms between the parties. The insurgents had been preparing for it more than thirty years, while the government had taken no steps to resist them. The former had carefully considered all the means which could be turned to their account. It undoubtedly was a well-pondered reliance with them that in their own unrestricted effort to destroy Union, Constitution and law, all together, the government would, in great degree, be restrained by the same Constitution and law from arresting their progress. Their sympathizers pervaded all departments of the government and nearly all communities of the people. From this material, under cover of "liberty of speech," "liberty of the press," and "*habeas corpus*," they hoped to keep on foot amongst us a most efficient corps of spies, informers, suppliers, and aiders and abettors of their cause in a thousand ways. They knew that in times such as they were inaugurating, by the Constitution itself the "*habeas corpus*" might be suspended; but they also knew they had friends who would make a question as to who was to suspend it; meanwhile their spies and others might remain at large to help on their cause. Or if, as has happened, the Executive should suspend the writ without ruinous waste of time, instances of arresting innocent persons might occur, as are always likely to occur in such cases; and then a clamor could be raised in regard to this, which might be at least of some service to the insurgent cause. It needed no very keen perception to discover this part of the enemy's programme, so soon as by open hostilities their machinery was fairly put in motion. Yet, thoroughly imbued with a reverence for the guaranteed rights of individuals, I was slow to adopt the strong measures which by degrees I have been forced to regard as being within the exceptions of the Constitution, and as indispensable to the public safety. Nothing is better known to history than that courts of justice are utterly incompetent to such cases. Civil courts are organized chiefly for trials of individuals, or, at most, a few individuals acting in concert—and this in quiet times, and on charges of crimes well defined in the law. Even in times of peace bands of horse-thieves and robbers frequently grow too numerous and powerful for the ordinary courts of justice. But what comparison, in numbers, have such bands ever borne to the insurgent sympathizers even in many of the loyal States? Again, a jury too frequently has at least one member more ready to hang the panel than to hang the traitor. And yet again, he who dissuades one man from volunteering, or induces one soldier to desert, weakens the Union cause as much as he who kills a Union soldier in battle. Yet this dissuasion or inducement may be so conducted as to be no defined crime of which any civil court would take cognizance. Ours is a case of rebellion—so called by the resolutions before me—in fact, a clear, flagrant, and gigantic case of rebellion; and the provision of the Constitution that "the privilege of the writ of *habeas corpus* shall not be suspended unless when, in cases of rebellion or invasion, the public safety may require it," is the provision which specially applies to our present case. This provision plainly attests the understanding of those who made the Constitution that ordinary courts of justice are inadequate to "cases of rebellion"—attests their purpose that, in such cases, men may be held in custody whom the courts, acting on ordinary rules, would discharge. *Habeas corpus* does not discharge men who are proved to be guilty of defined crime; and its suspension is allowed by the Constitution on purpose that men may be arrested and held who cannot be proved to be guilty of defined crime, "when, in cases of rebellion or invasion, the public safety may require it."

This is precisely our present case—a case of rebellion wherein the public Safety does require the suspension. Indeed, arrests by process of courts and arrests in cases of rebellion do not proceed altogether upon the same basis. The former is directed at the small percentage of ordinary and continuous perpetration of crime, while the latter is directed at sudden and extensive uprisings against the government, which, at most, will succeed or fail in no great length of time. In the latter case arrests are made not so much for what has been done, as for what probably would be done. The latter is more for the preventive and less for the vindictive than the former. In such cases the purposes of men are much more easily understood than in cases of ordinary crime. The man who stands by and says nothing when the peril of his government is discussed, cannot be misunderstood. If not hindered, he is sure to help the enemy; much more if he talks ambiguously—talks for his country with "buts," and "ifs" and "ands." Of how little value the constitutional provision I have quoted will be rendered if arrests shall never be made until defined crimes shall have been committed, may be illustrated by a few notable examples: General John C. Breckienridge, General Robert E. Lee, General Joseph E. Johnston, General John B. Magruder, General William B. Preston, General Simon B. Buckner, and Comodore Franklin Buchanan, now occupying the very highest places in the rebel war service, were all within the power of the government since the rebellion began, and were nearly as well known to be traitors then as now. Unquestionably if we had seized and held them, the insurgent cause would be much weaker. But no one of them had then committed any crime defined in the law.[4] Every one of them, if arrested, would have been discharged on *habeas corpus* were the writ allowed to operate. In view of these and similar cases, I think the time not unlikely to come when I shall be blamed for having made too few arrests rather than too many. By the third resolution the meeting indicated their opinion that military arrests may be constitutional in localities where rebellion actually exists, but that such arrests are unconstitutional in localities where rebellion or insurrection does not actually exist. They insist that such arrests shall not be made "outside of the lines of necessary military occupation and the scenes of insurrection." Inasmuch, however, as the Constitution itself makes no such distinction, I am unable to believe that there is any such constitutional distinction. I concede that the class of arrests complained of can be constitutional only when, in cases of rebellion or invasion, the public safety may require them; and I insist that in such cases they are constitutional *wherever* the public safety does require them, as well in places to which they may prevent the rebellion extending, as in those where it may be already prevailing; as well where they may restrain mischievous interference with the raising and supplying of armies to suppress the rebellion, as where the rebellion may actually

[4]Citing the confederate generals whom he might have incapacitated by arresting them at the beginning of the war, Lincoln argues that he had made too few arrests rather than too many.

be; as well where they may restrain the enticing men out of the army, as where they would prevent mutiny in the army; equally constitutional at all places where they will conduce to the public safety, as against the dangers of rebellion or invasion. Take the particular case mentioned by the meeting. They assert in substance, that Mr. Vallandigham was, by a military commander, seized and tried "for no other reason than words addressed to a public meeting in criticism of the course of the administration, and in condemnation of the military orders of the general." Now, if there be no mistake about this, if this assertion is the truth and the whole truth, if there was no other reason for the arrest, then I concede that the arrest was wrong. But the arrest, as I understand, was made for a very different reason. Mr. Vallandigham avows his hostility to the war on the part of the Union; and his arrest was made because he was laboring, with some effect, to prevent the raising of troops, to encourage desertions from the army, and to leave the rebellion without an adequate military force to suppress it. He was not arrested because he was damaging the political prospects of the administration or the personal interests of the commanding general, but because he was damaging the army, upon the existence and vigor of which the life of the nation depends. He was warring upon the military, and this gave the military constitutional jurisdiction to lay hands upon him.[5] If Mr. Vallandigham was not damaging the military power of the country, then his arrest was made on mistake of fact, which I would be glad to correct on reasonably satisfactory evidence. I understand the meeting whose resolutions I am considering to be in favor of suppressing the rebellion by military force—by armies. Long experience has shown that armies cannot be maintained unless desertion shall be punished by the severe penalty of death. The case requires, and the law and the Constitution sanction, this punishment. Must I shoot a simple-minded soldier boy who deserts, while I must not touch a hair of a wiley agitator who induces him to desert?[6] This is none the less injurious when effected by getting a father, or brother, or friend into a public meeting, and there working upon his feelings till he is persuaded to write the soldier boy that he is fighting in a bad cause, for a wicked administration of a contemptible government, too weak to arrest and punish him if he shall desert. I think that, in such a case, to silence the agitator and save the boy is not only constitutional, but withal a great mercy. If I be wrong on this question of constitutional power, my error lies in believing that certain proceedings are constitutional when, in cases of rebellion or invasion, the public safety requires them, which would not be constitutional when, in absence

[5]Lincoln indicates that Vallandigham was not arrested simply for voicing disagreements with the administration but for speech that directly interfered with military recruiting, which was thought necessary to the success of the Union effort.

[6]Lincoln, who was known for commuting the sentences of many deserting soldiers, questions how fair it would be to shoot them and not arrest those who goaded them to such actions.

of rebellion or invasion, the public safety does not require them: in other words, that the Constitution is not in its application in all respects the same in cases of rebellion or invasion involving the public safety, as it is in times of profound peace and public security. The Constitution itself makes the distinction, and I can no more be persuaded that the government can constitutionally take no strong measures in time of rebellion, because it can be shown that the same could not be lawfully taken in time of peace, than I can be persuaded that a particular drug is not good medicine for a sick man because it can be shown to not be good food for a well one. Nor am I able to appreciate the danger apprehended by the meeting, that the American people will by means of military arrests during the rebellion lose the right of public discussion, the liberty of speech and the press, the law of evidence, trial by jury, and *habeas corpus* throughout the indefinite peaceful future which I trust lies before them, any more than I am able to believe that a man could contract so strong an appetite for emetics during temporary illness as to persist in feeding upon them during the remainder of his healthful life. In giving the resolutions that earnest consideration which you request of me, I cannot overlook the fact that the meeting speak as "Democrats." Nor can I, with full respect for their known intelligence, and the fairly presumed deliberation with which they prepared their resolutions, be permitted to suppose that this occurred by accident, or in any way other than that they preferred to designate themselves "Democrats" rather than "American citizens." In this time of national peril I would have preferred to meet you upon a level one step higher than any party platform, because I am sure that from such more elevated position we could do better battle for the country we all love than we possibly can from those lower ones, where, from the force of habit, the prejudices of the past, and selfish hopes of the future, we are sure to expend much of our ingenuity and strength in finding fault with and aiming blows at each other.[7] But since you have denied me this, I will yet be thankful for the country's sake that not all Democrats have done so. He on whose discretionary judgment Mr. Vallandigham was arrested and tried is a Democrat, having no old party affinity with me, and the judge who rejected the constitutional view expressed in these resolutions, by refusing to discharge Mr. Vallandigham on *habeas corpus*, is a Democrat of better days than these, having received his judicial mantle at the hands of President Jackson.[8] And still more, of all those Democrats who are nobly exposing their lives and shedding their blood on the battle-field, I have learned that many approve the course taken with Mr. Vallandigham, while I have not heard of a

[7]Lincoln is appealing beyond party platforms to what he believes to be the greater good.

[8]Again, Lincoln is stressing that Mr. Vallandigham had been arrested not for his party affiliation, which differed from the president's, but for actions that directly interfered with the war effort.

single one condemning it. I cannot assert that there are none such. And the name of President Jackson recalls an instance of pertinent history. After the battle of New Orleans, and while the fact that the treaty of peace had been concluded was well known in the city, but before official knowledge of it had arrived, General Jackson still maintained martial or military law. Now that it could be said the war was over, the clamor against martial law, which had existed from the first, grew more furious.[9] Among other things, a Mr. Louaillier published a denunciatory newspaper article. General Jackson arrested him. A lawyer by the name of Morel procured the United States Judge Hall to order a writ of *habeas corpus* to release Mr. Louaillier. General Jackson arrested both the lawyer and the judge. A Mr. Hollander ventured to say of some part of the matter that "it was a dirty trick." General Jackson arrested him. When the officer undertook to serve the writ of *habeas corpus*, General Jackson took it from him, and sent him away with a copy. Holding the judge in custody a few days, the general sent him beyond the limits of his encampment, and set him at liberty with an order to remain till the ratification of peace should be regularly announced, or until the British should have left the southern coast. A day or two more elapsed, the ratification of the treaty of peace was regularly announced, and the judge and others were fully liberated. A few days more, and the judge called General Jackson into court and fined him $1000 for having arrested him and the others named. The general paid the fine, and then the matter rested for nearly thirty years, when Congress refunded principal and interest. The late Senator Douglas, then in the House of Representatives, took a leading part in the debates in which the constitutional question was much discussed. I am not prepared to say whom the journals would show to have voted for the measure.

It may be remarked:—first, that we had the same Constitution then as now; secondly, that we then had a case of invasion, and that now we have a case of rebellion; and, thirdly, that the permanent right of the people to public discussion, the liberty of speech and the press, the trial by jury, the law of evidence, and the *habeas corpus*, suffered no detriment whatever by that conduct of General Jackson, or its subsequent approval by the American Congress.

And yet, let me say that, in my own discretion, I do not know whether I would have ordered the arrest of Mr. Vallandigham. While I shift the responsibility from myself, I hold that, as a general rule, the

[9]Lincoln further reminds Corning of the resolve of an earlier Democrat president (Andrew Jackson) to preserve the Union, including the suspension of the writ of habeas corpus in New Orleans during the War of 1812.

commander in the field is the better judge of the necessity in any particular case. Of course I must practice a general directory and revisory power in the matter.

One of the resolutions expresses the opinion of the meeting that arbitrary arrests will have the effect to divide and distract those who should be united in suppressing the rebellion, and I am specifically called on to discharge Mr. Vallandigham. I regard this as, at least, a fair appeal to me on the expediency of exercising a constitutional power which I think exists. In response to such appeal I have to say, it gave me pain when I learned that Mr. Vallandigham had been arrested (that is, I was pained that there should have seemed to be a necessity for arresting him), and that it will afford me great pleasure to discharge him so soon as I can by any means believe the public safety will not suffer by it.[10]

I further say that, as the war progress, it appears to me, opinion and action, which were in great confusion at first, take shape and fall into more regular channels, so that the necessity for arbitrary dealing with them gradually decreases. I have every reason to desire that it should cease altogether, and far from the least is my regard for the opinions and wishes of those who, like the meeting at Albany, declare their purpose to sustain the government in every constitutional and lawful measure to suppress the rebellion. Still, I must continue to do so much as may seem to be required by the public safety.

A. Lincoln.

Source: Edward McPherson, *The Political History of the United States of America during the Great Rebellion*, 2nd ed. Washington, DC: Philp & Solomons, 1865, 163–167.

Abraham Lincoln's Proclamation on Troop Quotas

October 17, 1863

INTRODUCTION

At the beginning of the war, Lincoln had issued a call for 50,000 volunteers, but the war had lasted longer than most people on both sides had anticipated, and Lincoln had to ask for more in 1863.

Whereas the term of service of a part of the volunteer forces of the United States will expire during the coming year; and

Whereas, in addition to the men raised by the present draft, it is deemed expedient to call out 300,000 volunteers to serve for three years or the war, not, however, exceeding three years:

Now, therefore, I, Abraham Lincoln, President of the United States and Commander in Chief of the Army and Navy thereof and of the militia of the several States when called into actual service, do issue this my proclamation, calling upon the governors of the different States to raise and have enlisted into the United States service for the various companies and regiments in the field from their respective States their quotas of 300,000 men.[1]

I further proclaim that all volunteers thus called out and duly enlisted shall receive advance pay, premium, and bounty, as heretofore communicated to the governors of States by the War Department through the Provost-Marshal-General's Office by special letters.

I further proclaim that all volunteers received under this call, as well as all others not heretofore credited, shall be duly credited on and deducted from the quotas established for the next draft.

I further proclaim that if any State shall fail to raise the quota assigned to it by the War Department under this call, then a draft for the deficiency in said quota shall be made on said State, or on the

[1] Although the Southern states were known for their emphasis on state sovereignty, Lincoln's own call for troops is strikingly reminiscent of the system under the Articles of Confederation, which Congress had to requisition individual states to raise troops.

[2] Here Lincoln moves from state quotas to the possibility that the national government will have to draft individuals directly without going through the states.

districts of said State, for their due proportion of said quota; and the said draft shall commence on the 5th day of January, 1864.[2]

And I further proclaim that nothing in this proclamation shall interfere with existing orders, or those which may be issued, for the present draft in the States where it is now in progress or where it has not yet commenced.

The quotas of the States and districts will be assigned by the War Department, through the Provost-Marshal-General's Office, due regard being had for the men heretofore furnished, whether by volunteering or drafting, and the recruiting will be conducted in accordance with such instructions as have been or may be issued by that Department.

In issuing this proclamation I address myself not only to the governors of the several States, but also to the good and loyal people thereof, invoking them to lend their willing, cheerful, and effective aid to the measures thus adopted, with a view to reenforce our victorious armies now in the field and bring our needful military operations to a prosperous end, thus closing forever the fountains of sedition and civil war.

In witness whereof I have hereunto set my hand and caused the seal of the United States to be affixed.

Done at the city of Washington, this 17th day of October, A.D. 1863, and of the Independence of the United States the eighty-eighth.

ABRAHAM LINCOLN.

By the President:

WILLIAM H. SEWARD, *Secretary of State.*

Source: James D. Richardson, *A Compilation of the Messages and Papers of the Presidents*, Vol. 6. Washington, DC: Bureau of National Literature, 1897, 173–174.

Louis Lambert (Patrick Gilmore)'s "When Johnny Comes Marching Home Again"

1863

INTRODUCTION

Wars often begin with great anticipation and end with muted disappointment and sorrow, even among victors. By 1863, both North and South realized that the war would last longer, and cost more in lives and treasure, than either side anticipated. This song, which would be sung in later wars, was written by Patrick Gilmore, an American band leader, under the pen name Louis Lambert, and was first published in 1863. Individuals in both North and South sang this song. Although only Northern troops returned victorious, both sides welcomed their veterans as heroes.

When Johnny comes marching home again
Hurrah! Hurrah!

We'll give him a hearty welcome then
Hurrah! Hurrah!

The men will cheer and the boys will shout
The ladies they will all turn out
And we'll all feel gay[1]

When Johnny comes marching home.

The old church bell will peal with joy
Hurrah! Hurrah!

To welcome home our darling boy,
Hurrah! Hurrah!

The village lads and lassies say
With roses they will strew the way,
And we'll all feel gay

[1] More optimistic than "Johnny I Hardly Knew Ye," the Irish folk song that appears to have supplied the tune, in which a soldier returns home wounded, this song anticipates the joy of a healthy and triumphal return.

When Johnny comes marching home.

Get ready for the Jubilee,
Hurrah! Hurrah![2]

We'll give the hero three times three,
Hurrah! Hurrah!

The laurel wreath is ready now
To place upon his loyal brow
And we'll all feel gay

When Johnny comes marching home.

Let love and friendship on that day,
Hurrah, hurrah!

Their choicest pleasures then display,
Hurrah, hurrah!

And let each one perform some part,
To fill with joy the warrior's heart,
And we'll all feel gay

When Johnny comes marching home.

Source: Louis Lambert, "When Johnny Comes Marching Home." Boston: Henry Tolman, 1863.

[2]The Old Testament (Hebrew Scriptures) outlined a year of Jubilee (every 50th year) in which all slaves would be freed from bondage. Although the term "Jubilee," like the term "gay" as used in this song, was a term for "levity" and "rejoicing," Northerners might have had this Biblical reference in mind as they sang this song.

Abraham Lincoln's Gettysburg Address

November 19, 1863

INTRODUCTION

With the possible exception of the Declaration of Independence, there is no more iconic document in U.S. history than this speech, which Lincoln delivered at the site of a Union victory at Gettysburg, Pennsylvania, that stopped General Robert E. Lee's northward advance. Its most notable quality is arguably its length—a mere 278 words. Like Pericles's funeral oration at Athens, it crystalized the ideals to which Lincoln thought the nation was committed.

Four score and seven years ago our fathers brought forth on this continent, a new nation, conceived in Liberty, and dedicated to the proposition that all men are created equal.[1]

Now we are engaged in a great civil war, testing whether that nation, or any nation so conceived and so dedicated, can long endure. We are met on a great battle-field of that war. We have come to dedicate a portion of that field, as a final resting place for those who here gave their lives that that nation might live. It is altogether fitting and proper that we should do this.

But, in a larger sense, we can not dedicate—we can not consecrate—we can not hallow—this ground. The brave men, living and dead, who struggled here, have consecrated it, far above our poor power to add or detract. The world will little note, nor long remember what we say here, but it can never forget what they did here. It is for us the living, rather, to be dedicated here to the unfinished work which they who fought here have thus far so nobly advanced. It is rather for us to be here dedicated to the great task remaining before us—that from these honored dead we take increased devotion to that cause for which they gave the last full measure of devotion—that we here

[1] The opening phrase is evocative on the language of the King James Bible. This sentence dates the Union not to the Constitution of 1787 but to the Declaration of Independence of 1776. Its affirmation of human equality stands in clear contradiction to the practice of chattel slavery.

[2] Lincoln conceptualizes Union losses as willing sacrifices for the larger causes of freedom and democracy ("government of the people, by the people, for the people"), which should inspire those who remain to continue the task.

highly resolve that these dead shall not have died in vain—that this nation, under God, shall have a new birth of freedom—and that government of the people, by the people, for the people, shall not perish from the earth.[2]

Source: Abraham Lincoln, Transcript of the "Nicolay Copy" of the Gettysburg Address, 1863. Library of Congress.

Law Equalizing the Pay of Black Soldiers

June 15, 1864

INTRODUCTION

Even after the Union decided to allow black soldiers to serve, it did not pay them equally. This law, a clear precursor not only to the equal protection clause of the Fourteenth Amendment but also to future laws dealing with equal pay for women, sought to remedy that situation. It was not until the Korean War that President Harry S. Truman would eliminate segregated units within the armed forces.

CHAP. CXXIV.—An Act making Appropriations for the Support of the Army for the Year ending the thirtieth June, eighteen hundred and sixty-five, and for other Purposes.

. . . .

SEC. 2. *And be it further enacted*, That all persons of color who have been or may be mustered into the military service of the United States shall receive the same uniform, clothing, arms, equipments, camp equipage, rations, medical and hospital attendance, pay and emoluments, other than bounty, as other soldiers of the regular or volunteer forces of the United States of like arm of the service, from and after the first day of January, eighteen hundred and sixty-four; and that every person of color who shall hereafter be mustered into the service shall receive such sums in bounty as the President shall order in the different states and parts of the United States, not exceeding one hundred dollars.[1]

[1]This is the core provision of the act.

SEC. 3. *And be it further enacted*, That all persons enlisted and mustered into service as volunteers under the call, dated October seventeen, eighteen hundred and sixty-three, for three hundred thousand volunteers, who were at the time of enlistment actually enrolled and subject to draft in the state in which they volunteered, shall receive from the United States the same amount of bounty without regard to color.

SEC. 4. *And be it further enacted*, That all persons of color who were free on the nineteenth day of April, eighteen hundred and sixty-one, and who have been enlisted and mustered into the military service of the United States, shall, from the time of their enlistment, be entitled to receive the pay, bounty, and clothing allowed to such persons by the laws existing at the time of their enlistment. And the Attorney-General of the United States is hereby authorized to determine any question of law arising under this provision. And if the Attorney-General aforesaid shall determine that any of such enlisted persons are entitled to receive any pay, bounty, or clothing, in addition to what they have already received, the Secretary of War shall make all necessary regulations to enable the pay department to make payment in accordance with such determination.

SEC. 5. *And be it further enacted*, That all enlistments hereafter made in the regular army of the United States, during the continuance of the present rebellion, may be for the term of three years.

APPROVED, June 15, 1864.

Source: *U.S. Statutes at Large, Treaties, and Proclamations of the United States*, vol. 13 (Boston, 1866), 126–130.

The Wade-Davis Bill

July 2, 1864

INTRODUCTION

The period of congressional reconstruction of Southern states left a lasting legacy of resentment by disaffected whites, many of whom maintained their racial prejudices, who saw Northern attempts to guarantee the rights of freedmen as punitive actions directed against former rebels. Especially as Southern states adopted repressive black codes to limit the freedoms of former slaves, Congress increasingly came to think that nothing short of military rule would be sufficient, at least for a period when blacks could be enfranchised and educated.

A Bill to guarantee to certain States whose Governments have been usurped or overthrown a Republican Form of Government.

Be it enacted by the Senate and House of Representatives of the United States of America in Congress assembled, That in the states declared in rebellion against the United States, the President shall, by and with the advice and consent of the Senate, appoint for each a provisional governor, whose pay and emoluments shall not exceed that of a brigadier-general of volunteers, who shall be charged with the civil administration of such state until a state government therein shall be recognized as hereinafter provided.

SEC. 2. And be it further enacted, That so soon as the military resistance to the United States shall have been suppressed in any such state, and the people thereof shall have sufficiently returned to their obedience to the constitution and the laws of the United States, the provisional governor shall direct the marshal of the United States, as speedily as may be, to name a sufficient number of deputies, and to enroll all white male citizens of the United States, resident in the state in their respective counties, and to request each one to take the oath to support the constitution of the United States,[1] and in his enrolment to designate those who take and those who refuse to take that oath, which rolls shall be forthwith returned to the provisional

[1] Oaths, which are still used in inaugurations and judicial proceedings, were taken very seriously during this time period. Just as the Constitution required officeholders to affirm their support of the document, so this would require a similar oath, commonly administered to naturalized citizens, of voters.

governor; and if the persons taking that oath shall amount to a majority of the persons enrolled in the state, he shall, by proclamation, invite the loyal people of the state to elect delegates to a convention charged to declare the will of the people of the state relative to the reestablishment of a state government subject to, and in conformity with, the constitution of the United States.

SEC. 3. And be it further enacted, That the convention shall consist of as many members as both houses of the last constitutional state legislature, apportioned by the provisional governor among the counties, parishes, or districts of the state, in proportion to the white population, returned as electors, by the marshal, in compliance with the provisions of this act. The provisional governor shall, by proclamation, declare the number of delegates to be elected by each county, parish, or election district; name a day of election not less than thirty days thereafter; designate the places of voting in each county, parish, or district, conforming as nearly as may be convenient to the places used in the state elections next preceding the rebellion; appoint one or more commissioners to hold the election at each place of voting, and provide an adequate force to keep the peace during the election.

[2]Like provisions that would later appear in the Fourteenth Amendment, the law did not extend voting rights either to women or to those under the age of 21.

SEC. 4. And be it further enacted, That the delegates shall be elected by the loyal white male citizens of the United States of the age of twenty-one years, and resident at the time in the county, parish, or district in which they shall offer to vote,[2] and enrolled as aforesaid, or absent in the military service of the United States, and who shall take and subscribe the oath of allegiance to the United States in the form contained in the act of congress of July two, eighteen hundred and sixty-two; and all such citizens of the United States who are in the military service of the United States shall vote at the headquarters of their respective commands, under such regulations as may be prescribed by the provisional governor for the taking and return of their votes; but no person who has held or exercised any office, civil or military, state or confederate, under the rebel usurpation, or who has voluntarily borne arms against the United States, shall vote, or be eligible to be elected as delegate, at such election.

SEC. 5. And be it further enacted, That the said commissioners, or either of them, shall hold the election in conformity with this act, and, so far as may be consistent therewith, shall proceed in the manner used in the state prior to the rebellion. The oath of allegiance shall be taken and subscribed on the poll-book by every voter in the form above prescribed, but every person known by or proved to, the commissioners to have held or exercised any office, civil or military, state or confederate, under the rebel usurpation, or to have voluntarily borne arms against the United States, shall be excluded, though he offer to take the oath;[3] and in case any person who shall have borne arms against the United States shall offer to vote he shall be deemed to have borne arms voluntarily unless he shall prove the contrary by the testimony of a qualified voter. The poll-book, showing the name and oath of each voter, shall be returned to the provisional governor by the commissioners of election or the one acting, and the provisional governor shall canvass such returns, and declare the person having the highest number of votes elected.

SEC. 6. And be it further enacted, That the provisional governor shall, by proclamation, convene the delegates elected as aforesaid, at the capital of the state, on a day not more than three months after the election, giving at least thirty days' notice of such day. In case the said capital shall in his judgment be unfit, he shall in his proclamation appoint another place. He shall preside over the deliberations of the convention, and administer to each delegate, before taking his seat in the convention, the oath of allegiance to the United States in the form above prescribed.

SEC. 7. And be it further enacted, That the convention shall declare, on behalf of the people of the state, their submission to the constitution and laws of the United States, and shall adopt the following provisions, hereby prescribed by the United States in the execution of the constitutional duty to guarantee a republican form of government to every state, and incorporate them in the constitution of the state, that is to say:

First. No person who has held or exercised any office, civil or military, except offices merely ministerial, and military offices below the grade of colonel, state or confederate, under the usurping power, shall vote for or be a member of the legislature, or governor.

Second. Involuntary servitude is forever prohibited, and the freedom of all persons is guaranteed in said state.[4]

Third. No debt, state or confederate, created by or under the sanction of the usurping power, shall be recognized or paid by the state.[5]

[3]Those who had borne arms against the United States were presumptively excluded from participation.

[4]Lincoln doubted that Congress had the power, absent a constitutional amendment, to require states to prohibit slavery.

[5]Section 4 of the Fourteenth Amendment would later constitutionalize the provision prohibiting the repayment of Confederate debt.

SEC. 8. And be it further enacted, That when the convention shall have adopted those provisions, it shall proceed to re-establish a republican form of government, and ordain a constitution containing those provisions, which, when adopted the convention shall by ordinance provide for submitting to the people of the state, entitled to vote under this law, at an election to be held in the manner prescribed by the act for the election of delegates;[6] but at a time and place named by the convention, at which election the said electors, and none others, shall vote directly for or against such constitution and form of state government, and the returns of said election shall be made to the provisional governor, who shall canvass the same in the presence of the electors, and if a majority of the votes cast shall be for the constitution and form of government, he shall certify the same, with a copy thereof, to the President of the United States, who, after obtaining the assent of congress, shall, by proclamation, recognize the government so established, and none other, as the constitutional government of the state, and from the date of such recognition, and not before, Senators and Representatives, and electors for President and Vice President may be elected in such state, according to the laws of the state and of the United States.

SEC. 9. And be it further enacted, That if the convention shall refuse to reestablish the state government on the conditions aforesaid, the provisional governor shall declare it dissolved; but it shall be the duty of the President, whenever he shall have reason to believe that a sufficient number of the people of the state entitled to vote under this act, in number not less than a majority of those enrolled, as aforesaid, are willing to reestablish a state government on the conditions aforesaid, to direct the provisional governor to order another election of delegates to a convention for the purpose and in the manner prescribed in this act, and to proceed in all respects as hereinbefore provided, either to dissolve the convention, or to certify the state government reestablished by it to the President.

SEC. 10. And be it further enacted, That, until the United States shall have recognized a republican form of state government,[7] the provisional governor in each of said states shall see that this act, and the laws of the United States, and the laws of the state in force when the state government was overthrown by the rebellion, are faithfully executed within the state; but no law or usage whereby any person was heretofore held in involuntary servitude shall be recognized or

[6]Whereas a number of Confederate state governments had been created by state legislators, this law sought to put the reconstructed governments on the firmer footing of popular approval.

[7]Article V, Section 4, of the U.S. Constitution guarantees to each state a "republican," or representative, form of government.

enforced by any court or officer in such state, and the laws for the trial and punishment of white persons shall extend to all persons, and jurors shall have the qualifications of voters under this law for delegates to the convention. The President shall appoint such officers provided for by the laws of the state when its government was overthrown as he may find necessary to the civil administration of the slate, all which officers shall be entitled to receive the fees and emoluments provided by the state laws for such officers.

SEC. 11. And be it further enacted, That until the recognition of a state government as aforesaid, the provisional governor shall, under such regulations as he may prescribe, cause to be assessed, levied, and collected, for the year eighteen hundred and sixty-four, and every year thereafter, the taxes provided by the laws of such state to be levied during the fiscal year preceding the overthrow of the state government thereof, in the manner prescribed by the laws of the state, as nearly as may be; and the officers appointed, as aforesaid, are vested with all powers of levying and collecting such taxes, by distress or sale, as were vested in any officers or tribunal of the state government aforesaid for those purposes. The proceeds of such taxes shall be accounted for to the provisional governor, and be by him applied to the expenses of the administration of the laws in such state, subject to the direction of the President, and the surplus shall be deposited in the treasury of the United States to the credit of such state, to be paid to the state upon an appropriation therefor, to be made when a republican form of government shall be recognized therein by the United States.

SEC. 12. And be it further enacted, that all persons held to involuntary servitude or labor in the states aforesaid are hereby emancipated and discharged therefrom, and they and their posterity shall be forever free. And if any such persons or their posterity shall be restrained of liberty, under pretence of any claim to such service or labor, the courts of the United States shall, on *habeas corpus*, discharge them.[8]

[8]Note that this provision is included prior to the ratification of the Thirteenth Amendment (1865) prohibiting involuntary servitude.

SEC. 13. And be it further enacted, That if any person declared free by this act, or any law of the United States, or any proclamation of the President, be restrained of liberty, with intent to be held in or reduced to involuntary servitude or labor, the person convicted before a court of competent jurisdiction of such act shall be punished by fine of not less than fifteen hundred dollars, and be imprisoned not less than five nor more than twenty years.

SEC. 14. And be it further enacted, That every person who shall hereafter hold or exercise any office, civil or military, except offices merely ministerial, and military offices below the grade of colonel, in the rebel service, state or confederate, is hereby declared not to be a citizen of the United States.

Source: Records of Legislative Proceedings, Records of the U.S. House of Representatives 1789–1946, RG 233, National Archives.

An Act to Encourage Immigration

July 4, 1864

INTRODUCTION

Throughout its first hundred years, the United States depended on immigrants to provide labor in Eastern cities as many of their citizens moved westward. In the nineteenth century, many immigrants purchased their way by indenturing themselves to work for a fixed period as payment for their transit. This law, adopted in 1864, but largely repealed in 1868, sought to protect such agreements, with the intention of continuing the immigrant flow.

Be it enacted by the Senate and House of Representatives of the United States of America in Congress assembled, That the President of the United States is hereby authorized, by and with the advice and consent of the Senate, to appoint a commissioner of immigration, who shall be subject to the direction of the Department of State, shall hold his office for four years, and shall receive a salary at the rate of two thousand five hundred dollars a year. . . .

SEC. 2. *And be it further enacted.* That all contracts that shall be made by emigrants to the United States in foreign countries, in conformity to regulations that may be established by the said commissioner, whereby emigrants shall pledge the wages of their labor for a term not exceeding twelve months, to repay the expenses of their emigration, shall be held to be valid in law, and may be enforced in the courts of the United States, or of the several states and territories; and such advances, if so stipulated in the contract, and the contract be recorded in the recorder's office in the county where the emigrant shall settle, shall operate as a lien upon any land thereafter acquired by the emigrant; but nothing herein contained shall be deemed to authorize any contract contravening the Constitution of the United States, or creating in any way the relation of slavery or servitude.[1]

SEC 3. [Exempted incoming immigrants from compulsory military service.

[1] The law recognized that although there was a legal distinction between indenture (contracting one's labor for a fixed period) and slavery, it was a line that needed to be continually monitored.

SEC. 4. *And be it further enacted,* That there shall be established in the city of New York² an office to be known as the United States Emigrant Office; and there shall be appointed, by and with the advice and consent of the Senate, an officer for said city, to be known as superintendent of immigration. . . .

SEC. 5. [Provided that no one filling offices under the act should be otherwise directly or indirectly engaged in immigrant trafficking. Remaining sections omitted.]

Source: 13 Stat. 385, 38th Cong., 1st Sess., 246 (July 4, 1864).

Abraham Lincoln Explains His Veto of the Wade-Davis Bill

July 8, 1864

INTRODUCTION

Lincoln used a pocket veto to disapprove this bill written by Senator Benjamin Wade of Ohio and Representative Henry Winter Davis of Maryland. Lincoln thought it was too onerous to require half of the qualified white voters in the state to approve (he had previously supported plans involving oaths by only 10 percent of the white citizens), wanted to recognize the legitimacy of those who had already sought to restore governments in some of these states, and doubted the authority of Congress to eliminate slavery on its own (his own Emancipation Proclamation was issued as a war measure that might not remain effective at the end of the war). Lincoln's successor, Andrew Johnson, would take a far less flexible approach to the issue than Lincoln.

BY THE PRESIDENT OF THE UNITED STATES: A PROCLAMATION (July 8, 1864)

WHEREAS, at the late session, congress passed a bill to "guarantee to certain states, whose governments have been usurped or overthrown, a republican form of government," a copy of which is hereunto annexed;

And whereas the said bill was presented to the President of the United States for his approval less than one hour before the sine die adjournment of said session, and was not signed by him;[1]

And whereas the said bill contains, among other things, a plan for restoring the states in rebellion to their proper practical relation in the Union, which plan expresses the sense of congress upon that subject, and which plan it is now thought fit to lay before the people for their consideration;

Now, therefore, I, ABRAHAM LINCOLN, President of the United States, do proclaim, declare, and make known, that, while I am

[1] The Constitution specifies that if a president decided not to sign a bill that Congress passes in the last 10 days of a session, it does not become law. This is known as a pocket veto.

[2]Lincoln explains that he exercised this pocket veto because he thought the law was too inflexible, because he wanted to recognize reconstructed governments in states where Unionists had already proceeded under a different set of rules, and because he wanted to ensure the end of involuntary servitude through the passage of the Thirteenth Amendment.

(as I was in December last, when by proclamation I propounded a plan for restoration) unprepared by a formal approval of this bill, to be inflexibly committed to any single plan of restoration; and, while I am also unprepared to declare that the free state constitutions and governments already adopted and installed in Arkansas and Louisiana shall be set aside and held for nought, thereby repelling and discouraging the loyal citizens who have set up the same as to further effort, or to declare a constitutional competency in congress to abolish slavery in states, but am at the same time sincerely hoping and expecting that a constitutional amendment abolishing slavery throughout the nation may be adopted,[2] nevertheless I am truly satisfied with the system for restoration contained in the bill as one very proper plan for the loyal people of any state choosing to adopt it, and that I am, and at all times shall be, prepared to give the executive aid and assistance to any such people, so soon as the military resistance to the United States shall have been suppressed in any such state, and the people thereof shall have sufficiently returned to their obedience to the constitution and the laws of the United States, in which cases military governors will be appointed, with directions to proceed according to the bill.

In testimony whereof; I have hereunto set my hand, and caused the seal of the United States to be affixed.

Done at the city of Washington this eighth day of July, in the year of our [L S.] Lord one thousand eight hundred and sixty-four, and of the Independence of the United States the eighty-ninth.

ABRAHAM LINCOLN.

Source: Records of Legislative Proceedings, Records of the U.S. House of Representatives 1789–1946, RG 233, National Archives.

Abraham Lincoln's Memorandum on the Possibility of Electoral Failure

August 23, 1864

INTRODUCTION

Because we know that Lincoln was reelected, it is easy to assume that he anticipated victory, but the early years of the Civil War were full of dark days and battlefield defeats. Lincoln faced strong electoral opposition from General George B. McClellan, who seemed willing to end the war without achieving Union.

Executive Mansion
Washington, Aug. 23, 1864

This morning, as for some days past, it seems exceedingly probable that this Administration will not be re-elected. Then it will be my duty to so co-operate with the President elect, as to save the Union between the election and the inauguration;[1] as he will have secured his election on such ground that he can not possibly save it afterward.

A. LINCOLN

Source: Abraham Lincoln Papers, Manuscript Division, Library of Congress.

[1]Lincoln was prepared to try to use his authority prior to the inauguration of a successor, to secure the Union.

Abraham Lincoln's Response to a Serenade

November 10, 1864

INTRODUCTION

In the nineteenth century, long before the tradition was established for presidential candidates to give acceptance and concession speeches, it was common for supporters to gather outside the home of a winning candidate and clamor for a speech. The following is the text of the speech that Lincoln delivered to friends who gathered outside the White House after his 1864 presidential victory over General George B. McClellan, who had served for a time as commander of Union forces.

[1]Lincoln, who had himself been criticized for suspending the writ of habeas corpus, respected civil liberties and recognized that some individuals had questioned whether free government could survive emergencies.

[2]The most amazing aspect of the presidential election of 1864 is that it proceeded despite the intense conflict of the day.

[3]Lincoln had not used the excuse of war to perpetuate his own power by attempting to suspend the election. He set a wise precedent that was later continued during World Wars I and II.

It has long been a grave question whether any government, not too strong for the liberties of its people, can be strong enough to maintain its own existence, in great emergencies.[1] On this point the present rebellion brought our republic to a severe test; and a presidential election occurring in regular course during the rebellion added not a little to the strain.

If the loyal people, united, were put to the utmost of their strength by the rebellion, must they not fail when divided, and partially paralyzed, by a political war among themselves? But the election was a necessity. We can not have free government without elections; and if the rebellion could force us to forego, or postpone a national election, it might fairly claim to have already conquered and ruined us.[2] The strife of the election is but human nature practically applied to the facts of the case. What has occurred in this case must ever occur in similar cases. Human nature will not change. In any future great national trial, compared with the men of this, we shall have as weak and as strong, as silly and as wise, as bad and as good. Let us, therefore, study of the incidents of this as philosophy to learn wisdom from, and none of them as wrongs to be revenged. But the election, along with its incidental, and undesirable strife, has done good too. It has demonstrated that a people's government can sustain a national election in the midst of a great civil war. Until now it has not been known to the world that this was a possibility. It shows, also, how sound and how strong we still are.[3] It shows that, even among candidates of the same party, he who is most devoted to the Union and most opposed to treason can receive most of the people's votes. It shows, also, to the extent yet known, that we have more men now than we had when the war began. Gold is good in its place, but living, brave, patriotic men are better than gold.

But the rebellion continues, and now that the election is over, may not all having a common interest reunite in a common effort to save our common country? For my own part I have striven and shall strive to avoid placing any obstacle in the way. So long as I have been here I have not willingly planted a thorn in any man's bosom. While I am deeply sensible to the high compliment of re-election; and duly grateful, as I trust, to Almighty God for having directed my countrymen to a right conclusion, as I think, for their own good, it adds nothing to my satisfaction that any other man may be disappointed or pained by the result.[4]

[4] It generally demonstrates a lack of grace to gloat over one's victory. Lincoln expresses sensitivity to the feelings of the losing presidential candidate.

May I ask those who have not differed from me to join with me, in this same spirit toward those who have? And now let me close by asking three hearty cheers for our brave soldiers and seamen and their gallant and skillful commanders.[5]

[5] With the fate of the Union continuing to hang on the success of the military, it was appropriate for Lincoln to end his speech with a tribute to those in the armed forces.

Source: John G. Nicolay and John Hay, *Complete Works of Abraham Lincoln*, vol. 10. Harrogate, TN: Lincoln Memorial University, 1864, 263–265.

Law Creating the Freedmen's Bureau

March 3, 1865

INTRODUCTION

As the end of the Civil War approached, it became clear that the plight of newly freed slaves was paramount. No longer legally obligated to their masters, most faced unemployment and many faced dislocation. The national government assumed responsibility for what was arguably the largest welfare project in the nation's history.

CHAP. XC.–*An Act to establish a Bureau for the Relief of Freedmen and Refugees.*

Be it enacted by the Senate and House of Representatives of the United States of America in Congress assembled, That there is hereby established in the War Department, to continue during the present war of rebellion, and for one year thereafter, a bureau of refugees, freedmen, and abandoned lands, to which shall be committed, as hereinafter provided, the supervision and management of all abandoned lands, and the control of all subjects relating to refugees and freedmen from rebel states, or from any district of country within the territory embraced in the operations of the army, under such rules and regulations as may be prescribed by the head of the bureau and approved by the President. The said bureau shall be under the management and control of a commissioner to be appointed by the President, by and with the advice and consent of the Senate, whose compensation shall be three thousand dollars per annum, and such number of clerks as may be assigned to him by the Secretary of War, not exceeding one chief clerk, two of the fourth class, two of the third class, and five of the first class. And the commissioner and all persons appointed under this act, shall, before entering upon their duties, take the oath of office prescribed in an act entitled "An act to prescribe an oath of office, and for other purposes," approved July second, eighteen hundred and sixty-two, and the commissioner and the chief clerk shall, before entering upon their duties, give bonds to the treasurer of the United States, the former in the sum of fifty thousand dollars, and the latter in the sum of ten thousand dollars, conditioned for the faithful discharge of their duties respectively, with securities to be approved as sufficient by the Attorney-General, which bonds shall be filed in the office of the first comptroller of the treasury, to be by him put in suit for the benefit of any injured party upon any breach of the conditions thereof.

SEC. 2. *And be it further enacted,* That the Secretary of War may direct such issues of provisions, clothing, and fuel, as he may deem needful for the immediate and temporary shelter and supply of destitute and suffering refugees and freedmen and their wives and children, under such rules and regulations as he may direct.[1]

SEC. 3. *And be it further enacted,* That the President may, by and with the advice and consent of the Senate, appoint an assistant commissioner for each of the states declared to be in insurrection, not exceeding ten in number, who shall, under the direction of the commissioner, aid in the execution of the provisions of this act; and he shall give a bond to the Treasurer of the United States, in the sum of twenty thousand dollars, in the form and manner prescribed in the first section of this act. Each of said commissioners shall receive an annual salary of two thousand five hundred dollars in full compensation for all his services. And any military officer may be detailed and assigned to duty under this act without increase of pay or allowances. The commissioner shall, before the commencement of each regular session of congress, make full report of his proceedings with exhibits of the state of his accounts to the President, who shall communicate the same to congress, and shall also make special reports whenever required to do so by the President or either house of congress; and the assistant commissioners shall make quarterly reports of their proceedings to the commissioner, and also such other special reports as from time to time may be required.

SEC. 4. *And be it further enacted,* That the commissioner, under the direction of the President, shall have authority to set apart, for the use of loyal refugees and freedmen, such tracts of land within the insurrectionary states as shall have been abandoned, or to which the United States shall have acquired title by confiscation or sale,[2] or otherwise, and to every male citizen, whether refugee or freedman, as aforesaid, there shall be assigned not more than forty acres of such land,[3] and the person to whom it was so assigned shall be protected

[1] At the end of the Civil War, there were literally millions of former slaves, typically uneducated, who were now on their own in an environment in which the war had itself caused additional hardship and devastation. This bill was designed to provide for their needs until they could establish themselves within this new environment.

[2] With some exceptions, most notably Robert E. Lee's property that has since become the nation's national cemetery, the North chose not to confiscate the property of former slave owners, many of whom sought to reduce former slaves back into virtual peonage through a system of sharecropping.

[3] This appears to be the basis for the rumor that began circulating after the war that every former slave was to be entitled to "forty acres and a mule."

in the use and enjoyment of the land for the term of three years at an annual rent not exceeding six per centum upon the value of such land, as it was appraised by the state authorities in the year eighteen hundred and sixty, for the purpose of taxation, and in case no such appraisal can be found, then the rental shall be based upon the estimated value of the land in said year, to be ascertained in such manner as the commissioner may by regulation prescribe. At the end of said term, or at any time during said term, the occupants of any parcels so assigned may purchase the land and receive such title thereto as the United States can convey, upon paying therefor the value of the land, as ascertained and fixed for the purpose of determining the annual rent aforesaid.

SEC. 5. *And be it further enacted*, That all acts and parts of acts inconsistent with the provisions of this act, are hereby repealed.

APPROVED, March 3, 1865.

Source: *U.S. Statutes at Large, Treaties, and Proclamations of the United States of America*, vol. 13 (Boston, 1866), 507–509.

Abraham Lincoln's Second Inaugural Address

March 4, 1865

INTRODUCTION

At the time of Lincoln's Second Inaugural Address, he was able to anticipate a positive outcome for the war even as he wrestled with the terrible toll that it had taken on human life. Almost more a meditation than an oration, this speech remains among the most remarkable legacies of one of America's greatest presidents.

Fellow-Countrymen:

At this second appearing to take the oath of the Presidential office there is less occasion for an extended address than there was at the first. Then a statement somewhat in detail of a course to be pursued seemed fitting and proper. Now, at the expiration of four years, during which public declarations have been constantly called forth on every point and phase of the great contest which still absorbs the attention and engrosses the energies of the nation, little that is new could be presented. The progress of our arms, upon which all else chiefly depends, is as well known to the public as to myself, and it is, I trust, reasonably satisfactory and encouraging to all. With high hope for the future, no prediction in regard to it is ventured.

On the occasion corresponding to this four years ago all thoughts were anxiously directed to an impending civil war. All dreaded it, all sought to avert it. While the inaugural address was being delivered from this place, devoted altogether to saving the Union without war, insurgent agents were in the city seeking to destroy it without war— seeking to dissolve the Union and divide effects by negotiation. Both parties deprecated war, but one of them would make war rather than let the nation survive, and the other would accept war rather than let it perish, and the war came.[1]

One-eighth of the whole population were colored slaves, not distributed generally over the Union, but localized in the southern part of it. These slaves constituted a peculiar and powerful interest. All knew

[1] This passage is especially notable for its matter-of-fact retelling of the events that had led to the war. Consistent with his reflections on Divine Providence, Lincoln almost paints the coming of the war as an event beyond human control.

131

that this interest was somehow the cause of the war. To strengthen, perpetuate, and extend this interest was the object for which the insurgents would rend the Union even by war, while the Government claimed no right to do more than to restrict the territorial enlargement of it. Neither party expected for the war the magnitude or the duration which it has already attained. Neither anticipated that the cause of the conflict might cease with or even before the conflict itself should cease. Each looked for an easier triumph, and a result less fundamental and astounding. Both read the same Bible and pray to the same God, and each invokes His aid against the other. It may seem strange that any men should dare to ask a just God's assistance in wringing their bread from the sweat of other men's faces, but let us judge not, that we be not judged. The prayers of both could not be answered. That of neither has been answered fully. The Almighty has His own purposes.[2] "Woe unto the world because of offenses; for it must needs be that offenses come, but woe to that man by whom the offense cometh." If we shall suppose that American slavery is one of those offenses which, in the providence of God, must needs come, but which, having continued through His appointed time, He now wills to remove, and that He gives to both North and South this terrible war as the woe due to those by whom the offense came, shall we discern therein any departure from those divine attributes which the believers in a living God always ascribe to Him? Fondly do we hope, fervently do we pray, that this mighty scourge of war may speedily pass away. Yet, if God wills that it continue until all the wealth piled by the bondsman's two hundred and fifty years of unrequited toil shall be sunk, and until every drop of blood drawn with the lash shall be paid by another drawn with the sword, as was said three thousand years ago, so still it must be said "the judgments of the Lord are true and righteous altogether."[3]

With malice toward none, with charity for all, with firmness in the right as God gives us to see the right, let us strive on to finish the work we are in, to bind up the nation's wounds, to care for him who shall have borne the battle and for his widow and his orphan, to do all which may achieve and cherish a just and lasting peace among ourselves and with all nations.[4]

[2]One does not normally expect presidents to be theologians in chief, and yet this is a profound statement about how individuals who worship the same God can have diametrically opposed notions of God's will.

[3]Lincoln suggests that God's purpose in the war might be that of erasing the wealth that the nation had achieved through the institution of slavery.

[4]Although Lincoln died before the period of Southern reconstruction began, this passage suggests that he would have adopted a conciliatory policy toward the former slaveholding states. He also thought it important to provide for the families of those who had died in the conflict.

Source: Abraham Lincoln, Second Inaugural Address, endorsed by Lincoln, April 10, 1865, March 4, 1865, Series 3, General Correspondence, 1837–1897, The Abraham Lincoln Papers at the Library of Congress, Manuscript Division.

Confederate Law Authorizing the Enlistment of Black Soldiers

March 23, 1865

INTRODUCTION

Desperate times often result in desperate measure. It is difficult to imagine anything other than the thought of an impending defeat that would have prompted the Confederate states to enlist African Americans. It is also difficult to imagine many African Americans being willing to fight for a government that was committed to their continuing enslavement, but this law is a reminder that in the waning days of the Civil War, the South actually authorized African Americans to serve.

ADJT. AND INSP. GENERAL'S OFFICE,
Richmond, Va., March 23, 1865.
GENERAL ORDERS, No. 14.

I. The following act of Congress and regulations are published for the information and direction of all concerned:

AN ACT to increase the military force of the Confederate States.

The Congress of the Confederate States of America do enact, That, in order to provide additional forces to repel invasion, maintain the rightful possession of the Confederate States, secure their independence, and preserve their institutions, the President be, and he is hereby, authorized to ask for and accept from the owners of slaves, the services of such number of able-bodied negro men as he may deem expedient, for and during the war, to perform military service in whatever capacity he may direct.

SEC 2. That the General-in-Chief be authorized to organize the said slaves into companies, battalions, regiments, and brigades, under such rules and regulations as the Secretary of War may prescribe, and to be commanded by such officers as the President may appoint.[1]

[1] The South was no more willing than the North to integrate black and white troops in the same units.

SEC 3. That while employed in the service the said troops shall receive the same rations, clothing, and compensation as are allowed to other troops in the same branch of the service.

SEC 4. That if, under the previous sections of this act, the President shall not be able to raise a sufficient number of troops to prosecute the war successfully and maintain the sovereignty of the States and the independence of the Confederate States, then he is hereby authorized to call on each State, whenever he thinks it expedient, for her quota of 300,000 troops, in addition to those subject to military service under existing laws, or so many thereof as the President may deem necessary to be raised from such classes of the population, irrespective of color, in each State, as the proper authorities thereof may determine: *Provided*, That not more than twenty-five per cent. of the male slaves between the ages of eighteen and forty-five, in any State, shall be called for under the provisions of this act.

²As in its constitution, the Confederate states continued to give positive recognition to the institution of slavery.

SEC 5. That nothing in this act shall be construed to authorize a change in the relation which the said slaves shall bear toward their owners, except by consent of the owners and of the States in which they may reside, and in pursuance of the laws thereof.[2]

Approved March 13, 1865.

II. The recruiting service under this act will be conducted under the supervision of the Adjutant and Inspector General, according to the regulations for the recruiting service of the Regular Army, in so far as they are applicable, and except when special directions may be given by the War Department.

III. There will be assigned or appointed for each State an officer who will be charged with the collection, enrollment, and disposition of all the recruits that may be obtained under the first section of this act. One or more general depots will be established in each State and announced in orders, and a suitable number of officers will be detailed for duty in the staff departments at the depots. There will be assigned at each general depot a quartermaster, commissary, and surgeon, and the headquarters of the superintendent will be at the principal depot in the State. The proper officers to aid the superintendent in enlisting, mustering, and organizing the recruits will be assigned by orders from this office or by the General-in-Chief.

IV. The enlistment of colored persons under this act will be made upon printed forms, to be furnished for the purpose, similar to those established for the regular service. They will be executed in duplicate, one copy to be returned to this office for file. No slave will be accepted as a recruit unless with his own consent and with the approbation of his master by a written instrument conferring, as far as he may, the rights of a freedman, and which will be filed with the superintendent. The enlistments will be made for the war, and the effect of the enlistment will be to place the slave in the military service conformably to this act. The recruits will be organized at the camps in squads and companies, and will be subject to the order of the General-in-Chief under the second section of this act.

V. The superintendent in each State will cause a report to be made on the first Monday of every month showing the expenses of the previous month, the number of recruits at the various depots in the State, the number that has been sent away, and the destination of each. His report will show the names of all the slaves recruited, with their age, description, and the names of their masters. One copy will be sent to the General-in-Chief and one to the adjutant and Inspector General.

VI. The appointment of officers to the companies to be formed of the recruits aforesaid will be made by the President.

VII. To facilitate the raising of volunteer companies, officers recruiting therefor are authorized to muster their men into service as soon as enrolled. As soon as enrolled and mustered, the men will be sent, with descriptive lists, to the depots of rendezvous, at which they will be instructed until assigned for service in the field. When the organization of any company remains incomplete at the expiration of the time specified for its organization, the companies or detachments already mustered into service will be assigned to other organizations at the discretion of the General-in-Chief.

VIII. It is not the intention of the President to grant any authority for raising regiments or brigades. The only organizations to be perfected at the depots or camps of instructions are those of companies and (in exceptional cases where the slaves are of one estate) of battalions consisting of four companies, and the only authority to be issued will be for the raising of companies or the aforesaid special battalions of four companies. All larger organizations will be left for future action as experience may determine.

IX. All officers who may be employed in the recruiting service, under the provisions of this act, or who may be appointed to the command of troops raised under it, or who may hold any staff appointment in connection with them, are enjoined to a provident, considerate, and humane attention to whatever concerns the health, comfort, instruction, and discipline of those troops, and to the uniform observance of kindness, forbearance, and indulgence to their treatment of them, and especially that they will protect them from injustice and oppression.[3]

By order:
S. COOPER,
Adjutant and Inspector General.

Source: U.S. War Department, *The War of the Rebellion: A Compendium of the Official Records of the Union and Confederate Armies*, 128 vols. (Washington, 1880–1901), series 4, vol. 3, 1161–1162.

[3]This provision may be interpreted as seeking fair treatment for African-American recruits, but it also has a paternalistic quality about it.

Correspondence between Ulysses S. Grant and Robert E. Lee

April 1865

INTRODUCTION

Wars are often much easier to start than to end. After years of replacing one general with another, Lincoln had finally found in Ulysses S. Grant a general who was willing to fight and ground down the enemy. After Lee's forces retreated to Appomattox after the fall of the Confederate Capital in Richmond, Virginia, Grant reached out to Lee and called upon him to surrender. After a loss at Appomattox Station on April 8, 1865, Lee decided that the time had finally come to do so.

APRIL 7, 1865
General R. E. LEE:

The result of the last week must convince you of the hopelessness of further resistance on the part of the Army of Northern Virginia in this struggle. I feel that it is so, and regard it as my duty to shift from myself the responsibility of any further effusion of blood, by asking of you the surrender of that portion of the C. S. Army known as the Army of Northern Virginia.[1]

U.S. GRANT,
Lieutenant-General

[1] Grant does not anticipate that Lee will change his views of Union but hopes that he is realistic enough to recognize that the South can no longer win the conflict and anxious to avoid further loss of life.

HEADQUARTERS ARMY OF NORTHERN VIRGINIA,
APRIL 7, 1865
Lieut. Gen. U.S. GRANT:

I have received your note of this date. Though not entertaining the opinion you express on the hopelessness of further resistance on the part of the Army of Northern Virginia, I reciprocate your desire to avoid useless effusion of blood, and therefore, before considering your proposition, ask the terms you will offer on condition of its surrender.

R.E. LEE,
General.

————————

APRIL 8, 1865
General R.E. LEE:

Your note of last evening, in reply to mine of same date, asking the condition on which I will accept the surrender of the Army of Northern Virginia, is just received. In reply I would say that, peace being my great desire, there is but one condition I would insist upon, namely, that the men and officers surrendered shall be disqualified for taking up arms again against the Government of the United States until properly exchanged.[2] I will meet you, or will designate officers to meet any officers you may name for the same purpose, at any point agreeable to yell, for the purpose of arranging definitely the terms upon which the surrender of the Army of Northern Virginia will be received.

U.S. GRANT,
Lieutenant-General.

————————

HEADQUARTERS ARMY OF NORTHERN VIRGINIA,
APRIL 8, 1865
Lieut. Gen. U.S. GRANT:

I received at a late hour your note of to-day. In mine of yesterday I did not intend to propose the surrender of the Army of Northern Virginia, but to ask the terms of your proposition. To be frank, I do not think the emergency has arisen to call for the surrender of this army, but as the restoration of peace should be the sole object of all, I desired to know whether your proposals would lead to that

[2] Grant wanted to see that those who surrendered did not resume conflict, perhaps in an underground or guerilla capacity.

end. I cannot, therefore, meet you with a view to surrender the Army of Northern Virginia, but as far as your proposal may affect the C.S. forces under my command, and tend to the restoration of peace, I should be pleased to meet you at 10 a.m., tomorrow; on the old stage road to Richmond, between the picket-lines of the two armies.

R.E. LEE,
General.

———————

APRIL 9, 1865
General R.E. LEE:

Your note of yesterday is received. I have no authority to treat on the subject of peace; the meeting proposed for 10 a.m. to-day could lead to no good. I will state, however, general, that I am equally anxious for peace with yourself, and the whole North entertains the same feeling. The terms upon which peace can be had are well under-stood.[3] By the South laying down their arms they will hasten that most desirable event, save thousands of human lives, and hundreds of millions of property not yet destroyed. Seriously hoping that all our difficulties may be set-tied without the loss of another life, I subscribe myself, &c.,

U.S. GRANT,
Lieutenant-General.

———————

HEADQUARTERS ARMY OF NORTHERN VIRGINIA,
APRIL 9, 1865
Lieut. Gen. U.S. GRANT:

I received your note of this morning on the picket-line, whither I had come to meet you and ascertain definitely what terms were embraced in your proposal of yesterday with reference to the surrender of this

[3]Grant appears to hedge as to his authority to negotiate peace and yet still proceeds to make suitable arrangements.

army. I now ask an interview in accordance with the offer contained in your letter of yesterday for that purpose.

R. E. LEE,
General.

———————

APPOMATTOX COURT-HOUSE, VA.
April 9, 1865
General R. E. LEE:

In accordance with the substance of my letter to you of the 8th instant, I propose to receive the surrender of the Army of Northern Virginia on the following terms, to wit: Rolls of all the officers and men to be made in duplicate, one copy to be given to an officer to be designated by me, the other to be retained by such officer or officers as you may designate. The officers to give their individual paroles not to take up arms against the Government of the United States until properly exchanged; and each company or regimental commander sign a like parole for the men of their commands. The arms, artillery, and public property to be parked and stacked, and turned over to the officers appointed by me to receive them. This will not embrace the side-arms of the officers, nor their private horses or baggage. This done, each officer and man will be allowed to return to his home, not to be disturbed by U.S. authority so long as they observe their paroles and the laws in force where they may reside.[4]

U.S. GRANT,
Lieutenant-General.

———————

HEADQUARTERS ARMY OF NORTHERN VIRGINIA,
April 9, 1865
Lieut. Gen. U.S. GRANT:

I have received your letter of this date containing the terms of surrender of the Army of Northern Virginia as proposed by you. As they are substantially the same as those expressed in your letter of

[4] Soldiers on both sides had left family members behind, so the prospect of being able to return home rather than be imprisoned was important. So too, being able to take side arms and horses (at a time when the latter was a primary source of transportation) meant that returning officers would be better able to provide for their families.

the 8th instant, they are accepted. I will proceed to designate the proper officers to carry the stipulations into effect.

R.E. LEE,
General.

> **Source:** *The War of the Rebellion: A Compilation of the Official Records of the Union and Confederate Armies*, Series 1—vol. 34 (Part I). Washington, DC: Government Printing Office, 1891, 54–56.

Robert E. Lee's Explanation of Surrender

April 10, 1865

INTRODUCTION

Robert E. Lee (1807–1870), a Virginia native and graduate of the military academy at West Point, had turned down offers to lead Northern forces in order to command the Army of Northern Virginia. Although he was a relatively successful general, his forces were ultimately overwhelmed by those of the more populous North. When Lee decided that the time had come to surrender to General Ulysses S. Grant at the Appomattox Court House on April 9, 1865, he felt it necessary to explain his actions to his faithful troops.

Headquarters, Army of Northern Virginia,
April 10, 1865

After four years of arduous service, marked by unsurpassed courage and fortitude, the Army of Northern Virginia has been compelled to yield to overwhelming numbers and resources. I need not tell the brave survivors of so many hard fought battles who have remained steadfast to the last, that I have consented to this result for no distrust of them; but feeling that valor and devotion could accomplish nothing that could compensate for the loss that would have attended the continuance of the contest, I determined to avoid the useless sacrifice of those whose past services have endeared them to their countrymen.[1] By the terms of the agreement, officers and men can return to their homes and remain until exchanged. You will take with you the satisfaction that proceeds from the consciousness of duty faithfully performed and I earnestly pray that a merciful God will extend to you His blessing and protection.

With an unceasing admiration for your constancy and devotion to your country, and a grateful remembrance of your kind and generous consideration of myself, I bid you all an affectionate farewell.

R.E. Lee, General

[1] It would be difficult to find words that would be more likely to sooth the feelings of individuals who had fought in a losing cause. Lee makes it clear that his surrender was not based on any lack of confidence in those who served but simply on the reality of overwhelming numbers.

CONCLUSION

Lee subsequently worked for reconciliation between North and South, serving as president of Washington College (today's Washington and Lee University).

Source: Robert I. Lee, Jr., *Recollections and Letters of General Robert E. Lee.* New York: Doubleday, Page, 1905, 153–154.

Death of Lincoln to Inauguration of Grant

William Lloyd Garrison's Comments at Calhoun's Grave

April 1865

INTRODUCTION

William Lloyd Garrison (1805–1879) had been one of the earliest and most implacable foes of slavery. When he founded the antislavery newspaper *The Liberator*, he had announced that he was unwilling to compromise on this issue. In his early years, Garrison regarded the U.S. Constitution itself as "an agreement with hell, a covenant with death." Initially unimpressed with Lincoln, Garrison's spirits were renewed with the Emancipation Proclamation and the prospect of the Thirteenth Amendment.

In April 1865, Garrison visited Charleston, South Carolina, where hostilities had begun with the attack on Fort Sumter, but from which the U.S. flag was now flying. The occasion was bittersweet, because news had arrived that Lincoln was on his deathbed, the casualty of an assassin's bullet. Seeking out the grave of former vice president and South Carolina senator John C. Calhoun, who had defended the institution of slavery and the doctrines of nullification and secession, Garrison placed his hand on the marble slab atop the tomb and uttered the following words.

Down into a deeper grave than this slavery has gone, and for it there is no resurrection.[1]

[1] The hope of a bodily resurrection is a mainstay of the Christian faith, which was predominate in both North and South. Much like Lincoln, Garrison was convinced that the sacrifices brought about by the Civil War were sufficient to assure that chattel slavery would never be restored, or resurrected, in the United States.

Source: Frazar Kirkland, *The Pictorial Book of Anecdotes and Incidents of the War of the Rebellion*. Hartford, CT: Hartford Publishing, 1866, 151.

Walt Whitman's "O Captain! My Captain!"

1865

INTRODUCTION

Few events in U.S. history have been more traumatic than the assassination of President Abraham Lincoln shortly after the end of the Civil War. Gunned down by actor John Wilkes Booth in Ford's Theatre in the nation's capital on April 14, 1865, Lincoln's death the next day was an occasion for national mourning. The poet Walt Whitman (1819–1892) wrote this poem, which was published as part of his *Leaves of Grass*.

[1] Whitman plays on the common conception of the nation as a ship of state. As president and commander-in-chief, Lincoln was the captain, who had guided the ship through the nation's greatest crisis, only to die after the ship reaches its harbor (Union).

O Captain! my Captain! our fearful trip is done;
The ship has weathered every rack, the prize we sought is won;[1]
The port is near, the bells I hear, the people all exulting,
While follow eyes the steady keel, the vessel grim and daring.

But O heart! heart! heart!
O the bleeding drops of red!
Where on the deck my Captain lies,
Fallen cold and dead.

O Captain! my Captain! rise up and hear the bells;
Rise up! for you the flag is flung, for you the bugle trills;
For you bouquets and ribboned wreaths, for you the shores
a-crowding;
For you they call, the swaying mass, their eager faces turning.

[2] Whitman unites the imagery of the captain to that of Father Abraham. Contemporary iconography sometimes portrayed George Washington, also identified in the public mind as "father" of the nation, with open arms welcoming Lincoln into heaven.

O Captain! dear father![2]
This arm beneath your head;
It is some dream that on the deck
You've fallen cold and dead.

My Captain does not answer, his lips are pale and still;
My father does not feel my arm, he has no pulse nor will.

The ship is anchored safe and sound, its voyage closed and done;
From fearful trip the victor ship comes in with object won!

Exult, O shores! and ring, O bells!³
But I, with silent tread,
Walk the spot my Captain lies,
   Fallen cold and dead.

  Source: Walt Whitman, "O Captain! My Captain!," Proof sheet with corrections in ink, 1888. Manuscript Division, Library of Congress.

[3] Although bells commonly ring for the dead, they might also be intended to evoke the Liberty Bell, which the public often associated with emancipation.

Gordon Granger's General Orders, Number 3

June 19, 1865

INTRODUCTION

Each June 19, many African Americans celebrate Juneteenth. This celebration commemorates an order issued by Major General Gordon Granger (1822–1876) from Galveston, Texas, proclaiming that all slaves in Texas were free. Although the Emancipation Proclamation had gone into effect on January 1, 1863, it applied only behind rebel lines, and word got to Texas quite slowly. Indeed, many slaveholders from Mississippi and Louisiana had migrated there with their slaves as the war drew to a close.

General Orders, Number 3; Headquarters District of Texas, Galveston, June 19, 1865

The people of Texas are informed that, in accordance with a proclamation from the Executive of the United States, all slaves are free. This involves an absolute equality of personal rights and rights of property between former masters and slaves, and the connection heretofore existing between them becomes that between employer and hired labor. The freedmen are advised to remain quietly at their present homes and work for wages.[1] They are informed that they will not be allowed to collect at military posts and that they will not be supported in idleness either there or elsewhere.

[1] Although the order proclaimed "absolute equality," it was clear that officials expected former slaves to remain on plantations as hired workers. Moreover, the order itself did nothing to remedy the inequality of wealth between plantation owners and former slaves.

CONCLUSION

Even this order did not bring an immediate end to slavery, which largely had to await the arrival of individuals from the Freedman's Bureau, but like the earlier Emancipation Proclamation, this order provided a date to which one-time slaves could date their freedom.

Source: *The War of the Rebellion: A Compilation of Official Records.* Series I, Volume 48, Part II. Washington, DC: Government Printing Office, 1896, 929.

Thirteenth Amendment to the U.S. Constitution

December 6, 1865

Although the U.S. Constitution had never used the terms "slave" or "slavery," it had permitted the institution and informally recognized it in sections providing that slave states would receive representation in the House of Representatives by counting three-fifths of "such other persons" for such purposes, by providing for the continuing importation of slaves for 20 years, and by providing for the return of fugitive slaves. Lincoln had issued his Emancipation Proclamation under his power as commander in chief, and it applied only behind enemy lines. This amendment finally eliminated chattel slavery. Unlike the law that Congress had adopted for the District of Columbia in 1862, it did not provide for compensation for slave owners.

Section 1.

[1]This amendment represented a giant step toward achieving the principle "that all men are created equal" that the nation had announced in the Declaration of Independence of 1776. The nation would no longer be a "house divided" between slave states and free states although other regional and political differences would remain.

Neither slavery nor involuntary servitude, except as a punishment for crime whereof the party shall have been duly convicted, shall exist within the United States, or any place subject to their jurisdiction.[1]

Section 2.

Congress shall have power to enforce this article by appropriate legislation.

Source: Charters of Freedom, National Archives.

Black Codes

1865–1866

The end of slavery was a bitter pill for white residents of Southern states who had been raised on the ideology that blacks were inferior to whites and who had little desire to mingle socially with them. The following selections provide examples of some state laws that were clearly designed to keep blacks in a subordinate position prior to the adoption of the Fourteenth Amendment.

Alabama

AN ACT concerning vagrants and vagrancy.

SECTION 1. *Be it enacted* . . . That the commissioner's court of any county in this State . . . may cause to be hired out such as are vagrants, to work in chain-gangs, or otherwise, for the length of time for which they are sentenced, and the proceeds of such hiring must be paid into the county treasury for the benefit of the helpless in said poor-house, or house of correction.

SEC. 2. *Be it further enacted,* That the following persons are vagrants, in addition to those already declared to be vagrants by law . . .: A stubborn or refractory servant; a laborer or servant who loiters away his time, or refuses to comply with any contract for any term of service without just cause;[1] and any such person may be sent to the house of correction in the county in which such offence is committed; and for want of such house of correction the common jail of the county may be used for that purpose.

SEC. 3. *Be it further enacted,* That when a vagrant is found any justice of the peace must . . . issue his warrant . . . to bring such person before him; and if, upon examination and hearing of testimony, it appears to the justice that such person is a vagrant, he shall assess a fine of fifty dollars and costs against such vagrant, and in default of

[1] It is easy to imagine that former slave masters might regard freedmen who no longer wanted to continue working for them as vagrants.

153

payment he must commit such vagrant to the house of correction, or, if no such house, to the common jail of the county, for a term not exceeding six months, or until such costs, fine, and charges are paid, or such party is otherwise discharged by law: *Provided,* That when committed to jail under this section, the commissioner's court may cause him to be hired out in like manner as in section one of this act.[2]

[2]Being hired out by the state for inability to pay a fine would seem very much like slavery to those freedmen.

SEC. 4. *Be it further enacted,* That when any person shall be convicted of vagrancy as provided for in this act, the justice of the peace before whom such conviction is had may, at his discretion, either commit such person to jail, to the house of correction, or hire such person to any person who will hire the same for a period hot longer than six months for cash, giving three days' notice of the time and place of hiring; and the proceeds of such hiring, after paying all costs and charges, shall be paid into the county treasury for the benefit of the helpless in the poor-house. . . .

Approved December 15, 1865.

AN ACT to define the relative duties of master and apprentice.

SECTION 1. *Be it enacted* . . . That it shall be the duty of the sheriffs, justices of the peace, and other civil officers . . . in this State to report to the probate courts of their respective counties, at any time, all minors under the age of eighteen years, within their respective counties, beats or districts, who are orphans, without visible means of support, or whose parent or parents have not the means, or who refuse to provide for and support said minors, and thereupon it shall be the duty of said probate court to apprentice said minor to some suitable and competent person,[3] on such terms as the court may direct, having a particular care to the interest of said minor: *Provided,* If said minor be a child of a freedman, the former owner of said minor shall have the preference; when proof shall be made that he or she shall be a suitable person for that purpose. . . .

[3]At a time when many freedmen would be unemployed, this law threatened the custody of their children, who would doubtless find that returning to their plantations as apprentices would be little different that the lives they had known under slavery.

SEC. 2. *Be it further enacted,* That when proof shall be fully made before such court that the person or persons to whom said minor shall be apprenticed shall be a suitable person to have the charge and care of said minor, and fully to protect the interest of said minor, the said court shall require the said master or mistress[4] to execute bond, with security, to the State of Alabama, conditioned that he or she shall furnish said minor with sufficient food or clothing, to treat said minor humanely, furnish medical attention in case of sickness, teach, or cause to be taught, him or her to read and write, if under fifteen years old, and will conform to any law that may be hereafter passed for the regulation of the duties and relation of the master and apprentice.

SEC. 3. *Be it further enacted,* That in the management and control of said apprentices, said master or mistress shall have power to inflict such moderate corporal chastisement[5] as a father or guardian is allowed to inflict on his or her child or ward at common law: *Provided,* That in no case shall cruel or inhuman punishment be inflicted.

SEC. 4. *Be it further enacted,* That if any apprentice shall leave the employment of his or her master or mistress without his or her consent, said master or mistress may pursue and capture said apprentice . . .[6] and in the event of a refusal on the part of said apprentice so to return, then said justice [of the peace] shall commit said apprentice to the jail of said county, on failure to give bond, until the next term of the probate court; and it shall be the duty of said court at the next term thereafter to investigate said case, and if the court shall be of opinion that said apprentice left the employment of his or her master or mistress without good cause, to order him or her to receive such punishment as may be provided by the vagrant laws which may then be in force in this State, until he or she shall agree to return to his or her master or mistress: *Provided,* That if the court shall believe that said apprentice had good cause to quit the employment of his or her master or mistress, the court shall discharge such apprentice from said indenture, and may also enter a judgment against the master or mistress for not more than one hundred dollars, for the use and benefit of said apprentice, to be collected on execution, as in other cases. . . .

Approved February 23, 1866.

Florida

AN ACT prescribing additional penalties for the commission of offences against the State, and for other purposes.

[4]Notably, although the law designated such youth as apprentices, it continued to call their employers masters.

[5]The whip and the lash were among the most hated symbols of a slave society. Here, it is translated into "corporal punishment."

[6]One need look no further for precedents for this law than the fugitive slave laws in effect prior to the Thirteenth Amendment.

SEC. 12. *Be it further enacted,* That it shall not be lawful for any negro, mulatto, or other person of color to own, use, or keep in his possession . . . any bowie-knife, dirk, sword, fire-arms, or ammunition of any kind,[7] unless he first obtain a license to do so from the judge of probate of the county in which he may be a resident for the time being; and the said judge of probate is hereby authorized to issue such license upon the recommendation of two respectable citizens of the county, certifying to the peaceful and orderly character of the applicant; and any negro, mulatto, or other person of color so offending, shall be deemed to be guilty of a misdemeanor, and upon conviction shall forfeit to the use of the informer all such fire-arms and ammunition, and . . . shall be sentenced to stand in the pillory for one hour, or be whipped, not exceeding thirty-nine stripes, or both, at the discretion of the jury. . . .

SEC. 14. *Be it further enacted,* That if any negro, mulatto, or other person of color shall intrude himself into any religious or other public assembly of white persons, or into any railroad car or other public vehicle set apart for the exclusive accommodation of white people, he shall be deemed to be guilty of a misdemeanor,[8] and upon conviction shall be sentenced to stand in the pillory for one hour, or be whipped, not exceeding thirty-nine stripes, or both, at the discretion of the jury; nor shall it be lawful for any white person to intrude himself into any religious or other public assembly of colored persons, or into any railroad car or other public vehicle set apart for the exclusive accommodation of persons of color, under the same penalties.

Approved January 15, 1866.

Mississippi

AN ACT to amend the vagrant laws of the State.

SECTION 1. *Be it enacted* . . . That all rogues and vagabonds, idle and dissipated persons, beggars, jugglers, or persons practicing unlawful games or plays, runaways, common drunkards, common night-walkers, pilferers, lewd, wanton, or lascivious persons, in speech or behavior, common railers and brawlers, persons who neglect their calling or employment, misspend what they earn, or do not provide for the support of themselves or their families, or dependants, and all other idle and disorderly persons, including all who neglect all lawful business, habitually misspend their time by frequenting houses of ill-fame, gaming-houses, or tippling shops, shall be deemed and considered vagrants,[9] under the provisions of this act, and on conviction thereof shall be fined not exceeding one hundred dollars, with all accruing costs, and be imprisoned, at the discretion of the court, not exceeding ten days.

SEC. 2. *Be it further enacted,* That all freedmen, free negroes and mulattoes in this State, over the age of eighteen years, found on the second Monday in January, 1866, or thereafter, without lawful employment or business,[10] or found unlawfully assembling themselves together, either in the day or night time, and all white persons so assembling themselves with freedmen, free negroes or mulattoes, or usually associating with freedmen, free negroes or mulattoes, on terms of equality, or living in adultery or fornication with a freed woman, free negro or mulatto, shall be deemed vagrants, and on conviction thereof shall be fined in a sum not exceeding, in the case of a freedman, free negro, or mulatto, fifty dollars, and a white man two hundred dollars, and imprisoned, at the discretion of the court, the free negro not exceeding ten days, and the white man not exceeding six months. . . .

SEC. 5. *Be it further enacted,* That all fines and forfeitures collected under the provisions of this act shall be paid into the county treasury for general county purposes, and in case any freedman, free negro or mulatto shall fail for five days after the imposition of any fine or forfeiture upon him or her for violation of any of the provisions of this act to pay the same, that it shall be, and is hereby, made the duty of the sheriff of the proper county to hire out said freedman, free negro or mulatto, to any person who will, for the shortest period of service, pay said fine or forfeiture and all costs. . . .

SEC. 6. *Be it further enacted,* That the same duties and liabilities existing among white persons of this State shall attach to freedmen, free negroes and mulattoes, to support their indigent families and all colored paupers; and that in order to secure a support for such indigent freedmen, free negroes, and mulattoes, it shall be lawful, and it is hereby made the duty of the boards of county police of each county in this State, to levy a poll or capitation tax on each and every freedman, free negro, or mulatto, between the ages of eighteen and sixty years, not to exceed the sum of one dollar annually to each

[9]Mississippi undoubtedly expected such laws to apply with particular force to newly freed slaves. The terminology would give a great deal of discretion to arresting officers, most of whom would undoubtedly have been white.

[10]This law effectively made unemployment a crime, especially for those who, as former slaves, would be mostly illiterate (Southern states had imposed penalties on individuals who sought to teach blacks to read or write) and have relatively few marketable skills other than farming.

person so taxed, which tax . . . shall . . . constitute a fund to be called the Freedmen's Pauper Fund, which shall be applied by the commissioners of the poor for the maintenance of the poor of the freedmen, free negroes, and mulattoes of this State, under such regulations as may be established by the boards of county police in the respective counties of this State.

Approved November 24, 1865.

South Carolina

AN ACT to amend the criminal law. . . .

14. It shall not be lawful for a person of color to be owner, in whole or in part, of any distillery where spirituous liquors of any kind are made, or of any establishment where spirituous liquors of any kind are sold by retail; nor for a person of color to be engaged in distilling spirituous liquors, or in retailing the same, in a shop or elsewhere.[11] A person of color who shall do anything contrary to the provisions herein contained shall be guilty of a misdemeanor, and upon conviction may be punished by fine or corporal punishment and hard labor,[12] as to the district judge or magistrate before whom he may be tried shall seem meet. . . .

22. No person of color shall migrate into and reside in this State[13] unless, within twenty days after his arrival within the same, he shall enter into a bond, with two freeholders as sureties, to be approved by the judge of the district court or a magistrate, in a penalty of one thousand dollars, conditioned for his good behavior and for his support, if he should become unable to support himself. And in case any such person shall fail to execute the bond as aforesaid, the district judge or any magistrate is hereby authorized and required, upon complaint and due proof thereof, to issue his warrant, commanding such person of color to leave the State within ten days thereafter. . . .

Approved December 19, 1865.

AN ACT to establish and regulate the domestic relations of persons of color, and to amend the law in relation to paupers and vagrancy.

[11]This law limited occupational licenses on the basis of race and stereotypes.

[12]Again, the reference to "corporal punishment" seems very similar to that of the lash and the whip that had previously been used on slaves.

[13]Freedom of movement is an essential right of free people, but this law would limit this right to whites.

72. No person of color shall pursue or practice the art, trade, or business of an artisan, mechanic, or shop-keeper, or any other trade, employment, or business (besides that of husbandry or that of a servant under a contract for service or labor)[14] on his own account and for his own benefit, or in partnership with a white person, or as agent or servant of any person, until he shall have obtained a licence therefor from the judge of the district court,[15] which licence shall be good for one year only. This licence the judge may grant upon petition of the applicant, and upon being satisfied of his skill and fitness, and of his good moral character, and upon payment by the applicant to the clerk of the district court of one hundred dollars, if a shop-keeper or peddler, to be paid annually, and ten dollars if a mechanic, artisan, or to engage in any other trade, also to be paid annually: *Provided, however,* That upon complaint being made, and proved to the district judge, of an abuse of such license, he shall revoke the same: *And provided also,* That no person of color shall practice any mechanical art or trade unless he shows that he has served an apprenticeship in such art or trade, or is now practicing such art or trade. . . .

Approved December 21, 1865.

> **Source:** Compiled by 39th Cong., 2d Sess., in Senate Executive Document No. 6, *Laws in Relation to Freedman* (1867).

[14]The right to pursue an occupation is another right generally associated with freedom.

[15]This law would grant discretion to ruling whites, some of whom might be in competition, as to whether to license African-American establishments.

Ex Parte Milligan

April 3, 1866

INTRODUCTION

The Civil War presented unique issues involving civil liberties. In this case, Lambdin P. Milligan, a citizen of Indiana who had aided the Confederate war effort, had been tried and sentenced to death under the authority of a military commission that President Lincoln had created for such circumstances. Although this case may be portrayed as a ringing endorsement of civil liberties, the Court did not issue its decision until after the war was over and passions on the subject had cooled.

Mr. Justice DAVIS delivered the opinion of the court.

. . .

Milligan insists that said military commission had no jurisdiction to try him upon the charges preferred, or upon any charges whatever, because he was a citizen of the United States and the State of Indiana, and had not been, since the commencement of the late Rebellion, a resident of any of the States whose citizens were arrayed against the government, and that the right of trial by jury was guaranteed to him by the Constitution of the United States. . . .

The controlling question in the case is this: upon the facts stated in Milligan's petition and the exhibits filed, had the military commission mentioned in it jurisdiction legally to try and sentence him? Milligan, not a resident of one of the rebellious states or a prisoner of war, but a citizen of Indiana for twenty years past and never in the military or naval service, is, while at his home, arrested by the military power of the United States, imprisoned, and, on certain criminal charges preferred against him, tried, convicted, and sentenced to be hanged by a military commission, organized under the direction of the military commander of the military district of Indiana. Had this tribunal the legal power and authority to try and punish this man?

No graver question was ever considered by this court, nor one which more nearly concerns the rights of the whole people, for it is the birthright of every American citizen when charged with crime to be tried and punished according to law. The power of punishment is alone through the means which the laws have provided for that purpose, and, if they are ineffectual, there is an immunity from punishment, no matter how great an offender the individual may be or how much his crimes may have shocked the sense of justice of the country or endangered its safety. By the protection of the law, human rights are secured; withdraw that protection and they are at the mercy of wicked rulers or the clamor of an excited people. If there was law to justify this military trial, it is not our province to interfere; if there was not, it is our duty to declare the nullity of the whole proceedings. The decision of this question does not depend on argument or judicial precedents, numerous and highly illustrative as they are. These precedents inform us of the extent of the struggle to preserve liberty and to relieve those in civil life from military trials. The founders of our government were familiar with the history of that struggle, and secured in a written constitution every right which the people had wrested from power during a contest of ages. By that Constitution and the laws authorized by it, this question must be determined. The provisions of that instrument on the administration of criminal justice are too plain and direct to leave room for misconstruction or doubt of their true meaning. Those applicable to this case are found in that clause of the original Constitution which says "That the trial of all crimes, except in case of impeachment, shall be by jury," and in the fourth, fifth, and sixth articles of the amendments.[1] The fourth proclaims the right to be secure in person and effects against unreasonable search and seizure, and directs that a judicial warrant shall not issue "without proof of probable cause supported by oath or affirmation." The fifth declares "that no person shall be held to answer for a capital or otherwise infamous crime unless on presentment by a grand jury, except in cases arising in the land or naval forces, or in the militia, when in actual service in time of war or public danger, nor be deprived of life, liberty, or property without due process of law."

And the sixth guarantees the right of trial by jury, in such manner and with such regulations that, with upright judges, impartial juries, and an able bar, the innocent will be saved and the guilty punished. It is in these words: "In all criminal prosecutions the accused shall

[1] Because this trial involved a U.S. military tribunal, rather than a state court, it was subject to the provisions of the Bill of Rights, which applied directly to the national government. Davis accordingly cites provisions of the Fourth through Sixth Amendments.

enjoy the right to a speedy and public trial by an impartial jury of the state and district wherein the crime shall have been committed, which district shall have been previously ascertained by law, and to be informed of the nature and cause of the accusation, to be confronted with the witnesses against him, to have compulsory process for obtaining witnesses in his favor, and to have the assistance of counsel for his defence."

These securities for personal liberty thus embodied were such as wisdom and experience had demonstrated to be necessary for the protection of those accused of crime. And so strong was the sense of the country of their importance, and so jealous were the people that these rights, highly prized, might be denied them by implication, that, when the original Constitution was proposed for adoption, it encountered severe opposition, and, but for the belief that it would be so amended as to embrace them, it would never have been ratified.

Time has proven the discernment of our ancestors, for even these provisions, expressed in such plain English words that it would seem the ingenuity of man could not evade them, are now, after the lapse of more than seventy years, sought to be avoided. Those great and good men foresaw that troublous times would arise when rulers and people would become restive under restraint, and seek by sharp and decisive measures to accomplish ends deemed just and proper, and that the principles of constitutional liberty would be in peril unless established by irrepealable law. The history of the world had taught them that what was done in the past might be attempted in the future. The Constitution of the United States is a law for rulers and people, equally in war and in peace, and covers with the shield of its protection all classes of men, at all times and under all circumstances. No doctrine involving more pernicious consequences was ever invented by the wit of man than that any of its provisions can be suspended during any of the great exigencies of government. Such a doctrine leads directly to anarchy or despotism, but the theory of necessity on which it is based is false, for the government, within the Constitution, has all the powers granted to it which are necessary to preserve its existence, as has been happily proved by the result of the great effort to throw off its just authority.

Have any of the rights guaranteed by the Constitution been violated in the case of Milligan?, and, if so, what are they?

Every trial involves the exercise of judicial power, and from what source did the military commission that tried him derive their authority? Certainly no part of judicial power of the country was conferred on them, because the Constitution expressly vests it "in one supreme court and such inferior courts as the Congress may from time to time ordain and establish," and it is not pretended that the commission was a court ordained and established by Congress. They cannot justify on the mandate of the President, because he is controlled by law, and has his appropriate sphere of duty, which is to execute, not to make, the laws, and there is "no unwritten criminal code to which resort can be had as a source of jurisdiction."

But it is said that the jurisdiction is complete under the "laws and usages of war."

It can serve no useful purpose to inquire what those laws and usages are, whence they originated, where found, and on whom they operate; they can never be applied to citizens in states which have upheld the authority of the government, and where the courts are open and their process unobstructed.[2] This court has judicial knowledge that, in Indiana, the Federal authority was always unopposed, and its courts always open to hear criminal accusations and redress grievances, and no usage of war could sanction a military trial there for any offence whatever of a citizen in civil life in nowise connected with the military service. Congress could grant no such power, and, to the honor of our national legislature be it said, it has never been provoked by the state of the country even to attempt its exercise. One of the plainest constitutional provisions was therefore infringed when Milligan was tried by a court not ordained and established by Congress and not composed of judges appointed during good behavior.

Why was he not delivered to the Circuit Court of Indiana to be proceeded against according to law? No reason of necessity could be urged against it, because Congress had declared penalties against the offences charged, provided for their punishment, and directed that court to hear and determine them. And soon after this military tribunal was ended, the Circuit Court met, peacefully transacted its business, and adjourned. It needed no bayonets to protect it, and required no military aid to execute its judgments. It was held in a state, eminently distinguished for patriotism, by judges commissioned during the Rebellion, who were provided with juries, upright, intelligent, and

[2] The court does not deny that war might create conditions under which the government might have to operate outside regular channels, but Milligan was living in Indiana, which had not been invaded, and its civilian courts had remained open.

selected by a marshal appointed by the President. The government had no right to conclude that Milligan, if guilty, would not receive in that court merited punishment, for its records disclose that it was constantly engaged in the trial of similar offences, and was never interrupted in its administration of criminal justice. If it was dangerous, in the distracted condition of affairs, to leave Milligan unrestrained of his liberty because he "conspired against the government, afforded aid and comfort to rebels, and incited the people to insurrection," the law said arrest him, confine him closely, render him powerless to do further mischief, and then present his case to the grand jury of the district, with proofs of his guilt, and, if indicted, try him according to the course of the common law. If this had been done, the Constitution would have been vindicated, the law of 1863 enforced, and the securities for personal liberty preserved and defended.

Another guarantee of freedom was broken when Milligan was denied a trial by jury. The great minds of the country have differed on the correct interpretation to be given to various provisions of the Federal Constitution, and judicial decision has been often invoked to settle their true meaning; but, until recently, no one ever doubted that the right of trial by jury was fortified in the organic law against the power of attack. It is *now* assailed, but if ideas can be expressed in words and language has any meaning, *this right*—one of the most valuable in a free country—is preserved to everyone accused of crime who is not attached to the army or navy or militia in actual service. The sixth amendment affirms that, "in all criminal prosecutions, the accused shall enjoy the right to a speedy and public trial by an impartial jury," language broad enough to embrace all persons and cases; but the fifth, recognizing the necessity of an indictment or presentment before anyone can be held to answer for high crimes, "*excepts* cases arising in the land or naval forces, or in the militia, when in actual service, in time of war or public danger," and the framers of the Constitution doubtless meant to limit the right of trial by jury in the sixth amendment to those persons who were subject to indictment or presentment in the fifth.

[3]Consistent with the Fifth Amendment, the court recognizes a role for military tribunals to deal with infractions my members of the military.

The discipline necessary to the efficiency of the army and navy required other and swifter modes of trial than are furnished by the common law courts, and, in pursuance of the power conferred by the Constitution, Congress has declared the kinds of trial, and the manner in which they shall be conducted, for offences committed while the party is in the military or naval service.[3] Everyone connected with these branches of the public service is amenable to the jurisdiction which Congress has created for their government, and, while thus serving, surrenders his right to be tried by the civil courts. *All other persons,* citizens of states where the courts are open, if charged with crime, are guaranteed the inestimable privilege of trial by jury.[4] This privilege is a vital principle, underlying the whole administration of criminal justice; it is not held by sufferance, and cannot be frittered away on any plea of state or political necessity. When peace prevails, and the authority of the government is undisputed, there is no difficulty of preserving the safeguards of liberty, for the ordinary modes of trial are never neglected, and no one wishes it otherwise; but if society is disturbed by civil commotion—if the passions of men are aroused and the restraints of law weakened, if not disregarded— these safeguards need, and should receive, the watchful care of those intrusted with the guardianship of the Constitution and laws. In no other way can we transmit to posterity unimpaired the blessings of liberty, consecrated by the sacrifices of the Revolution.

It is claimed that martial law covers with its broad mantle the proceedings of this military commission. The proposition is this: that, in a time of war, the commander of an armed force (if, in his opinion, the exigencies of the country demand it, and of which he is to judge) has the power, within the lines of his military district, to suspend all civil rights and their remedies and subject citizens, as well as soldiers to the rule of *his will,* and, in the exercise of his lawful authority, cannot be restrained except by his superior officer or the President of the United States.

If this position is sound to the extent claimed, then, when war exists, foreign or domestic, and the country is subdivided into military departments for mere convenience, the commander of one of them can, if he chooses, within his limits, on the plea of necessity, with the approval of the Executive, substitute military force for and to the exclusion of the laws, and punish all persons as he thinks right and proper, without fixed or certain rules.

The statement of this proposition shows its importance, for, if true, republican government is a failure, and there is an end of liberty regulated by law. Martial law established on such a basis destroys every guarantee of the Constitution, and effectually renders the "military independent of and superior to the civil power"—the attempt to do which by the King of Great Britain was deemed by our fathers

[4]The court does not think that this same authority extends to civilians.

such an offence that they assigned it to the world as one of the causes which impelled them to declare their independence. Civil liberty and this kind of martial law cannot endure together; the antagonism is irreconcilable, and, in the conflict, one or the other must perish.

This nation, as experience has proved, cannot always remain at peace, and has no right to expect that it will always have wise and humane rulers sincerely attached to the principles of the Constitution. Wicked men, ambitious of power, with hatred of liberty and contempt of law, may fill the place once occupied by Washington and Lincoln, and if this right is conceded, and the calamities of war again befall us, the dangers to human liberty are frightful to contemplate.[5] If our fathers had failed to provide for just such a contingency, they would have been false to the trust reposed in them. They knew—the history of the world told them—the nation they were founding, be its existence short or long, would be involved in war; how often or how long continued human foresight could not tell, and that unlimited power, wherever lodged at such a time, was especially hazardous to freemen. For this and other equally weighty reasons, they secured the inheritance they had fought to maintain by incorporating in a written constitution the safeguards which time had proved were essential to its preservation. Not one of these safeguards can the President or Congress or the Judiciary disturb, except the one concerning the writ of habeas corpus.

It is essential to the safety of every government that, in a great crisis like the one we have just passed through, there should be a power somewhere of suspending the writ of habeas corpus. In every war, there are men of previously good character wicked enough to counsel their fellow-citizens to resist the measures deemed necessary by a good government to sustain its just authority and overthrow its enemies, and their influence may lead to dangerous combinations. In the emergency of the times, an immediate public investigation according to law may not be possible, and yet the period to the country may be too imminent to suffer such persons to go at large. Unquestionably, there is then an exigency which demands that the government, if it should see fit in the exercise of a proper discretion to make arrests, should not be required to produce the persons arrested in answer to a writ of habeas corpus. The Constitution goes no further.[6] It does not say, after a writ of habeas corpus is denied a citizen, that he shall

[5] The court is seeking to temper its decision by acknowledging the good will of President Lincoln while indicating that even leaders of good will need to be subject to constitutional principles.

[6] Lincoln had suspended the writ of habeas corpus (which required the government to detail charges against individuals it detailed), and the court recognizes that such a power may be necessary in times of war but that it was still limited.

be tried otherwise than by the course of the common law; if it had intended this result, it was easy, by the use of direct words, to have accomplished it. The illustrious men who framed that instrument were guarding the foundations of civil liberty against the abuses of unlimited power; they were full of wisdom, and the lessons of history informed them that a trial by an established court, assisted by an impartial jury, was the only sure way of protecting the citizen against oppression and wrong. Knowing this, they limited the suspension to one great right, and left the rest to remain forever inviolable. But it is insisted that the safety of the country in time of war demands that this broad claim for martial law shall be sustained. If this were true, it could be well said that a country, preserved at the sacrifice of all the cardinal principles of liberty, is not worth the cost of preservation. Happily, it is not so.

It will be borne in mind that this is not a question of the power to proclaim martial law when war exists in a community and the courts and civil authorities are overthrown. Nor is it a question what rule a military commander, at the head of his army, can impose on states in rebellion to cripple their resources and quell the insurrection. The jurisdiction claimed is much more extensive. The necessities of the service during the late Rebellion required that the loyal states should be placed within the limits of certain military districts and commanders appointed in them, and it is urged that this, in a military sense, constituted them the theater of military operations, and as, in this case, Indiana had been and was again threatened with invasion by the enemy, the occasion was furnished to establish martial law. The conclusion does not follow from the premises. If armies were collected in Indiana, they were to be employed in another locality, where the laws were obstructed and the national authority disputed. On her soil there was no hostile foot; if once invaded, that invasion was at an end, and, with it, all pretext for martial law. Martial law cannot arise from a *threatened* invasion. The necessity must be actual and present, the invasion real, such as effectually closes the courts and deposes the civil administration.

It is difficult to see how the *safety* for the country required martial law in Indiana. If any of her citizens were plotting treason, the power of arrest could secure them until the government was prepared for their trial, when the courts were open and ready to try them. It was as easy to protect witnesses before a civil as a military tribunal, and as there could be no wish to convict except on sufficient legal evidence, surely an ordained and establish court was better able to judge of this than a military tribunal composed of gentlemen not trained to the profession of the law.

It follows from what has been said on this subject that there are occasions when martial rule can be properly applied. If, in foreign invasion or civil war, the courts are actually closed, and it is impossible to administer criminal justice according to law, *then*, on the theatre of active military operations, where war really prevails, there is a necessity to furnish a substitute for the civil authority, thus overthrown, to preserve the safety of the army and society,[7] and as no power is left but the military, it is allowed to govern by martial rule until the laws can have their free course. As necessity creates the rule, so it limits its duration, for, if this government is continued *after* the courts are reinstated, it is a gross usurpation of power. Martial rule can never exist where the courts are open and in the proper and unobstructed exercise of their jurisdiction. It is also confined to the locality of actual war. Because, during the late Rebellion, it could have been enforced in Virginia, where the national authority was overturned and the courts driven out, it does not follow that it should obtain in Indiana, where that authority was never disputed and justice was always administered. And so, in the case of a foreign invasion, martial rule may become a necessity in one state when, in another, it would be "mere lawless violence." . . .

The two remaining questions in this case must be answered in the affirmative. The suspension of the privilege of the writ of habeas corpus does not suspend the writ itself. The writ issues as a matter of course, and, on the return made to it, the court decides whether the party applying is denied the right of proceeding any further with it.

If the military trial of Milligan was contrary to law, then he was entitled, on the facts stated in his petition, to be discharged from custody by the terms of the act of Congress of March 3d, 1863. The provisions of this law having been considered in a previous part of this opinion, we will not restate the views there presented. Milligan avers he was a citizen of Indiana, not in the military or naval service, and was detained in close confinement, by order of the President, from the 5th day of October, 1864, until the 2d day of January, 1865, when the Circuit Court for the District of Indiana, with a grand jury, convened in session at Indianapolis, and afterwards, on the 27th day

7 Just as the court believed the right to suspect the writ of habeas corpus was limited, so too it believed that martial law should be limited to areas that were under military occupation.

of the same month, adjourned without finding an indictment or presentment against him. If these averments were true (and their truth is conceded for the purposes of this case), the court was required to liberate him on taking certain oaths prescribed by the law, and entering into recognizance for his good behavior.

But it is insisted that Milligan was a prisoner of war, and therefore excluded from the privileges of the statute. It is not easy to see how he can be treated as a prisoner of war when he lived in Indiana for the past twenty years, was arrested there, and had not been, during the late troubles, a resident of any of the states in rebellion.[8] If in Indiana he conspired with bad men to assist the enemy, he is punishable for it in the courts of Indiana; but, when tried for the offence, he cannot plead the rights of war, for he was not engaged in legal acts of hostility against the government, and only such persons, when captured, are prisoners of war. If he cannot enjoy the immunities attaching to the character of a prisoner of war, how can he be subject to their pains and penalties? . . .

The CHIEF JUSTICE delivered the following opinion.

. . .

We do not doubt that the positive provisions of the act of Congress require such answers. We do not think it necessary to look beyond these provisions. In them, we find sufficient and controlling reasons for our conclusions.

But the opinion which has just been read goes further, and, as we understand it, asserts not only that the military commission held in Indiana was not authorized by Congress, but that it was not in the power of Congress to authorize it, from which it may be thought to follow that Congress has no power to indemnify the officers who composed the commission against liability in civil courts for acting as members of it.

We cannot agree to this.

We agree in the proposition that no department of the government of the United States—neither President, nor Congress, nor the Courts—possesses any power not given by the Constitution.

[8] Because Milligan was a civilian, the court denied that he could be considered to be a prisoner of war.

[9] The dissenting opinion agrees that Lincoln did not have the authority to create military tribunals to try civilians on his own authority, but argued that he could have if Congress had consented. Twentieth-century decisions have also suggested that the president's powers are at their maximum when Congress has authorized such actions.

We assent fully to all that is said in the opinion of the inestimable value of the trial by jury, and of the other constitutional safeguards of civil liberty. And we concur also in what is said of the writ of habeas corpus and of its suspension, with two reservations: (1) that, in our judgment, when the writ is suspended, the Executive is authorized to arrest, as well as to detain, and (2) that there are cases in which, the privilege of the writ being suspended, trial and punishment by military commission, in states where civil courts are open, may be authorized by Congress, as well as arrest and detention.

We think that Congress had power, though not exercised, to authorize the military commission which was held in Indiana. . . .[9]

Source: Ex parte Milligan, 71 U.S. (4 Wall.) 2 (1866).

Civil Rights Act

April 5, 1866

INTRODUCTION

Freeing the slaves did not, by itself, guarantee freedmen the same rights as others. This law is best known as a precursor to the language of the Fourteenth Amendment with its provision of citizenship to all persons born in the United States. Congress adopted it over President Andrew Johnson's veto.

Be it enacted by the Senate and House of Representatives of the United States of America in Congress assembled, That all persons born in the United States and not subject to any foreign power, excluding Indians not taxed, are hereby declared to be citizens of the United States; and such citizens, of every race and color,[1] without regard to any previous condition of slavery or involuntary servitude, except as a punishment for crime whereof the party shall have been duly convicted, shall have the same right, in every State and Territory in the United States, to make and enforce contracts, to sue, be parties, and give evidence, to inherit, purchase, lease, sell, hold, and convey real and personal property,[2] and to full and equal benefit of all laws and proceedings for the security of person and property, as is enjoyed by white citizens,[3] and shall be subject to like punishment, pains, and penalties, and to none other, any law, statute, ordinance, regulation, or custom, to the contrary notwithstanding.

SEC. 2. And be it further enacted, That any person who, under color of any law, statute, ordinance, regulation, or custom, shall subject, or cause to be subjected, any inhabitant of any State or Territory to the deprivation of any right secured or protected by this act . . . shall be deemed guilty of a misdemeanor, and, on conviction, shall be punished by fine not exceeding one thousand dollars, or imprisonment not exceeding one year, or both, in the discretion of the court.

[1] Like the Fourteenth Amendment, this law sought to guarantee citizenship to individuals born in the United States, regardless of their race.

[2] The law actually articulates property rights more clearly than that amendment.

[3] This provision for "full and equal benefit of all laws" is a predecessor to the equal protection clause of the Fourteenth Amendment.

SEC. 6. And be it further enacted, That any person who shall knowingly and wilfully obstruct, hinder, or prevent any officer, or other person charged with the execution of any warrant or process issued under the provisions of this act . . . [shall] be subject to a fine not exceeding one thousand dollars, and imprisonment not exceeding six months.

Source: Statutes at Large, 39th Cong., 1st Sess., 31, 27.

The Reconstruction Acts

March 1867

INTRODUCTION

The war was over, but what should be done with those states that had led the rebellion? Should Congress seat their representatives immediately, or should they first be required to alter their governments so as to guarantee rights to the newly freed slaves?

Andrew Johnson, a Southerner who had become president upon Abraham Lincoln's assassination, and Congress, led by radical Republicans who were committed to securing equal liberty for all, clashed over this issue. Between March and July of 1867, Congress ultimately adopted three acts calling for Southern reconstruction, all of which were adopted over President Johnson's veto.

Act of March 2, 1867

An Act to provide for the more efficient Government of the Rebel States[1]

Whereas no legal State governments or adequate protection for life or property now exists in the rebel States of Virginia, North Carolina, South Carolina, Georgia, Mississippi, Alabama, Louisiana, Florida. Texas and Arkansas; and whereas it is necessary that peace and good order should be enforced in said States until loyal and republican State governments can be legally established: Therefore,

Be it enacted by the Senate and House of Representatives of the United States of America in Congress assembled, That said rebel States shall be divided into military districts and made subject to the military authority of the United States[2] as hereinafter prescribed, and for that purpose Virginia shall constitute the first district; North Carolina and South Carolina the second district; Georgia, Alabama and Florida the third district; Mississippi and Arkansas the fourth district; and Louisiana and Texas the fifth district.

[1] Passed over President Johnson's veto, March 2, 1867.

[2] Military occupation was considered to be strong medicine but necessary in light of the unwillingness of former rebels to guarantee rights to newly freed slaves.

173

Sec. 2 And be it further enacted, That it shall be the duty of the President to assign to the command of each of the said districts an officer of the army, not below the rank of brigadier-general, and to detail a sufficient military force to enable such officer to perform his duties and enforce his authority within the district to which he is assigned.

Sec. 3 And be it further enacted, That it shall be the duty of each officer assigned as aforesaid, to protect all persons in their rights of person and property, to suppress insurrection, disorder, and violence, and to punish, or cause to be punished, all disturbers of the public peace and criminals;[3] and to this end he may allow local civil tribunals to take jurisdiction of and to try offenders, or, when in his judgment it may be necessary for the trial of offenders, he shall have power to organize military commissions or tribunals for that purpose, and all interference under color of State authority with the exercise of military authority under this act, shall be null and void.

[3]The law clearly focused on the need to guarantee rights and maintain law and order.

Sec. 4 And be it further enacted, That all persons put under military arrest by virtue of this act shall be tried without unnecessary delay, and no cruel or unusual punishment shall be inflicted, and no sentence of any military commission or tribunal hereby authorized, affecting the life or liberty of any person, shall be executed until it is approved by the officer in command of the district, and the laws and regulations for the government of the army shall not be affected by this act, except in so far as they conflict with its provisions: Provided, That no sentence of death under the provisions of this act shall be carried into effect without the approval of the President.

Sec. 5 And be it further enacted, That when the people of any one of said rebel States shall have formed a constitution of government in conformity with the Constitution of the United States in all respects,[4] framed by a convention of delegates elected by the male citizens of said State, twenty-one years old and upward, of whatever race, color, or previous condition, who have been resident in said State for one year previous to the day of such election, except such as may be disfranchised for participation in the rebellion or for felony at common law, and when such constitution shall provide that the elective franchise shall be enjoyed by all such persons as have the qualifications herein stated for electors of delegates, and when such constitution shall be ratified by a majority of the persons voting on the question of ratification who are qualified as electors for delegates,

[4]The laws were called Reconstruction Acts because they were designed to affect changes in the governments of states that that participated in the rebellion. Article IV of the U.S. Constitution guarantees each state a "republican" form of government.

and when such constitution shall have been submitted to Congress for examination and approval, and Congress shall have approved the same, and when said State, by a vote of its legislature elected under said constitution, shall have adopted the amendment to the Constitution of the United States, proposed by the Thirty-ninth Congress, and known as article fourteen,[5] and when such article shall have become a part of the Constitution of the United States, said State shall be declared entitled to representation in Congress, and senators and representatives shall be admitted therefrom on their taking the oath prescribed by law,[6] and then and thereafter the preceding sections of this act shall be inoperative in said State: Provided, That no person excluded from the privilege of holding office by said proposed amendment to the Constitution of the United States, shall be eligible to election as a member of the convention to frame a constitution for any of said rebel States, nor shall any such person vote for members of such convention.

Sec. 6 And be it further enacted, That, until the people of said rebel States shall be by law admitted to representation in the Congress of the United States, any civil governments which may exist therein shall be deemed provisional only, and in all respects subject to the paramount authority of the United States at any time to abolish, modify, control, or supersede the same; and in all elections to any office under such provisional governments all persons shall be entitled to vote, and none others, who are entitled to vote under the provisions of the fifth section of this act; and no person shall be eligible to any office under any provisional governments who would be disqualified from holding office under the provisions of the third article of said constitutional amendment.

Chap. VI. An Act supplementary to an Act entitled "An Act to provide for the more efficient Government of the Rebel States," passed March second, eighteen hundred and sixty-seven, and to facilitate Restoration [Passed over President Johnson's veto March 23, 1867].

Be it enacted by the Senate and House of Representatives of the United States of America in Congress assembled, That before the first day of September, eighteen hundred and sixty-seven, the commanding general in each district defined by an act entitled "An act to provide for the more efficient government of the rebel States," passed March second, eighteen hundred and sixty-seven, shall cause

[5]Congress further required such states to ratify the Fourteenth Amendment as a condition of having their congressmen seated.

[6]Congress utilized its power by denying seats to representatives and senators who were not elected in states with acceptable constitutions.

a registration to be made of the male citizens of the United States, twenty-one years of age and upwards, resident in each county or parish in the State or States included in his district, which registration shall include only those persons who are qualified to vote for delegates by the act aforesaid, and who shall have taken and subscribed the following oath or affirmation: "I, _____, do solemnly swear (or affirm), in the presence of Almighty God, that I am a citizen of the State of _____; that I have resided in said State for _____ months next preceding this day, and now reside in the county of _____ or the parish of _____, in said State (as the case may be); that I am twenty-one years old; that I have not be disfranchised for participation in any rebellion or civil war against the United States, nor for felony committed against the laws of any State or of the United States; that I have never been a member of any State legislature, nor held any executive or judicial office in any State and afterwards engaged in insurrection or rebellion against the United States, or given aid or comfort to the enemies thereof; that I have never taken an oath as a member of Congress of the United States, or as an officer of the United States, or as a member of any State legislature, or as an executive or judicial officer of any State, to support the Constitution of the United States, and afterwards engaged in insurrection or rebellion against the United States, or given aid or comfort to the enemies thereof; that I will faithfully support the Constitution and obey the laws of the United States, and will to the best of my ability, encourage others so to do, so help me God"[7] which oath or affirmation may be administered by any registering officer.

Sec. 2. And be it further enacted, That after the completion of the registration hereby provided for in any State, at such time and places therein as the commanding general shall appoint and direct, of which at least thirty days' public notice shall be given, an election shall be held of delegates to a convention for the purpose of establishing a constitution and civil government for such State loyal to the Union, said convention in each State, except Virginia,[8] to consist of the same number of members as the most numerous branch of the State legislature of such State in the year eighteen hundred and sixty, to be apportioned among the several districts, counties, or parishes of such State by the commanding general, giving to each representation in the ratio of voters registered as aforesaid as nearly as may be. The convention in Virginia shall consist of the same number of members as represented the territory now constituting Virginia in

[7] This oath, applied retroactively, was designed to assure that only those who supported governments based on free principles would be participating.

[8] The current state of West Virginia had split from Virginia during the Civil War and become a separate state, so the number of representatives in 1860 would no longer be applicable.

the most numerous branch of the legislature of said State in the year eighteen hundred and sixty, to be apportioned as aforesaid.

Sec. 3. And be it further enacted, That at said election the registered voters of each State shall vote for or against a convention to form a constitution therefor under this act. Those voting in favor of such a convention shall have written or printed on the ballots by which they vote for delegates, as aforesaid, the words "For a convention," and those voting against such a convention shall have written or printed on such ballots the words "Against a convention." The persons appointed to superintend said election, and to make return of the votes given thereat, as herein provided, shall count and make return of the votes given for and against a convention; and the commanding general to whom the same shall have been returned shall ascertain and declare the total vote in each State for and against a convention. If a majority of the votes given on that question shall be for a convention, then such convention shall be held as hereinafter provided; but if a majority of said votes shall be against a convention, then no such convention shall be held under this act: Provided, That such convention shall not be held unless a majority of all such registered voters shall have voted on the question of holding such convention.

Sec. 4. And be it further enacted, That the commanding general of each district shall appoint as many boards of registration as may be necessary, consisting of three loyal officers or persons, to make and complete the registration, superintend the election, and make return to him of the votes, list of voters, and of the persons elected as delegates by a plurality of the votes cast at said election; and upon receiving said returns he shall open the same, ascertain the persons elected as delegates, according to the returns of the officers who conducted said election, make proclamation thereof; and if a majority of the votes given on that question shall be for a convention, the commanding general, within sixty days from the date of election, shall notify the delegates to assemble in convention, at a time and place to be mentioned in the notification, and said convention, when organized, shall proceed to frame a constitution and civil government according to the provisions of this act, and the act to which it is supplementary; and when the same shall have been so framed, said constitution shall be submitted by the convention for ratification to the persons registered under the provisions of this act at an election to be conducted by the officers or persons appointed or to be appointed by the commanding general, as hereinbefore provided, and to be held after the expiration of thirty days from the date of notice thereof, to be given by said convention; and the returns thereof shall be made to the commanding general of the district.

[9] Prior state constitutions had been ratified in a number of ways. This law was designed to provide popular support by providing for popular ratification of the result of state constitutional conventions.

Sec. 5. And be it further enacted, That if, according to said returns, the constitution shall be ratified by a majority of the votes of the registered electors qualified as herein specified, cast at said election, at least one half of all the registered voters voting upon the question of such ratification,[9] the president of the convention shall transmit a copy of the same, duly certified, to the President of the United States, who shall forthwith transmit the same to Congress, if then in session, and if not in session, then immediately upon its next assembling; and if it shall moreover appear to Congress that the election was one at which all the registered and qualified electors in the State had an opportunity to vote freely and without restraint, fear, or the influence of fraud, and if the Congress shall be satisfied that such constitution meets the approval of a majority of all the qualified electors in the State, and if the said constitution shall be declared by Congress to be in conformity with the provisions of the act to which this is supplementary, and the other provisions of said act shall have been complied with, and the said constitution shall be approved by Congress, the State shall be declared entitled to representation, and senators and representatives shall be admitted therefrom as therein provided.

Sec. 6. And be it further enacted, That all elections in the States mentioned in said "Act to provide for the more efficient government of the rebel States," shall, during the operation of said act, be by ballot; and all officers making the said registration of voters and conducting said elections shall, before entering upon the discharge of their duties, take and subscribe the oath prescribed by the act approved. . . .

Sec. 8. And be it further enacted, That the convention for each State shall prescribe the fees, salary, and compensation to be paid to all delegates and other officers and agents herein authorized or necessary to carry into effect the purposes of this act not herein otherwise provided for, and shall provide for the levy and collection of such taxes on the property in such State as may be necessary to pay the same.

Sec. 9. And be it further enacted, That the word "article," in the sixth section of the act to which this is supplementary, shall be construed to mean "section."

Act of March 23, 1867

Chap. XXX. An Act supplementary to an Act entitled "An Act to provide for the more efficient Government of the Rebel States," passed on the second day of March, eighteen hundred and sixty-seven, and the Act supplementary thereto, passed on the twenty-third day of March, eighteen hundred and sixty-seven.[10]

Be it enacted by the Senate and House of Representatives of the United States of America in Congress assembled, That it is hereby declared to have been the true intent and meaning of the act of the second day of March, one thousand eight hundred and sixty-seven, entitled "An act to provide for the more efficient government of the rebel States," and of the act supplementary thereto, passed on the twenty-third day of March, in the year one thousand eight hundred and sixty-seven, that the governments then existing in the rebel States of Virginia, North Carolina, South Carolina, Georgia, Mississippi, Alabama, Louisiana, Florida, Texas, and Arkansas were not legal State governments; and that thereafter said governments, if continued, were to be continued subject in all respects to the military commanders of the respective districts, and to the paramount authority of Congress.

Sec. 2. And be it further enacted, That the commander of any district named in said act shall have power, subject to the disapproval of the General of the army of the United States, and to have effect till disapproved, whenever in the opinion of such commander the proper administration of said act shall require it, to suspend or remove from office, or from the performance of official duties and the exercise of official powers, any officer or person holding or exercising, or professing to hold or exercise, any civil or military office or duty in such district under any power, election, appointment or authority derived from, or granted by, or claimed under, any so-called State or the government thereof, or any municipal or other division thereof, and upon such suspension or removal such commander, subject to the disapproval of the General as aforesaid, shall have power to provide

[10]Passed over President Johnson's veto July 19, 1867.

from time to time for the performance of the said duties of such officer or person so suspended or removed, by the detail of some competent officer or soldier of the army, or by the appointment of some other person, to perform the same, and to fill vacancies occasioned by death, resignation, or otherwise.

Sec. 3. And be it further enacted, That the General of the army of the United Sates shall be invested with all the powers of suspension, removal, appointment, and detail granted in the preceding section to district commanders.

Sec. 4. And be it further enacted, That the acts of the officers of the army already done in removing in said districts persons exercising the functions of civil officers, and appointing others in their stead, are hereby confirmed. . . .

Sec. 5. And be it further enacted, That the boards of registration provided for . . . shall have power, and it shall be their duty before allowing the registration of any person, to ascertain, upon such facts or information as they can obtain, whether such person is entitled to be registered under said act, and the oath required by said act shall not be conclusive on such question, and no person shall be registered unless such board shall decide that he is entitled thereto; and such board shall also have power to examine, under oath, (to be administered by any member of such board,) any one touching the qualification of any person claiming registration; but in every case of refusal by the board to register an applicant, and in every case of striking his name from the list as hereinafter provided, the board shall make a note or memorandum, which shall be returned with the registration list to the commanding general of the district, setting forth the grounds of such refusal or such striking from the list: Provided, That no person shall be disqualified as member of any board of registration by reason of race or color.

Sec. 6. And be it further enacted, That the true intent and meaning of the oath prescribed in said supplementary act is, (among other things,) that no person who has been a member of the legislature of any State, or who has held any executive or judicial office in any State, whether he has taken an oath to support the Constitution of the United Sates or not, and whether he was holding such office at the commencement of the rebellion, or had held it before, and who has afterwards engaged in insurrection or rebellion against the United States, or given aid or comfort to the enemies thereof, is entitled to be registered or to vote;[11] and the words "executive or judicial office in any State" in said oath mentioned shall be construed to include all civil offices created by law for the administration of any general law of a State, or for the administration of justice.

Sec. 7. And be it further enacted, That the time for completing the original registration provided for in said act may, in the discretion of the commander of any district be extended to the first day of October, eighteen hundred and sixty-seven. . . .

Sec. 8. And be it further enacted, That section four of said last-named act shall be construed to authorize the commanding general named therein, whenever he shall deem it needful, to remove any member of a board of registration and to appoint another in his stead, and to fill any vacancy in such board.

Sec. 9. And be it further enacted, That all members of said boards of registration and all persons hereafter elected or appointed to office in said military districts, under any so-called State or municipal authority, or by detail or appointment of the district commanders, shall be required to take and to subscribe the oath of office prescribed by law for officers of the United States.

Sec. 10. And be it further enacted, That no district commander or member of the board of registration, or any of the officers or appointees acting under them shall be bound in his action by any opinion of any civil officer of the United States.

Sec. 11. And be it further enacted, That all the provisions of this act and of the acts to which this is supplementary shall be construed liberally, to the end that all intents thereof may be fully and perfectly carried out.

Sources: Act of March 2, 1867, 39th Cong., 2d Sess., 153, 14 Statutes at Large, 428. Act of March 23, 1867, 40th Cong., 1st Sess., 6, 15 Statutes at Large, 2.

[11]The law reiterated that new government was to be founded on individuals who had not participated in the rebellion and who were committed to principles of free government.

Andrew Johnson's Veto of the First Reconstruction Act

March 2, 1867

INTRODUCTION

Although the Thirteenth Amendment had brought an end to slavery, many states began to enact so-called Black Codes, which seriously interfered with the freedom of newly freed slaves, who were considered to be dangerous vagrants. Northerners were concerned that white Southern majorities were likely to ignore the needs of newly freed slaves. Members of Congress from these states were therefore reluctant to seat delegates from states that did not have explicit constitutional protections providing for freedom for all. They wanted to make sure that such governments were thoroughly "reconstructed" before being given a place at the national table.

In this speech, Andrew Johnson presented his reasons for opposing the First Reconstruction Act, which was subsequently passed over his veto.

To the House of Representatives of the United States:

I have examined the bill to provide for the more efficient government of the Rebel States' with care and anxiety which its transcendent importance is calculated to awaken. I am unable to give it my assent for reasons so grave that I hope a statement of them may have some influence on the minds of the patriotic and enlightened men with whom the decision must ultimately rest.

The bill places all the people of the ten States therein named under the absolute domination of military rule; and the preamble undertakes to give the reason upon which the measure is based and the ground upon which it is justified. It declares that there exists in those States no legal governments and no adequate protection for life or property, and asserts the necessity of enforcing peace and good order within their limits. This is not true as a matter of fact.

It is not denied that the States in question have each of them an actual government, with all the powers—executive, judicial, and legislative—which properly belong to a free State. They are organized like the other States of the Union, and, like them, they make, administer, and execute the laws which concern their domestic affairs. An existing de facto government, exercising such functions as these, is itself the law of the State upon all matters within its jurisdiction. To pronounce the supreme law making power of an established State illegal is to say that law itself is unlawful.[1]

The provisions which these governments have made for the preservation of order, the suppression of crime, and the redress of private injuries are in substance and principle the same as those which prevail in the Northern States and in other civilized countries. They certainly have not succeeded in preventing the commission of all crime, nor has this been accomplished any where in the world. . . . But that people are maintaining local governments for themselves which habitually defeat the object of all government and render their own lives and property insecure is in itself utterly improbable, and the averment of the bill to that effect is not supported by any evidence which has come to my knowledge.

The bill, however, would seem to show upon its face that the establishment of peace and good order is not its real object. The fifth section declares that the preceding sections shall cease to operate in any State where certain events shall have happened. These events are, first, the selection of delegates to a State convention by an election at which Negroes shall be allowed to vote;[2] second, the formation of a State constitution by the convention so chosen; third, the insertion into the State constitution of a provision which will secure the right of voting at all elections to Negroes and to such white men as may not be disfranchised for rebellion or felony; fourth, the submission of the constitution for ratification by their vote; fifth, the submission of the State constitution to Congress for examination and approval, and the actual approval of it by that body; sixth, the adoption of a certain amendment to the Federal Constitution by a vote of Legislature elected under the new constitution;[3] seventh, the adoption of said amendment by a sufficient number of other States to make it a part of the Constitution of the United States. All these conditions must be fulfilled before the people of any of these States can be relieved from the bondage of military domination; but when they

[1] It has been said that if something looks, quacks, and waddles like a duck, it must be a duck. Johnson applies a similar test to existing state governments, which were organized very much like those that the Southern states had prior to the war. For him, this was sufficient to give them full privileges as states.

[2] Northern representatives did not believe a government could be legitimate in which individuals were excluded from participation on the basis of race.

[3] Northern representatives further thought it necessary that the states ratify the Fourteenth Amendment, which was designed to provide federal protections for former slaves.

are fulfilled, then immediately the pains and penalties of the bill are to cease, no matter whether there be peace and order or not, and without any reference to the security of life or property.

The excuse given for the bill in the preamble is one of necessity. The military rule which it establishes is plainly to be used, not for any purpose of order or for the prevention of crime, but solely as a means of coercing the people into the adoption of principles and measures to which it is known that they are opposed, and upon which they have an undeniable right to exercise their own judgment.[4]

I submit to Congress whether this measure is not in its whole character, scope, and object without precedent and without authority, in palpable conflict with the plainest provisions of liberty and humanity for which our ancestors on both sides of the Atlantic have shed so much blood, and expended so much treasure.

The ten States named in the bill are divided into five districts. For each district an officer of the Army, not below the rank of a brigadier-general, is to be appointed to rule over the people; and he is to be supported with an efficient military force to enable him to perform his duties and enforce his authority. Those duties and that authority, as defined by the third section of the bill, are "to protect all persons in their rights of person and property, to suppress insurrection, disorder, and violence, and to punish or cause to be punished all disturbers of the public peace or criminals." The power thus given to the commanding officer over all the people of each district is that of an absolute monarch. His mere will is to take the place of all law.[5] The law of the States is now the only rule applicable to the subjects placed under his control, and that is completely displaced by the clause which declares all interference of State authority to be null and void. He alone is permitted to determine what are rights of person or property, and he may protect them in such a way as in his discretion may seem proper. It places at his free disposal all the lands and goods in his district, and he may distribute them without let or hindrance to whom he pleases. Being bound by no State law, and there being no other law to regulate the subject, he may make a criminal code of his own; and he can make it as bloody as any recorded in history or he can reserve the privilege of acting upon the impulse of his private passions in each case that arises. He is bound by no rules of evidence; there is indeed no provision by which he is authorized or required

[4] Johnson did not think it was appropriate to attach such conditions of state representation in Congress.

[5] Johnson is critical of the idea of subjecting Southern states to military rulers.

to take any evidence at all. Every thing is a crime which he chooses to call so, and all persons are condemned whom he pronounces to be guilty. He is not bound to keep any record or make any report of his proceedings. He may arrest his victims wherever he finds them, without warrant, accusation, or proof of probable cause. If he gives them a trial before he inflicts the punishment, he gives it of his grace and mercy, not because he is commanded so to do.

Cruel or unusual punishment is not to be inflicted, but who is to decide what is cruel and what is unusual? . . . Each officer may define cruelty according to his own temper, and if it is not usual, he will make it usual. Corporal punishment, imprisonment, the gag, the ball and chain, and the almost insupportable forms of torture invented for military punishment lie within the range of choice. The sentence of a commission is not to be executed without being approved by the commander, if it affects life or liberty, and a sentence of death must be approved by the President. This applies to cases in which there has been a trial and sentence. I take it to be clear, under this bill, that the military commander may condemn to death without even the form of a trial by a military commission, so that the life of the condemned may depend upon the will of two men instead of one.

It is plain that the authority here given to the military officer amounts to absolute despotism. But to make it still more unendurable, the bill provides that it may be delegated to as many subordinates as he chooses to appoint, for it declares that he shall "punish or cause to be punished." Such a power has not been wielded by any Monarch in England for more than five hundred years. In all that time no people who speak the English language have borne such servitude. It reduces the whole population of the ten States—all persons, of every color, sex and condition, and every stranger within their limits—to the most abject and degrading slavery. No master ever had a control so absolute over the slaves as this bill gives to the military officers over both white and colored persons.

I come now to a question which is, if possible, still more important. Have we the power to establish and carry into execution a measure like this? I answer, "Certainly not," if we derive our authority from the Constitution and if we are bound by the limitations which it imposes.[6] This proposition is perfectly clear, that no branch of the Federal Government—executive, legislative, or judicial—can have

[6] Johnson is expounding a restrictive view of federal powers.

any just powers except those which it derives through and exercises under the organic laws of the Union. Outside of the Constitution we have no legal authority more than private citizens, and within it we have only so much as that instrument gives us. This broad principle limits all our functions and applies to all subjects. It protects not only the citizens of States which are within the Union, but it shields every human being who comes or is brought under our jurisdiction. We have no right to do in one place more than in another that which the Constitution says we shall not do at all. If, therefore, the Southern States were in truth out of the Union, we could not treat their people in a way which the fundamental law forbids.

[7]Johnson further argues that the Union victory in and of itself did not change constitutional relationships.

Some persons assume that the success of our arms in crushing the opposition which was made in some of the States to the execution of the Federal laws reduced those States and all their people—the innocent as well as the guilty—to the condition of vassalage and gave us a power over them which the Constitution does not bestow or define or limit. No fallacy can be more transparent than this.[7] Our victories subjected the insurgents to legal obedience, not to the yoke of an arbitrary despotism. When an absolute sovereign reduces his rebellious subjects, he may deal with them according to his pleasure, because he had that power before. But when a limited monarch puts down an insurrection, he must still govern according to law.

If an insurrection should take place in one of our States against the authority of the State government, and end in the overthrowing of those who planned it, would they take away the rights of all the people of the counties where it was favored by a part or a majority of the population? Could they for such a reason be wholly outlawed and deprived of their representation in the Legislature? I have always contended that the Government of the United States was sovereign within its constitutional sphere; that it executed its laws like the States themselves, by applying its coercive power directly to individuals; and that it could put down insurrection with the same effect as a State and no other. The opposite doctrine is the worst heresy of those who advocated secession, and can not be agreed to without admitting that heresy to be right.

This is a bill passed by Congress in time of peace. There is not in any one of the States brought under its operation either war or insurrection. The laws of the States and of the Federal Government are all in undisturbed and harmonious operation. The courts, State and Federal, are open and in the full exercise of their proper authority. Over every State comprised in these five military districts, life, and property are secured by State laws and Federal laws, and the National Constitution is every where in force and every where obeyed. What, then is the ground on which the bill proceeds?[8] The title of the bill announces that it is intended "for the more efficient government" of these ten States. It is recited by way of preamble that no legal State Governments "nor adequate protection for life or property" exist in those States, and that peace and good order should be thus recitals, which prepare the way for martial law, is this, that the only foundation upon which martial law can exist under our form of Government is not stated or so much as pretended. Actual war, foreign invasion, domestic insurrection—none of these appear, and none of these in fact exist. It is not even recited that any sort of war or insurrection is threatened. Let us pause to consider, upon this question of constitutional law and power of Congress, a recent decision of the Supreme Court of the United States in ex parte Milligan . . . [*Johnson continues by quoting from this decision.*]

This is sufficiently explicit. Peace exists in all the territory to which this bill applies. It asserts a power in Congress, in time of peace, to set aside the laws of peace and to substitute the laws of war. The minority, concurring with the majority, declares that Congress does not possess that power. . . . I need not say to the representatives of the American people that their Constitution forbids the exercise of judicial power in any way but one—that is, by the ordained and established courts. It is equally well known that in all criminal cases a trial by jury is made indispensable by the express words of that instrument.

I need not say to the Representatives of the American people that their Constitution forbids the exercise of judicial power in any way but one; that is, by the ordained and established courts. It is equally well known that, in all criminal cases, a trial by jury is made indispensable by the express words of that instrument. I will not enlarge on the inestimable value of the right thus secured to every freeman, or speak of the danger to public liberty, in all parts of the country, which must ensue from a denial of it anywhere, or upon any pretense.

The Constitution also forbids the arrest of the citizen without judicial warrant, founded on probable cause. This bill authorizes an arrest

[8] Just as the decision in *Ex Parte Milligan* limited the right of military courts to try civilians outside military zones, so too Johnson believes that the power of Congress over the South ended with the termination of this conflict.

without warrant, at pleasure of a military commander. The Constitution declares that "no person shall be held to answer for a capital or otherwise infamous crime unless on presentment of a grand jury." This bill holds every person not a soldier answerable for all crimes and all charges without any presentment. The Constitution declares that "no person shall be deprived of life, liberty, or property without due process of law." This bill sets aside all process of law, and makes the citizen answerable in his person and property to the will of one man, and as to his life to the will of two. Finally, the Constitution declares that "the privilege of the writ of habeas corpus shall not be suspended unless when, in case of rebellion or invasion, the public safety may require it"; whereas this bill declares martial law (which of itself suspends this great writ) in time of peace, and authorizes the military to make the arrest, and gives to the prisoner only one privilege, and that is trial "without unnecessary delay." He has no hope of release from custody, except the hope, such as it is, of release by acquittal before a military commission.

The United States are bound to guaranty to each State a republican form of government. Can it be pretended that this obligation is not palpably broken if we carry out a measure like this, which wipes away every vestige of republican government in ten States and puts the life, property, and honor of all people in each of them under domination of a single person clothed with unlimited authority?

Here is a bill of attainder[9] against 9,000,000 people at once. It is based upon an accusation so vague as to be scarcely intelligible and found to be true upon no credible evidence. Not one of the 9,000,000 was heard in his own defense. The representatives of the doomed parties were excluded from all participation in the trial.[10] The conviction is to be followed by the most ignominious punishment ever inflicted on large masses of men. It disfranchises them by hundreds of thousands and degrades them all, even those who are admitted to be guiltless, from the rank of freeman to the condition of slaves.

The purpose and object of the bill—the general intent which pervades it from beginning to end—is to change the entire structure and character of the State Governments and to compel them by force to the adoption of organic laws and regulations which they are unwilling to accept if left to themselves.[11] The Negroes have not asked for the privilege of voting; the vast majority of them have no idea what it means. This bill not only thrusts it into their hands, but compels

[9] A bill of attainder, forbidden in Article I, Section 9 of the Constitution, is a legislative punishment meted out to specific individuals without the benefit of a trial.

[10] Johnson believes that the Reconstruction Act effectively declared Southerners guilty with a trial.

[11] It is important to recognize that Johnson is writing prior to the ratification of the Fourteenth Amendment, when states exercised primary police powers, which Johnson thought Congress was attempting to usurp.

them, as well as the whites, to use it in a particular way. If they do not form a constitution with prescribed articles in it and afterwards elect a legislature which will act upon certain measures in a prescribed way, neither blacks nor whites can be relieved from the slavery which the bill imposes upon them. Without pausing here to consider the policy or impolicy of Africanizing the southern part of our territory,[12] I would simply ask the attention of Congress to the manifest, well-known, and universally acknowledged rule of Constitutional law which declares that the Federal Government has no jurisdiction, authority, or power to regulate such subjects for any State. To force the right of suffrage out of the hands of white people and into the hands of the Negroes is an arbitrary violation of this principle.[13]

This bill imposes martial law at once, and its operations will begin so soon as the General and his troops can be put in place. The dread alternative between its harsh rule and compliance with the terms of this measure is not suspended, nor are the people afforded any time for free deliberation. The bill says to them, Take martial law first, then deliberate.

The bill also denies the legality of the governments of ten of the States which participated in the ratification of the amendment to the Federal Constitution abolishing slavery forever within the jurisdiction of the United States, and practically excludes them from the Union.

That the measure proposed by this bill does violate the Constitution in the particulars mentioned and in many other ways which I forbear to enumerate is too clear to admit the least doubt. . . . It was to punish the gross crime of defying the Constitution and to vindicate its supreme authority that we carried on a bloody war of four years' duration. Shall we now acknowledge that we sacrificed a million of lives and expended billions of treasure[14] to enforce a Constitution which is not worthy of respect and preservation?

It is a part of our public history which can never be forgotten that both Houses of Congress, in July 1861, declared in the form of a solemn resolution that the war was and should be carried on for no purpose of subjugation, but solely to enforce the Constitutional rights of the States and of individuals unimpaired. This resolution was adopted and sent forth to the world unanimously by the Senate and with only two dissenting voices in the House. It was accepted

[12]His reference to "Africanizing the southern part of our territory" is an acknowledgment that the multiplicity of African Americans in these states might give them control.

[13]Many individuals who favored the elimination of slavery still supported voting qualifications, including literacy tests that would have excluded most blacks from voting.

[14]Johnson may be exaggerating a bit, but the Civil War was America's bloodiest conflict and is believed to have resulted in about 620,000 casualties among combatants.

by the friends of the Union in the South as well as in the North as expressing honestly and truly the object of the war. On the faith of it many thousands of persons in both sections gave their lives and their fortunes to the cause. To repudiate it now by refusing to the States and to the individuals within them the "rights" which the Constitution and laws of the Union would secure to them is a breach of our plighted honor for which I can imagine no excuse and to which I cannot voluntarily become a party.

I am thoroughly convinced that any settlement or compromise or plan of actions which is inconsistent with the principles of the Constitution will not only be unavailing, but mischievous; that it will but multiply the present evils, instead of removing them. The Constitution, in its whole integrity and vigor, throughout the length and breadth of the land, is the best of all compromises. Besides, our duty does not, in my judgment, leave us a choice between that and any other. I believe that it contains the remedy that is so much needed, and that if the coordinate branches of the Government would unite upon its provisions they would be found broad enough and strong enough to sustain in time of peace the Nation which they bore safely through the ordeal of a protracted civil war. Among the most sacred guaranties of that instrument are those which declare that "each State shall have at least one Representative," and that "no State, without its consent, shall be deprived of its equal suffrage in the Senate." Each House is made the "judge of the elections, returns and qualifications of its own members," and may, "with the concurrence of two-thirds, expel a member." Thus, as heretofore urged, "in the admission of Senators and Representatives from any and all of the States there can be no just ground of apprehension that persons who are disloyal will be clothed with the powers of legislation, for this could not happen when the Constitution and the laws are enforced by a vigilant and faithful Congress." When a Senator or Representative presents his certificate of election, he may at once be admitted or rejected, or, should there be any question as to his eligibility, his credentials may be referred for investigation to the appropriate committee. If admitted to a seat, it must be upon evidence satisfactory to the House of which he thus becomes a member that he possesses the requisite constitutional and legal qualifications. If refused admission as a member for want of due allegiance to the Government, and returned to his constituents, they are admonished that none but persons loyal to the United States will be allowed a voice in the legislative councils of the Nation, and the political power and moral influence of Congress are thus effectively exerted in the interests of loyalty to the Government and fidelity of the Union.[15]

And is it not far better that the work of restoration should be accomplished by simple compliance with the plain requirements of the Constitution, than by a recourse to measures which, in effect, destroy the States, and threaten the subversion of the General Government? All that is necessary to settle this simple but important question, without further agitation or delay, is a willingness, on the part of all, to sustain the Constitution, and carry its provisions into practical operation. If to-morrow either branch of Congress would declare that, upon the presentation of their credentials, members constitutionally elected, and loyal to the General Government, would be admitted to seats in Congress, while all others would be excluded, and their places remain vacant until the selection by the people of loyal and qualified persons; and if, at the same time, assurance were given that this policy would be continued until all the States were represented in Congress, it would send a thrill of joy throughout the entire land, as indicating the inauguration of a system which must speedily bring tranquility to the public mind.

While we are legislating upon subjects which are of great importance to the whole people, and which must affect all parts of the country, not only hurting the life of the present generation, but for ages to come, we should remember that all men are entitled at least to a hearing in the councils which decide upon the destiny of themselves and their children. At present ten States are denied representation, and when the Fortieth Congress assembles on the 4th day of the present month sixteen States will be without a voice in the House of Representatives.[16] This grave fact, with the important questions before us, should induce us to pause in a course of legislation which, looking solely to the attainment of political ends, fails to consider the rights it transgresses, the law which it violates, or the institutions which it imperils.

Source: James D. Richardson, *A Compilation of the Messages and Papers of the Presidents, Volume 6, Section 2: Andrew Johnson.* New York: Bureau of National Literature, 1897.

[15] Johnson is suggesting that it would be easier for Congress to refuse to seat members that they believe to be disloyal rather than requiring complete changes in their governments.

[16] Because Congress was meeting in an extra session, a number of states did not have representatives present at the time, but would when the Congress officially assembled.

Treaty with Russia Purchasing Alaska

June 20, 1867

INTRODUCTION

The purchase of Alaska from Russia turned out to be a remarkable acquisition that would later provide not only a source of great mineral wealth but also part of America's strategic defense. The fact that Russia negotiated with the United States rather than with Great Britain, which had authority over Canada at the time, suggested that Russia, which would have had difficulty defending Alaska, hoped that the United States would serve as something of a bulwark against British power.

CONVENTION between the United States of America and His Majesty the Emperor of Russia, for the Cession of the Russian Possessions in North America to the United States

The United States of America and His Majesty the Emperor of all the Russias, being desirous of strengthening, if possible, the good understanding which exists between them, have, for that purpose, appointed as their Plenipotentiaries, the President of the United States, William H. Seward, Secretary of State;[1] and His Majesty the Emperor of all the Russias, the Privy Counsellor Edward de Stoeckl, his Envoy Extraordinary and Minister Plenipotentiary to the United States; And the said Plenipotentiaries, having exchanged their full powers, which were found to be in due form, have agreed upon and signed the following articles:

Article I

His Majesty the Emperor of all the Russias, agrees to cede to the United States, by this convention, immediately upon the exchange of the ratifications thereof, all the territory and dominion now possessed by his said Majesty on the continent of America and in adjacent islands, the same being contained within the geographical limits herein set forth, to wit: The eastern limit is the line of demarcation

[1] The purchase of Alaska is often referred to as "Seward's folly," after the U.S. secretary of state who worked so hard to make the acquisition.

between the Russian and the British possessions in North America, as established by the convention between Russia and Great Britain, of February 28–16, 1825, and described in Articles III and IV of said convention. . . .

Article II

In the cession of territory and dominion made by the preceding article, are included the right of property in all public lots and squares, vacant lands, and all public buildings, fortifications, barracks, and other edifies which are not private individual property.[2] It is, however, understood and agreed, that the churches which have been built in the ceded territory by the Russian Government, shall remain the property of such members of the Greek Oriental Church resident in the territory as may choose to worship therein. Any Government archives, papers, and documents relative to the territory and dominion aforesaid, which may now be existing there, will be left in the possession of the agent of the United States; but an authenticated copy of such of them as may be required, will be, at all times, given by the United States to the Russian Government, or to such Russian officers or subjects as they may apply for.

[2]Along with the land, the purchase of Alaska gave the United States access to public buildings previously used by the Russian government.

Article III

The inhabitants of the ceded territory, according to their choice, reserving their natural allegiance, may return to Russia within three years; but if they should prefer to remain in the ceded territory, they, with the exception of uncivilized native tribes, shall be admitted to the enjoyment of all the rights, advantages, and immunities of citizens of the United States,[3] and shall be maintained and protected in the free enjoyment of their liberty, property, and religion. The uncivilized tribes will be subject to such laws and regulations as the United States may from time to time adopt in regard to aboriginal tribes of that country.

[3]This provision recognizes the rights of individuals from Russia to return there while essentially treating aborigines in the same way that the Constitution already provided for Native American Indians.

Article IV

His Majesty, the Emperor of all the Russias, shall appoint, with convenient despatch, an agent or agents for the purpose of formally delivering to a similar agent or agents, appointed on behalf of the United States, the territory, dominion, property, dependencies, and appurtenances which are ceded as above, and for doing any other act which may be necessary in regard thereto. But the cession, with the right of immediate possession, is nevertheless to be deemed complete and absolute on the exchange of ratifications, without waiting for such formal delivery.

Article V

Immediately after the exchange of the ratifications of this convention, any fortifications or military posts which may be in the ceded territory shall be delivered to the agent of the United States, and any Russian troops which may be in the territory shall be withdrawn as soon as may be reasonably and conveniently practicable.

Article VI

[4]This only amounted to about two cents an acre, but the money was welcomed in Russia, which was increasingly uncertain of its ability to hold on to the territory.

In consideration of the cession aforesaid, the United States agree to pay at the Treasury in Washington, within ten months after the exchange of the ratifications of this convention, to the diplomatic representative or other agent of His Majesty the Emperor of all the Russias, duly authorized to receive the same, seven million two hundred thousand dollars in gold.[4] The cession of territory and dominion herein made is hereby declared to be free and unincumbered by any reservations, privileges, franchises, grants, or possessions, by any associated companies, whether corporate or incorporate, Russian or any other; or by any parties, except merely private individual property-holders; and the cession hereby made conveys all the rights, franchises, and privileges now belonging to Russia in the said territory or dominion, and appurtenances thereto.

Article VII

When this convention shall have been duly ratified by the President, of the United States, by and with the advice and consent of the Senate, on the one part, and, on the other, by His Majesty the Emperor of all the Russias, the ratifications shall be exchanged at Washington within three months from the date thereof, or sooner if possible.

In faith whereof the respective Plenipotentiaries have signed this convention, and thereto affixed the seals of their arms.

Done at Washington, the thirtieth day of March, in the year of our Lord one thousand eight hundred and sixty-seven.

William H. Seward [L.S.]

Edward de Stoeckl [L.S.]

Source: *U.S. Statutes at Large*, Vol. XIV. Treaty with Russia, March 30, 1867. Boston: Little, Brown, 1868, 539–543.

Articles of Impeachment against Andrew Johnson

March 2, 1868

INTRODUCTION

The Constitution provides that the House of Representatives may bring articles of impeachment for bribery, treason, and "other high crimes and misdemeanors" against judicial and executive officers, which the Senate, acting as a jury, will then try. The House adopted the following resolutions on February 24, 1868, and presented them to the Senate on March 2, 1868.

Articles exhibited by the House of Representatives of the United States, in the name of themselves and all the people of the United States, against Andrew Johnson, President of the United States, in maintenance and support of their impeachment against him for high crimes and misdemeanors.

Article I

[1] The U.S. Constitution requires the president to appoint cabinet officers with "the advice and consent" of the Senate, but it does not specify who has the power to fire such executive individuals, and the Supreme Court had not yet issued its decision in *Myers v. United States*, 272 U.S. 52 (1926), in which it declared that this was a presidential power.

[2] Johnson's attempt to remove the Secretary of War Edwin M. Stanton, counter to the wishes of Congress, which had declared in the Tenure of Office Act of 1867 that such removal required senatorial consent, stirred considerable controversy.

That said Andrew Johnson, President of the United States, on the 21st day of February, in the year of our Lord, 1868, at Washington, in the District of Columbia, unmindful of the high duties of his office, of his oath of office, and of the requirement of the Constitution that he should take care that the laws be faithfully executed, did unlawfully and in violation of the Constitution and laws of the United States[1] issue and order in writing for the removal of Edwin M. Stanton from the office of Secretary for the Department of War, said Edwin M. Stanton having been theretofore duly appointed and commissioned, by and with the advice and consent of the Senate of the United States, as such Secretary. . . .[2]

Articles II–IX

[These articles dealt with issues related to Staunton's firing and Johnson's attempt to replace him with Brevet Major-General Lorenzo Thomas.]

Article X

That said Andrew Johnson, President of the United States, unmindful of the high duties of his office and the dignity and proprieties thereof, and of the harmony and courtesies which ought to exist and be maintained between the executive and legislative branches of the Government of the United States, designing and intending to set aside the rightful authorities and powers of Congress, did attempt to bring into disgrace, ridicule, hatred, contempt and reproach the Congress of the United States, and the several branches thereof, to impair and destroy the regard and respect of all the good people of the United States for the Congress and legislative power thereof, (which all officers of the government ought inviolably to preserve and maintain,)[3] and to excite the odium and resentment of all good people of the United States against Congress and the laws by it duly and constitutionally enacted; and in pursuance of his said design and intent, openly and publicly and before divers assemblages of citizens of the United States, convened in divers parts thereof, to meet and receive said Andrew Johnson as the Chief Magistrate of the United States, did, on the 18th day of August, in the year of our Lord 1866, and on divers other days and times, as well before as afterward, make and declare, with a loud voice certain intemperate, inflammatory, and scandalous harangues, and therein utter loud threats and bitter menaces, as well against Congress as the laws of the United States duly enacted thereby, amid the cries, jeers and laughter of the multitudes then assembled in hearing, which are set forth in the several specifications hereinafter written, in substance and effect, that it to say:

Specification First. In this, that at Washington, in the District of Columbia, in the Executive Mansion, to a committee of citizens who called upon the President of the United States, speaking of and concerning the Congress of the United States, heretofore, to wit: On the 18th day of August, in the year of our Lord, 1866, in a loud voice, declare in substance and effect, among other things, that is to say: "So far as the Executive Department of the government is concerned, the effort has been made to restore the Union, to heal the breach, to pour oil into the wounds which were consequent upon the struggle, and, to speak in a common phrase, to prepare, as the learned and wise physician would, a plaster healing in character and co-extensive with the wound. We thought and we think that we

[3]Supreme Court Justice Samuel Chase was impeached, albeit not convicted, during the Jefferson administration for inflammatory remarks that he made before a jury. As the following examples illustrate, Congress was again indicting a public official essentially for speaking in a demeaning fashion about a coordinate branch of the national government. However prudent or imprudent Johnson's language was understood to be, Congress probably should have recognized that the best way to combat disagreeable speech was with arguments.

had partially succeeded, but as the work progresses, as reconstruction seemed to be taking place, and the country was becoming reunited, we found a disturbing and moving element opposing it. In alluding to that element it shall go no further than your Convention, and the distinguished gentleman who has delivered the report of the proceedings, I shall make no reference that I do not believe, and the time and the occasion justify. "We have witnessed in one department of the government every endeavor to prevent the restoration of peace, harmony and union. We have seen hanging upon the verge of the government, as it were, a body called or which assumes to be the Congress of the United States, while in fact it is a Congress of only part of the States. We have seen this Congress pretend to be for the Union, when its every step and act tended to perpetuate disunion and make a disruption of States inevitable. "We have seen Congress gradually encroach, step by step, upon constitutional rights, and violate day after day, and month after month, fundamental principles of the government. We have seen a Congress that seemed to forget that there was a limit to the sphere and scope of legislation. We have seen a Congress in a minority assume to exercise power which, if allowed to be consummated, would result in despotism or monarchy itself."

Specification Second. In this, that at Cleveland, in the State of Ohio, heretofore to wit: On the third day of September, in the year of our Lord, 1866, before a public assemblage of citizens and others, said Andrew Johnson, President of the United States, speaking of and concerning the Congress of the United States, did, in a loud voice, declare in substance and effect, among other things, that is to say: "I will tell you what I did do? I called upon your Congress that is trying to break up the Government."

. . .

"In conclusion, beside that Congress had taken much pains to poison the constituents against him, what has Congress done? Have they done anything to restore the union of the States? No: On the contrary, they had done everything to prevent it: and because he stood now where he did when the rebellion commenced, he had been denounced as a traitor. Who had run greater risks or made greater sacrifices than himself? But Congress, factions and domineering, had undertaken to poison the minds of the American people."

Specification Third. In this case, that at St. Louis, in the State of Missouri, heretofore to wit: On the 8th day of September, in the year of our Lord 1866, before a public assemblage of citizens and others, said Andrew Johnson, President of the United States, speaking of acts concerning the Congress of the United States, did, in a loud voice, declare in substance and effect, among other things, that is to say: "Go on, perhaps if you had a word or two on the subject of New Orleans you might understand more about it than you do, and if you will go back and ascertain the cause of the riot at New Orleans, perhaps you will not be so prompt in calling out 'New Orleans.' If you will take up the riot of New Orleans and trace it back to its source and its immediate cause, you will find out who was responsible for the blood that was shed there. If you will take up the riot at New Orleans and trace it back to the Radical Congress, you will find that the riot at New Orleans was substantially planned. If you will take up the proceedings in their caucuses you will understand that they knew that a convention was to be called which was extinct by its powers having expired; that it was said that the intention was that a new government was to be organized, and on the organization of that government the intention was to enfranchise one portion of the population, called the colored population, and who had been emancipated, and at the same time disfranchise white men. When you design to talk about New Orleans you ought to understand what you are talking about. When you read the speeches that were made, and take up the facts on the Friday and Saturday before that convention sat, you will find that speeches were made incendiary in their character, exciting that portion of the population? the black population? to arm themselves and prepare for the shedding of blood. You will also find that convention did assemble in violation of law, and the intention of that convention was to supersede the organized authorities in the State of Louisiana, which had been organized by the government of the United States, and every man engaged in that rebellion, in the convention, with the intention of superseding and upturning the civil government which had been recognized by the Government of the United States, I say that he was a traitor to the Constitution of the United States, and hence you find that another rebellion was commenced, having its origin in the Radical Congress."

. . .

"So much for the New Orleans riot. And there was the cause and the origin of the blood that was shed, and every drop of blood that was shed is upon their skirts and they are responsible. I could test this thing a little closer, but will not do it here to-night. But when you talk about the causes and consequences that resulted from proceedings of that kind, perhaps, as I have been introduced here and you have provoked questions of this kind, though it does not provoke me, I will tell you a few wholesome things that have been done by this Radical Congress in connection with New Orleans and the extension of the elective franchise.

"I know that I have been traduced and abused. I know it has come in advance of me here, as elsewhere, that I have attempted to exercise an arbitrary power in resisting laws that were intended to be forced upon the government; that I had exercised that power; that I had abandoned the party that elected me, and that I was a traitor, because I exercised the veto power in attempting, and did arrest for a time, that which was called a 'Freedmen's Bureau' bill. Yes, that I was a traitor. And I have been traduced; I have been slandered; I have been maligned; I have been called Judas Iscariot, and all that. Now, my countrymen, here to-night, it is very easy to indulge in epithets; it is easy to call a man a Judas, and cry out traitor, but when he is called upon to give arguments and facts he is very often found wanting. Judas Iscariot? Judas! There was a Judas, and he was one of the twelve Apostles. O, yes, the twelve Apostles had a Christ, and he never could have had a Judas unless he had twelve Apostles. If I have played the Judas who has been my Christ that I have played the Judas with? Was it Thad. Stevens? Was it Wendell Phillips? Was it Charles Sumner? They are the men that stop and compare themselves with the Savior, and everybody that differs with them in opinion, and tries to stay and arrest their diabolical and nefarious policy is to be denounced as a Judas."[4]

. . .

"Well, let me say to you, if you will stand by me in this action, if you will stand by me in trying to give the people a fair chance? soldiers and citizens? to participate in these office, God be willing, I will kick them out. I will kick them out just as fast as I can.

"Let me say to you, in concluding, that what I have said is what I intended to say; I was not provoked into this, and care not for their

[4]The individuals named were prominent radical Republicans, with whom Johnson had vehemently disagreed on Reconstruction policies.

menaces, the taunts and the jeers. I care not for threats, I do not intend to be bullied by enemies, nor erawed by my friends. But, God willing, with your help, I will veto their measures whenever any of them come to me."

Which said utterances, declarations, threats and harangues, highly censurable in any, are peculiarly indecent and unbecoming in the Chief Magistrate of the United States, by means whereof the said Andrew Johnson has brought the high office of the President of the United States into contempt, ridicule and disgrace, to the great scandal of all good citizens, whereby said Andrew Johnson, President of the United States, did commit, and was then and there guilty of a high misdemeanor in office.

Article XI

That the said Andrew Johnson, President of the United States, unmindful of the high duties of his office and of his oath of office, and in disregard of the Constitution and laws of the United States, did, heretofore, to wit: On the 18th day of August, 1866, at the city of Washington, and in the District of Columbia, by public speech, declare and affirm in substance, that the Thirty-Ninth Congress of the United States was not a Congress of the United States authorized by the Constitution to exercise legislative power under the same; but, on the contrary, was a Congress of only part of the States, thereby denying and intending to deny, that the legislation of said Congress was valid or obligatory upon him,[5] the said Andrew Johnson, except in so far as he saw fit to approve the same, and also thereby denying the power of the said Thirty-Ninth Congress to propose amendments to the Constitution of the United States. And in pursuance of said declaration, the said Andrew Johnson, President of the United States, afterwards, to wit: On the 21st day of February, 1868, at the city of Washington, D.C., did, unlawfully and in disregard of the requirements of the Constitution that he should take care that the laws be faithfully executed, attempt to prevent the execution of an act entitled "An act regulating the tenure of certain civil office," passed March 2, 1867,[6] by unlawfully devising and contriving and attempting to devise and contrive means by which he should prevent Edwin M. Stanton from forthwith resuming the functions of the office of Secretary for the Department of War, notwithstanding the

[5] Johnson did not believe that Congress had properly excluded Southern representatives from their seats.

[6] The Tenure in Office Act was the one that had sought to limit President Johnson's authority to fire cabinet officers without the consent of the U.S. Senate.

refusal of the Senate to concur in the suspension therefore made by the said Andrew Johnson of said Edwin M. Stanton from said office of Secretary for the Department of War; and also by further unlawfully devising and contriving, and attempting to devise and contrive, means then and there to prevent the execution of an act entitled "An act making appropriations for the support of the army for the fiscal year ending June 30, 1868, and for other purposes," approved March 2, 1867. And also to prevent the execution of an act entitled "An act to provide for the more efficient government of the rebel States," passed March 2, 1867. Whereby the said Andrew Johnson, President of the United States, did then, to wit: on the 21st day of February, 1868, at the city of Washington, commit and was guilty of a high misdemeanor in office.

CONCLUSION

This was the first impeachment of a U.S. president and ultimately fell a single vote short of the two-thirds majority necessary to convict within the Senate.

Source: The Impeachment Trial of President Andrew Johnson. Supplement to the Congressional Globe, 40th Cong., 2d Sess., 3–4.

Fourteenth Amendment to the U.S. Constitution

July 9, 1868

INTRODUCTION

Like its immediate predecessor, the Fourteenth Amendment grew out of the conflict that had led to the Civil War. In 1857, the U.S. Supreme Court had decided in *Dred Scott v. Sandford* that blacks were not and could not become U.S. citizens. The Thirteenth Amendment (1865) abolished involuntary servitude without specifying whether they were citizens or clarifying what rights the new freedmen would have. Many Southern states adopted so-called Black Codes, which severely restricted their freedom and sought to reduce them to a state of peonage not that far removed from the slavery from which they had been freed. Congress initially sought to protect them through civil rights legislation, most notably the Civil Rights Act of 1866, but decided that their rights would be more secure if specifically incorporated into the constitutional text. The result was the longest amendment to the Constitution. Southern state governments were required to ratify this amendment before Congress agreed to seat their representatives.

Section 1

All persons born or naturalized in the United States, and subject to the jurisdiction thereof, are citizens of the United States and of the State wherein they reside.[1] No State shall make or enforce any law which shall abridge the privileges or immunities of citizens of the United States;[2] nor shall any State[3] deprive any person of life, liberty, or property,[4] without due process of law;[5] nor deny to any person within its jurisdiction the equal protection of the laws.[6]

Section 2

Representatives shall be apportioned among the several States according to their respective numbers, counting the whole number

[1] Prior to this amendment, the Constitution did not contain a formal definition of citizenship although it had specified that the president should be natural-born, and it had vested Congress with power over naturalization.

[2] Citizenship is important because it is associated with certain rights here called "privileges or immunities."

[3] Whereas the court had interpreted the first 10 amendments (the Bill of Rights) as limiting only the national government, this amendment specifically addresses states ("No State shall"). Later decisions, most notably the Civil Rights Cases of 1883, would distinguish between limits on "state action" and mere "private action," which they considered to be beyond the scope of this amendment.

4 This amendment identifies three central protections for all citizens. Although some supporters anticipated that the privileges and immunities clause might be the most substantive source of additional rights, it was also subject to the interpretation that it simply required states to treat out-of-state citizens like their own.

5 The due process clause would become not only an important guarantee of procedural protections, but also the vehicle through which the Supreme Court would ultimately apply most of the provisions of the first 10 amendments (the Bill of Rights) to the states.

6 The equal protection clause arguably incorporated the ideal of equality that the Declaration of Independence had embodied, and through which Lincoln had argued that the Constitution should be interpreted, into the Document. From 1896 to 1954, the U.S. Supreme Court narrowed the reach of this provision by upholding de jure (legally mandated) racial segregation under the doctrine of "separate but equal."

7 Under the original Constitution, states were represented in the U.S. House of Representatives according to their white population and three-fifths of "such other persons," namely slaves.

8 With slavery eliminated and African Americans not yet fully enfranchised, this led to the possibility that Southern states would actually have greater voting power in that body than before the war. This provision, never enforced, permitted a reduction of such representation if black men were disenfranchised.

9 Leaders of the women's suffrage movement, many of whom had supported the amendment, were incensed that the provision specifically used the term "male inhabitants," thus excluding them from its putative protection.

of persons in each State,[7] excluding Indians not taxed. But when the right to vote at any election for the choice of electors for President and Vice-President of the United States, Representatives in Congress, the Executive and Judicial officers of a State, or the members of the Legislature thereof, is denied to any of the male inhabitants of such State, being twenty-one years of age, and citizens of the United States, or in any way abridged, except for participation in rebellion, or other crime, the basis of representation therein shall be reduced in the proportion which the number of such male citizens shall bear[8] to the whole number of male citizens[9] twenty-one years of age in such State.

Section 3

No person shall be a Senator or Representative in Congress, or elector of President and Vice-President, or hold any office, civil or military, under the United States, or under any State, who, having previously taken an oath, as a member of Congress, or as an officer of the United States, or as a member of any State legislature, or as an executive or judicial officer of any State, to support the Constitution of the United States, shall have engaged in insurrection or rebellion against the same, or given aid or comfort to the enemies thereof. But Congress may by a vote of two-thirds of each House, remove such disability.[10]

Section 4

The validity of the public debt of the United States, authorized by law, including debts incurred for payment of pensions and bounties for services in suppressing insurrection or rebellion, shall not be questioned.[11] But neither the United States nor any State shall assume or pay any debt or obligation incurred in aid of insurrection or rebellion against the United States, or any claim for the loss or emancipation of any slave; but all such debts, obligations and claims shall be held illegal and void.[12]

Section 5

The Congress shall have power to enforce, by appropriate legislation, the provisions of this article.[13]

Source: Charters of Freedom, National Archives.

[10]Northern leaders regarded those who had joined the Confederate cause as traitors. This provision was designed to bar such individuals from office, unless and until a two-thirds majority of Congress voted otherwise. Congress removed most such restrictions in 1872.

[11]Congress hereby acknowledged the debts that it had incurred to fight the Civil War, while repudiating the debt that the Confederate states had amassed.

[12]Congress was making it clear that it would not then, or later, provide reimbursement for those who sought to dismantle the Union and lost their slaves in the process.

[13]Congress had already taken measures to provide for the rights of newly freed slaves, and the amendment indicated that it would have the right to do so. This provision thus serves, much like the necessary proper clause at the end of Article I, Section 8 of the Constitution, to indicate that Congress had discretion in interpreting the amendment.

Frederick Douglass's Letter to Josephine Sophie White Griffing

September 27, 1868

INTRODUCTION

Frederick Douglass (1818–1895), the one-time slave who had written an autobiography after escaping from slavery and given numerous speeches in favor of abolitionism, was also an advocate of women's rights who had attended the Seneca Falls Convention of 1848. At the end of the Civil War, women's rights advocates like Josephine Griffing were disappointed that Douglass did not devote more efforts to see that women were included within the language of the Fourteenth and Fifteenth Amendments. He explains in this letter that while he remained committed to women's rights, he thought the more serious issue at hand was that of black men who had previously been held as slaves.

My Dear Friend:

I am impelled by no lack of generosity in refusing to come to Washington to speak in behalf of woman's suffrage. The right of woman to vote is as sacred in my judgment as that of man, and I am quite willing at any time to hold up both hands in favor of this right. It does not however follow that I can come to Washington or go elsewhere to deliver lectures upon this special subject. I am now devoting myself to a cause not more sacred, certainly more urgent, because it is one of life and death to the long-enslaved people of this country, and this is: negro suffrage. While the negro is mobbed, beaten, shot, stabbed, hanged, burnt and is the target of all that is malignant in the North and all that is murderous in the South, his claims may be preferred by me without exposing in any wise myself to the imputation of narrowness or meanness toward the cause of women.[1] As you very well know, woman has a thousand ways to attach herself to the governing power of the land and already exerts an honorable influence on the course of legislation.[2] She is the victim of abuses, to be sure, but it cannot be pretended I think that her cause is as urgent as that of ours. I never suspect you of sympathizing with

[1] Douglass has grasped a basic principle of politics, which is that it is sometimes necessary to accept the practical better for the theoretical best.

[2] Douglass believes that white women would continue to have the sympathies of their husbands and fathers, while black men could not succeed unless they had the franchise.

Miss [Susan B.] Anthony and Mrs. [Elizabeth Cady] Stanton in their course. Their principle is: that no negro shall be enfranchised while woman is not. Now, considering that white men have been enfranchised always, and colored men have not, the conduct of these white women, whose husbands, fathers and brothers are voters, does not seem generous.

Very truly yours—
Fredk Douglass

CONCLUSION

This controversy resulted in a split between the National Woman Suffrage Association, which was led by Stanton and Anthony, and which had opposed the adoption of the Fourteenth and Fifteenth Amendments because they did not include women, and the American Woman Suffrage Association, which had supported the post-bellum amendments even though they did not extend suffrage to women. In 1890, both groups joined forces in the National American Woman Suffrage Association (NAWSA). Women finally secured national suffrage with the ratification of the Nineteenth Amendment in 1920.

Source: Griffing Papers, Columbia University Rare Book & Manuscript Library.

SECTION III

The Rest of Reconstruction

Ulysses S. Grant's First Inaugural Address

March 4, 1869

INTRODUCTION

Although his impeachment trial did not end in removal from office, Andrew Johnson's presidency had been tumultuous. It is not surprising that the nation turned to Ulysses S. Grant, who had led Union forces to victory in the Civil War, to replace him. Grant's position on Reconstruction was closer to that of Congress than Johnson's had been, and yet he did not share the animosity that some Northern members of Congress shared toward their Southern brothers.

Citizens of the United States

On all leading questions agitating the public mind I will always express my views to Congress and urge them according to my judgment, and when I think it advisable will exercise the constitutional privilege of interposing a veto to defeat measures which I oppose; but all laws will be faithfully executed, whether they meet my approval or not.

I shall on all subjects have a policy to recommend, but none to enforce against the will of the people. Laws are to govern all alike—those opposed as well as those who favor them. I know no method to secure the repeal of bad or obnoxious laws so effective as their stringent execution.

The country having just emerged from a great rebellion,[1] many questions will come before it for settlement in the next four years which preceding Administrations have never had to deal with. In meeting these it is desirable that they should be approached calmly, without prejudice, hate, or sectional pride, remembering that the greatest good to the greatest number is the object to be attained. This requires security of person, property, and free religious and political opinion in every part of our common country, without regard to local prejudice. All laws to secure these ends will receive my best efforts for their enforcement.[2]

[1] Notably, Grant, like Lincoln, referred to the conflict as a rebellion rather than as a war between the states.

[2] Although lacking the lyrical quality of Lincoln's rhetoric, this policy toward Southern Reconstruction sounds similar to Lincoln's words in his Second Inaugural Address.

A great debt has been contracted in securing to us and our posterity the Union. The payment of this, principal and interest, as well as the return to a specie[3] basis as soon as it can be accomplished without material detriment to the debtor class or to the country at large, must be provided for. To protect the national honor, every dollar of Government indebtedness should be paid in gold, unless otherwise expressly stipulated in the contract. Let it be understood that no repudiator of one farthing of our public debt will be trusted in public place, and it will go far toward strengthening a credit which ought to be the best in the world, and will ultimately enable us to replace the debt with bonds bearing less interest than we now pay. To this should be added a faithful collection of the revenue, a strict accountability to the Treasury for every dollar collected, and the greatest practicable retrenchment in expenditure in every department of Government.

4The national debt in 1869 was just over $76 million. Grant anticipated that the nation would better be able to pay off this debt as it healed from the wounds of war.

When we compare the paying capacity of the country now, with the ten States in poverty from the effects of war, but soon to emerge, I trust, into greater prosperity than ever before, with its paying capacity twenty-five years ago, and calculate what it probably will be twenty-five years hence, who can doubt the feasibility of paying every dollar then with more ease than we now pay for useless luxuries?[4] Why, it looks as though Providence had bestowed upon us a strong box in the precious metals locked up in the sterile mountains of the far West, and which we are now forging the key to unlock, to meet the very contingency that is now upon us.

Ultimately it may be necessary to insure the facilities to reach these riches and it may be necessary also that the General Government should give its aid to secure this access; but that should only be when a dollar of obligation to pay secures precisely the same sort of dollar to use now, and not before. . . .

It will be my endeavor to execute all laws in good faith, to collect all revenues assessed, and to have them properly accounted for and economically disbursed. I will to the best of my ability appoint to office those only who will carry out this design.

In regard to foreign policy, I would deal with nations as equitable law requires individuals to deal with each other, and I would protect the law-abiding citizen, whether of native or foreign birth, wherever his rights are jeopardized or the flag of our country floats. I would respect the rights of all nations, demanding equal respect for our own. If others depart from this rule in their dealings with us, we may be compelled to follow their precedent.

The proper treatment of the original occupants of this land—the Indians—is one deserving of careful study. I will favor any course toward them which tends to their civilization and ultimate citizenship.[5]

The question of suffrage is one which is likely to agitate the public so long as a portion of the citizens of the nation are excluded from its privileges in any State. It seems to me very desirable that this question should be settled now, and I entertain the hope and express the desire that it may be by the ratification of the fifteenth article of amendment to the Constitution.[6]

In conclusion I ask patient forbearance one toward another throughout the land, and a determined effort on the part of every citizen to do his share toward cementing a happy union; and I ask the prayers of the nation to Almighty God in behalf of this consummation.

Source: James D. Richardson, *A Compilation of the Messages and Papers of the Presidents, Volume 7, Part 1: Ulysses S. Grant.* New York: National Bureau of Literature, 1897.

[5] This part of the speech is an appropriate reminder that the Fourteenth Amendment, ratified the previous year, did not guarantee citizenship to Native-American Indians.

[6] The Fifteenth Amendment, prohibiting discrimination in voting on the basis of race or national origin, had been proposed but not yet ratified. The measure was considered to be not simply a matter of justice but also a way of perpetuating control by the Republican Party, which was its chief sponsor. Democrats were concentrated in the South, where African Americans were no longer counted as three-fifths of a person. If African Americans, who were predominately Republican, did not have the vote in such states, Democratic strength could actually be stronger after emancipation than before.

Texas v. White

April 12, 1869

INTRODUCTION

Southern states had sought to secede from the Union, which had denied their right to do so and won the battle of arms. In this case, involving Texas's attempt to sell bonds that it had received from the national government to support the Confederate cause (albeit without the required signature), the Court assessed the lessons of the Civil War and the continuing relationship between the nation and the states. If Texas had ceased to be a state, the Court would not have had jurisdiction over this case.

The CHIEF JUSTICE [Chase] delivered the opinion of the court.

. . .

Did Texas, in consequence of these acts, cease to be a State? Or, if not, did the State cease to be a member of the Union?

It is needless to discuss at length the question whether the right of a State to withdraw from the Union for any cause regarded by herself as sufficient is consistent with the Constitution of the United States.

The Union of the States never was a purely artificial and arbitrary relation. It began among the Colonies, and grew out of common origin, mutual sympathies, kindred principles, similar interests, and geographical relations. It was confirmed and strengthened by the necessities of war, and received definite form and character and sanction from the Articles of Confederation. By these, the Union was solemnly declared to "be perpetual."[1] And when these Articles were found to be inadequate to the exigencies of the country, the Constitution was ordained "to form a more perfect Union." It is difficult to convey the idea of indissoluble unity more clearly than by these words. What can be indissoluble if a perpetual Union, made more perfect, is not?

[1] Northern and Southern states had disagreed profoundly about the nature of the Union. Chase's argument for the perpetuity of the Union blends the idea, common in Great Britain, which does not have a single written constitution, that the state is an organic growth, with the idea implicit in a written document that it represents a type of social contract.

214

But the perpetuity and indissolubility of the Union by no means implies the loss of distinct and individual existence, or of the right of self-government, by the States. Under the Articles of Confederation, each State retained its sovereignty, freedom, and independence, and every power, jurisdiction, and right not expressly delegated to the United States. Under the Constitution, though the powers of the States were much restricted, still all powers not delegated to the United States nor prohibited to the States, are reserved to the States respectively, or to the people.[2] And we have already had occasion to remark at this term that the people of each State compose a State, having its own government, and endowed with all the functions essential to separate and independent existence, and that, "without the States in union, there could be no such political body as the United States." Not only, therefore, can there be no loss of separate and independent autonomy to the States through their union under the Constitution, but it may be not unreasonably said that the preservation of the States, and the maintenance of their governments, are as much within the design and care of the Constitution as the preservation of the Union and the maintenance of the National government. The Constitution, in all its provisions, looks to an indestructible Union composed of indestructible States.[3]

When, therefore, Texas became one of the United States, she entered into an indissoluble relation. All the obligations of perpetual union, and all the guaranties of republican government in the Union, attached at once to the State. The act which consummated her admission into the Union was something more than a compact; it was the incorporation of a new member into the political body.[4] And it was final. The union between Texas and the other States was as complete, as perpetual, and as indissoluble as the union between the original States. There was no place for reconsideration or revocation, except through revolution or through consent of the States.

Considered therefore as transactions under the Constitution, the ordinance of secession, adopted by the convention and ratified by a majority of the citizens of Texas, and all the acts of her legislature intended to give effect to that ordinance, were absolutely null.[5] They were utterly without operation in law. The obligations of the State, as a member of the Union, and of every citizen of the State, as a citizen of the United States, remained perfect and unimpaired. It certainly follows that the State did not cease to be a State, nor her citizens to be citizens of the Union. If this were otherwise, the State must

[2]Chase recognized that while the Civil War had denied the states the prerogative of nullification or secession, it had neither erased state boundaries nor their continuing individual existences.

[3]This sentence is arguably echoed in the Pledge "to the flag of the United States [plural] of America [singular]" and its reference to "one nation, indivisible."

[4]Southerners had pushed for the admission of Texas into the Union in part because it was a slave state. Even though it was a republic prior to becoming a state, this decision indicates that it had no more right to secede than did the other states.

[5]Because the Court did not believe states had the right to secede, it considered any efforts to do so to be void.

have become foreign, and her citizens foreigners. The war must have ceased to be a war for the suppression of rebellion, and must have become a war for conquest and subjugation.

Our conclusion therefore is that Texas continued to be a State, and a State of the Union, notwithstanding the transactions to which we have referred. And this conclusion, in our judgment, is not in conflict with any act or declaration of any department of the National government, but entirely in accordance with the whole series of such acts and declarations since the first outbreak of the rebellion.

Source: *Texas v. White*, 74 US 700 (1869).

Fifteenth Amendment to the U.S. Constitution

February 3, 1870

INTRODUCTION

Had it been enforced, this amendment might have been the most important of the three postbellum amendments because it sought to give African Americans the right to protect their own rights at the voting booth. Like its immediate predecessor, this amendment did not prohibit discrimination on the basis of sex.

Section 1. The right of citizens of the United States to vote shall not be denied or abridged by the United States or by any State on account of race, color, or previous condition of servitude.[1]

Section 2. The Congress shall have power to enforce this article by appropriate legislation.[2]

[1] Because the Constitution otherwise left voting qualifications to the states, this amendment was phrased as a prohibition rather than as a positive right.

[2] Like the two amendments that proceeded, it included a congressional enforcement clause.

CONCLUSION

Despite this amendment, states supplemented the intimidation exercised by groups like the Ku Klux Klan with such devices as poll taxes, grandfather clauses, literacy tests, all-white primaries, and other stratagems that effectively suppressed most Black voting until the civil rights revolution of the 1950s and 1960s, most notably the Voting Rights Act of 1965 and its successors.

Source: Charters of Freedom, National Archives.

Civil Rights Act (The Enforcement Act)

May 31, 1870

INTRODUCTION

Consistent with Section 2 of the Fifteenth Amendment, Congress adopted this act to prohibit the use of race as a qualification for voting.

[1]The U.S. Constitution does not affirmatively grant the right to vote to anyone (after the law, women were still not permitted to vote), but this law was designed to eliminate discrimination based on race, color, or prior slavery.

Be it enacted by the Senate and House of Representatives of the United States of America in Congress assembled, That all citizens of the United States who are or shall be otherwise qualified by law to vote at any election . . . shall be entitled and allowed to vote at all such elections, without distinction of race, color, or previous condition of servitude. . . .[1]

SEC. 2. And be it further enacted, That it shall be the duty of every person and officer to give to all citizens of the United States the same and equal opportunity to perform [any] prerequisite, and to become qualified to vote without distinction of race, color, or previous condition of servitude; and if any person or officer shall refuse or knowingly omit to give full effect to this section, he shall . . . be deemed guilty of a misdemeanor, and shall, on conviction thereof, be fined not less than five hundred dollars, or be imprisoned not less than one month and not more than one year, or both, at the discretion of the court.

[2]The use of force and other illegal actions sometimes undermine laws. This provision of the laws was designed to prohibit groups like the Ku Klux Klan from intimidating black voters.

SEC. 6. And be it further enacted, That if two or more persons shall band or conspire together, or go in disguise upon the public highway, or upon the premises of another, with intent to violate any provision of this act, or to injure, oppress, threaten, or intimidate any citizen with intent to prevent or hinder his free exercise and enjoyment of any right or privilege granted or secured to him by the Constitution or laws of the United States,[2] or because of his having exercised the same, such persons shall be held guilty of felony, and, on conviction thereof, shall be fined or imprisoned, or both, at the discretion of the court,—the fine not to exceed five thousand dollars, and the imprisonment not to exceed ten years,—and shall, moreover, be thereafter ineligible to, and disabled from holding, any office or place of honor, profit, or trust created by the Constitution or laws of the United States.

SEC. 17. And be it further enacted, That any person who, under color of any law, statute, ordinance, regulation, or custom, shall subject, or cause to be subjected, any inhabitant of any State or Territory to the deprivation of any right secured or protected by the last preceding section [giving all persons the same rights as white citizens] of this act,[3] or to different punishment, pains, or penalties on account of such person being an alien, or by reason of his color or race, than is prescribed for the punishment of citizens, shall be deemed guilty of a misdemeanor, and, on conviction, shall be punished by fine not exceeding one thousand dollars, or imprisonment not exceeding one year, or both, in the discretion of the court.

Source: *U.S. Statutes at Large*, 16 Stat. 140–146, 41st Cong., 2d Sess., 114.

[3] In *United States v. Cruikshank* (1875), the U.S. Supreme Court issued a very restrictive interpretation of this law that left it to states to provide most protections against physical intimidation.

Civil Rights Act (Second Enforcement Act)

April 20, 1871

INTRODUCTION

Even after the adoption of the three postbellum amendments, Congress continued to express concern that laws were being flouted by acts of violence, especially by members of the Ku Klux Klan, many of whose members were former Confederate soldiers who were collectively acting as conspirators against African Americans.

[1]Note the emphasis of the law on conspiracies to commit violence against individuals either upholding the law or attempting to enforce it.

SEC. 2. That if two or more persons within any State or Territory of the United States shall conspire together to overthrow, or to put down, or to destroy by force the government of the United States, or to levy war against the United States, or to oppose by force the authority of the government of the United States, or by force, intimidation, or threat to prevent, hinder, or delay the execution of any law of the United States, or by force to seize, take, or possess any property of the United States contrary to the authority thereof, or by force, intimidation, or threat to prevent any person from accepting or holding any office or trust or place of confidence under the United States, or from discharging the duties thereof, or by force, intimidation, or threat to induce any officer of the United States to leave any State, district, or place where his duties as such officer might lawfully be performed, or to injure him in his person or property on account of his lawful discharge of the duties of his office, or to injure his person while engaged in the lawful discharge of the duties of his office,[1] or to injure his property so as to molest, interrupt, hinder, or impede him in the discharge of his official duty, or by force, intimidation, or threat to deter any party or witness in any court of the United States from attending such court, or from testifying in any matter pending in such court fully, freely, and truthfully, or to injure any such party or witness in his person or property on account of his having so attended or testified, or by force, intimidation, or threat to influence the verdict, presentment, or indictment, of any juror or grand juror in any court of the United States, or to injure such juror in his person or property on account of any verdict, presentment, or indictment lawfully assented to by him, or on account of his being or having been such juror, or shall conspire together, or go in disguise upon the public highway or upon the premises of another for the purpose, either directly or indirectly, of depriving any person or any class of persons of the equal protection of the laws, or of equal privileges or immunities under the laws, or for the purpose of preventing or hindering the constituted authorities of any State from giving or securing to all persons within such State the equal protection of the laws, or shall conspire together for the purpose of in any manner impeding, hindering, obstructing, or defeating the due course of justice in any State or Territory, with intent to deny to any citizen of the United States the due and equal protection of the laws, or to injure any person in his person or his property for lawfully enforcing the right of any person or class of persons to the equal protection of the laws, or by force, intimidation, or threat to prevent any citizen of the United States lawfully entitled to vote from giving his support or advocacy in a lawful manner towards or in favor of the election of any lawfully qualified person as an elector of President or Vice-President of the United States, or as a member of the Congress of the United States, or to injure any such citizen in his person or property on account of such support or advocacy, each and every person so offending shall be deemed guilty of a high crime, and, upon conviction thereof in any district or circuit court of the United States or district or supreme court of any Territory of the United States having jurisdiction of similar offences, shall be punished by a fine not less than five hundred nor more than five thousand dollars, or by imprisonment, with or without hard labor, as the court may determine, for a period of not less than six months nor more than six years, as the court may determine, or by both such fine and imprisonment as the court shall determine.[2]

[2]Like the preceding Civil Rights Act of the previous year, this law was chiefly aimed at the private use of intimidation and force.

CONCLUSION

In *United States v. Cruikshank* (1876), the Supreme Court decided that the post-bellum amendments only gave authority to Congress to prevent acts of state discrimination; citizens would have to look to state governments, which typically closed their eyes to such white-on-black violence, for protections against acts by private individuals.

Source: *U.S. Statutes at Large*, 17 Stat. 13, 42nd Cong., 1st Sess., 22.

The Law Creating Yellowstone Park

March 1, 1872

INTRODUCTION

The United States has not always been heedful of its natural resources (consider the decimation of the passenger pigeon and the near destruction of American bison on the Great Plains), but the law designating Yellowstone as the first national park was an important milestone.

CHAP. XXIV.—*An Act to set apart a certain Tract of Land lying near the Head-waters of the Yellowstone River as a public Park.*

Be it enacted by the Senate and House of Representatives of the United States of America in Congress assembled, That the tract of land in the Territories of Montana and Wyoming, lying near the head-waters of the Yellowstone river, and described as follows,[1] to wit, commencing at the junction of Gardiner's river with the Yellowstone river and running east to the median passing ten miles to the eastward of the most eastern point of Yellowstone lake; thence south along said meridian to the parallel of latitude passing fifteen miles west of the most western point of Madison lake; thence north along said meridian to the latitude of the junction of the Yellowstone and Gardiner's rivers; thence east to the place of beginning, is hereby reserved and withdrawn from settlement, occupancy, or sale under the laws of the United States, and dedicated and set apart as a public park or pleasuring-ground for the benefit and enjoyment of the people;[2] and all persons who shall locate or settle upon or occupy the same, or any part thereof, except as hereinafter provided, shall be considered trespassers and removed therefrom.

SEC. 2. That said public park shall be under the exclusive control of the Secretary of the Interior, whose duty it shall be, as soon as practicable, to make and publish such rules and regulations as he may deem necessary or proper for the care and management of the same. Such regulations shall provide for the preservation, from

[1] This area, known for its great natural beauty, which includes hot springs, geysers, and waterfalls, is now known to be sitting on one of the world's largest underground volcanoes.

[2] Millions of people visit the park each year.

injury or spoliation, of all timber, mineral deposits, natural curiosities, or wonders within said park, and their retention in their natural condition. . . .

APPROVED, March 1, 1872

CONCLUSION

Fortunately, the government was able to designate this unique landscape as a park prior to extensive settlement. Other parks, for example the Shenandoah National Park, would later require the government to use its power of eminent domain to force settlers to sell the land to the government.

Source: *Statutes at Large*, 42nd Cong., 2d Sess., XXIV, 32–33.

The Slaughterhouse Cases

April 14, 1873

INTRODUCTION

The postbellum amendments contained some vital principles, but how would they be interpreted and who would enforce them? This was the issue in the Slaughterhouse Cases. At issue was a Louisiana regulation, shaped by an unlikely mix of public health concerns (pollution from slaughterhouses had fouled the city's drinking water) and political favoritism, which limited the slaughterhouses where butchers could carry out their trade in New Orleans.

Butchers who were forced to work at places other than their own businesses objected that the law interfered with their livelihood and hence with the "privileges and immunities" as U.S. citizens. The Supreme Court had to decide precisely what privileges and immunities were covered by the Fourteenth Amendment.

Mr. Justice MILLER, now, April 14th, 1873, delivered the opinion of the court.

. . .

The wisdom of the monopoly granted by the legislature may be open to question, but it is difficult to see a justification for the assertion that the butchers are deprived of the right to labor in their occupation, or the people of their daily service in preparing food, or how this statute, with the duties and guards imposed upon the company, can be said to destroy the business of the butcher, or seriously interfere with its pursuit.

[1] States had long been recognized as having "police powers" over local matters involving economic issues.

The power here exercised by the legislature of Louisiana is, in its essential nature, one which has been, up to the present period in the constitutional history of this country, always conceded to belong to the States, however it may now be questioned in some of its details....[1]

It may, therefore, be considered as established that the authority of the legislature of Louisiana to pass the present statute is ample

224

unless some restraint in the exercise of that power be found in the constitution of that State or in the amendments to the Constitution of the United States, adopted since the date of the decisions we have already cited.

If any such restraint is supposed to exist in the constitution of the State, the Supreme Court of Louisiana having necessarily passed on that question, it would not be open to review in this court.

The plaintiffs in error, accepting this issue, allege that the statute is a violation of the Constitution of the United States in these several particulars:

That it creates an involuntary servitude forbidden by the thirteenth article of amendment;

That it abridges the privileges and immunities of citizens of the United States;

That it denies to the plaintiffs the equal protection of the laws; and,

That it deprives them of their property without due process of law, contrary to the provisions of the first section of the fourteenth article of amendment.[2]

This court is thus called upon for the first time to give construction to these articles.

We do not conceal from ourselves the great responsibility which this duty devolves upon us. No questions so far-reaching and pervading in their consequences, so profoundly interesting to the people of this country, and so important in their bearing upon the relations of the United States, of the several States to each other, and to the citizens of the States and of the United States, have been before this court during the official life of any of its present members. . . .

Twelve articles of amendment were added to the Federal Constitution soon after the original organization of the government under it in 1789. Of these, all but the last were adopted so soon afterwards as to justify the statement that they were practically contemporaneous with the adoption of the original; and the twelfth, adopted in eighteen hundred and three, was so nearly so as to have become, like all the others, historical and of another age. But within the first

[2]Although this decision focused chiefly on the privileges and immunities clause, the plaintiffs had also invoked the Thirteenth Amendment and other provisions of the Fourteenth Amendment.

eight years, three other articles of amendment of vast importance have been added by the voice of the people to that now venerable instrument.

[3]By focusing on the chief object of the postbellum amendments to provide for the rights of freedmen, the Court was minimizing the impact that these provisions would have in other circumstances, like the one at issue in this case.

The most cursory glance at these articles discloses a unity of purpose, when taken in connection with the history of the times, which cannot fail to have an important bearing on any question of doubt concerning their true meaning.[3] Nor can such doubts, when any reasonably exist, be safely and rationally solved without a reference to that history, for in it is found the occasion and the necessity for recurring again to the great source of power in this country, the people of the States, for additional guarantees of human rights, additional powers to the Federal government; additional restraints upon those of the States. Fortunately, that history is fresh within the memory of us all, and its leading features, as they bear upon the matter before us, free from doubt.

The institution of African slavery, as it existed in about half the States of the Union, and the contests pervading the public mind for many years between those who desired its curtailment and ultimate extinction and those who desired additional safeguards for its security and perpetuation, culminated in the effort, on the part of most of the States in which slavery existed, to separate from the Federal government and to resist its authority. This constituted the war of the rebellion, and whatever auxiliary causes may have contributed to bring about this war, undoubtedly the overshadowing and efficient cause was African slavery.[4]

[4]The Court clearly attributes the Civil War largely to the issue of slavery.

In that struggle, slavery, as a legalized social relation, perished. It perished as a necessity of the bitterness and force of the conflict. When the armies of freedom found themselves upon the soil of slavery, they could do nothing less than free the poor victims whose enforced servitude was the foundation of the quarrel. And when hard-pressed in the contest, these men (for they proved themselves men in that terrible crisis) offered their services and were accepted by thousands to aid in suppressing the unlawful rebellion, slavery was at an end wherever the Federal government succeeded in that purpose. The proclamation of President Lincoln expressed an accomplished fact as to a large portion of the insurrectionary districts when he declared slavery abolished in them all. But the war being over, those who had succeeded in reestablishing the authority of the Federal government were not content to permit this great act of emancipation to rest on the actual results of the contest or the proclamation of the Executive, both of which might have been questioned in after times, and they determined to place this main and most valuable result in the Constitution of the restored Union as one of its fundamental articles. Hence, the thirteenth article of amendment of that instrument.

Its two short sections seem hardly to admit of construction, so vigorous is their expression and so appropriate to the purpose we have indicated.

"1. Neither slavery nor involuntary servitude, except as a punishment for crime, whereof the party shall have been duly convicted, shall exist within the United States or any place subject to their jurisdiction."

"2. Congress shall have power to enforce this article by appropriate legislation."

To withdraw the mind from the contemplation of this grand yet simple declaration of the personal freedom of all the human race within the jurisdiction of this government—a declaration designed to establish the freedom of four millions of slaves—and with a microscopic search endeavor to find in it a reference to servitudes which may have been attached to property in certain localities requires an effort, to say the least of it.

That a personal servitude was meant is proved by the use of the word "involuntary," which can only apply to human beings. The exception of servitude as a punishment for crime gives an idea of the class of servitude that is meant. The word servitude is of larger meaning than slavery, as the latter is popularly understood in this country, and the obvious purpose was to forbid all shades and conditions of African slavery. It was very well understood that, in the form of apprenticeship for long terms, as it had been practiced in the West India Islands, on the abolition of slavery by the English government, or by reducing the slaves to the condition of serfs attached to the plantation, the purpose of the article might have been evaded if only the word slavery had been used. The case of the apprentice slave, held under a law of Maryland, liberated by Chief Justice Chase on a writ of habeas corpus under this article, illustrates this course of observation. And it is all that we deem necessary to say on the application of that article to the statute of Louisiana, now under consideration.

[5]Justice Miller associates the adoption of the Thirteenth and Fourteenth Amendments with the desire to end chattel slavery and provide freedoms for the newly freed slaves. He finds it difficult to apply the law to cover white butchers unhappy with a state regulation of their businesses.

[6]Miller is describing the black codes that Southern states had enacted prior to the adoption of the Fourteenth Amendment.

The process of restoring to their proper relations with the Federal government and with the other States those which had sided with the rebellion, undertaken under the proclamation of President Johnson in 1865 and before the assembling of Congress, developed the fact that, notwithstanding the formal recognition by those States of the abolition of slavery, the condition of the slave race would, without further protection of the Federal government, be almost as bad as it was before. Among the first acts of legislation adopted by several of the States in the legislative bodies which claimed to be in their normal relations with the Federal government were laws which imposed upon the colored race onerous disabilities and burdens and curtailed their rights in the pursuit of life, liberty, and property to such an extent that their freedom was of little value, while they had lost the protection which they had received from their former owners from motives both of interest and humanity.[5]

They were in some States forbidden to appear in the towns in any other character than menial servants. They were required to reside on and cultivate the soil without the right to purchase or own it. They were excluded from many occupations of gain, and were not permitted to give testimony in the courts in any case where a white man was a party. It was said that their lives were at the mercy of bad men, either because the laws for their protection were insufficient or were not enforced.[6]

These circumstances, whatever of falsehood or misconception may have been mingled with their presentation, forced upon the statesmen who had conducted the Federal government in safety through the crisis of the rebellion, and who supposed that, by the thirteenth article of amendment, they had secured the result of their labors, the conviction that something more was necessary in the way of constitutional protection to the unfortunate race who had suffered so much. They accordingly passed through Congress the proposition for the fourteenth amendment, and they declined to treat as restored to their full participation in the government of the Union the States which had been in insurrection until they ratified that article by a formal vote of their legislative bodies.

Before we proceed to examine more critically the provisions of this amendment, on which the plaintiffs in error rely, let us complete and dismiss the history of the recent amendments, as that history relates to the general purpose which pervades them all. A few years' experience satisfied the thoughtful men who had been the authors of the other two amendments that, notwithstanding the restraints of those articles on the States and the laws passed under the additional powers granted to Congress, these were inadequate for the protection of life, liberty, and property, without which freedom to the slave was no boon. They were in all those States denied the right of suffrage. The laws were administered by the white man alone. It was urged that a race of men distinctively marked, as was the negro, living in the midst of another and dominant race, could never be fully secured in their person and their property without the right of suffrage.

Hence, the fifteenth amendment, which declares that "the right of a citizen of the United States to vote shall not be denied or abridged by any State on account of race, color, or previous condition of servitude."

The negro having, by the fourteenth amendment, been declared to be a citizen of the United States, is thus made a voter in every State of the Union.

We repeat, then, in the light of this recapitulation of events, almost too recent to be called history, but which are familiar to us all, and on the most casual examination of the language of these amendments, no one can fail to be impressed with the one pervading purpose found in them all, lying at the foundation of each, and without which none of them would have been even suggested; we mean the freedom of the slave race, the security and firm establishment of that freedom, and the protection of the newly made freeman and citizen from the oppressions of those who had formerly exercised unlimited dominion over him.[7] It is true that only the fifteenth amendment, in terms, mentions the negro by speaking of his color and his slavery. But it is just as true that each of the other articles was addressed to the grievances of that race, and designed to remedy them as the fifteenth.

We do not say that no one else but the negro can share in this protection. Both the language and spirit of these articles are to have their fair and just weight in any question of construction. Undoubtedly while negro slavery alone was in the mind of the Congress which proposed the thirteenth article, it forbids any other kind of slavery, now or hereafter. If Mexican peonage or the

[7]Again, the Court is attempting to limit the scope of the Fourteenth Amendment by associating it with the primary purpose of protecting the rights of freedmen rather than focusing on its more universalistic language.

8While acknowledging that the Fourteenth Amendment is not limiting to protecting blacks, Miller is wary of interpreting it beyond what he believed to be its central objective.

Chinese coolie labor system shall develop slavery of the Mexican of Chinese race within our territory, this amendment may safely be trusted to make it void. And so, if other rights are assailed by the States which properly and necessarily fall within the protection of these articles, that protection will apply, though the party interested may not be of African descent.[8] But what we do say, and what we wish to be understood, is that, in any fair and just construction of any section or phrase of these amendments, it is necessary to look to the purpose which we have said was the pervading spirit of them all, the evil which they were designed to remedy, and the process of continued addition to the Constitution, until that purpose was supposed to be accomplished as far as constitutional law can accomplish it.

The first section of the fourteenth article to which our attention is more specially invited opens with a definition of citizenship—not only citizenship of the United States, but citizenship of the States. No such definition was previously found in the Constitution, nor had any attempt been made to define it by act of Congress. It had been the occasion of much discussion in the courts, by the executive departments, and in the public journals. It had been said by eminent judges that no man was a citizen of the United States except as he was a citizen of one of the States composing the Union. Those, therefore, who had been born and resided always in the District of Columbia or in the Territories, though within the United States, were not citizens. Whether this proposition was sound or not had never been judicially decided. But it had been held by this court, in the celebrated Dred Scott case, only a few years before the outbreak of the civil war, that a man of African descent, whether a slave or not, was not and could not be a citizen of a State or of the United States. This decision, while it met the condemnation of some of the ablest statesmen and constitutional lawyers of the country, had never been overruled, and if was to be accepted as a constitutional limitation of the right of citizenship, then all the negro race who had recently been made freemen were still not only not citizens, but were incapable of becoming so by anything short of an amendment to the Constitution.

To remove this difficulty primarily, and to establish clear and comprehensive definition of citizenship which should declare what should constitute citizenship of the United States and also citizenship of a State, the first clause of the first section was framed.

"All persons born or naturalized in the United States, and subject to the jurisdiction thereof, are citizens of the United States and of the State wherein they reside."

The first observation we have to make on this clause is that it puts at rest both the questions which we stated to have been the subject of differences of opinion. It declares that persons may be citizens of the United States without regard to their citizenship of a particular State, and it overturns the Dred Scott decision by making all persons born within the United States and subject to its jurisdiction citizens of the United States.[9] That its main purpose was to establish the citizenship of the negro can admit of no doubt. The phrase, "subject to its jurisdiction" was intended to exclude from its operation children of ministers, consuls, and citizens or subjects of foreign States born within the United States.

The next observation is more important in view of the arguments of counsel in the present case. It is that the distinction between citizenship of the United States and citizenship of a State is clearly recognized and established.

Not only may a man be a citizen of the United States without being a citizen of a State, but an important element is necessary to convert the former into the latter. He must reside within the State to make him a citizen of it, but it is only necessary that he should be born or naturalized in the United States to be a citizen of the Union.

It is quite clear, then, that there is a citizenship of the United States, and a citizenship of a State, which are distinct from each other, and which depend upon different characteristics or circumstances in the individual.[10]

We think this distinction and its explicit recognition in this amendment of great weight in this argument, because the next paragraph of this same section, which is the one mainly relied on by the plaintiffs in error, speaks only of privileges and immunities of citizens of the United States, and does not speak of those of citizens of the several States. The argument, however, in favor of the plaintiffs rests wholly on the assumption that the citizenship is the same, and the privileges and immunities guaranteed by the clause are the same.

[9]Miller has acknowledged that the Fourteenth Amendment overturned the Dred Scott Decision, which had declared that blacks were not and could not be U.S. citizens.

[10]Miller did not believe that the amendment had abolished the distinction between state and national citizenship.

The language is, "No State shall make or enforce any law which shall abridge the privileges or immunities of citizens of the United States." It is a little remarkable, if this clause was intended as a protection to the citizen of a State against the legislative power of his own State, that the word citizen of the State should be left out when it is so carefully used, and used in contradistinction to citizens of the United States in the very sentence which precedes it. It is too clear for argument that the change in phraseology was adopted understandingly and, with a purpose.

Of the privileges and immunities of the citizen of the United States, and of the privileges and immunities of the citizen of the State, and what they respectively are, we will presently consider; but we wish to state here that it is only the former which are placed by this clause under the protection of the Federal Constitution, and that the latter, whatever they may be, are not intended to have any additional protection by this paragraph of the amendment.[11]

[11] Deferring to earlier ideas of federalism, the Court is confining the scope of the privileges and immunities clause to the rights of U.S. citizenship, which it will subsequently interpret quite narrowly.

If, then, there is a difference between the privileges and immunities belonging to a citizen of the United States as such and those belonging to the citizen of the State as such, the latter must rest for their security and protection where they have heretofore rested, for they are not embraced by this paragraph of the amendment.

The first occurrence of the words "privileges and immunities" in our constitutional history is to be found in the fourth of the articles of the old Confederation.

It declares "that the better to secure and perpetuate mutual friendship and intercourse among the people of the different States in this Union, the free inhabitants of each of these States, paupers, vagabonds, and fugitives from justice excepted, shall be entitled to all the privileges and immunities of free citizens in the several States, and the people of each State shall have free ingress and regress to and from any other State, and shall enjoy therein all the privileges of trade and commerce, subject to the same duties, impositions, and restrictions as the inhabitants thereof respectively."

In the Constitution of the United States, which superseded the Articles of Confederation, the corresponding provision is found in section two of the fourth article, in the following words: "The citizens of each State shall be entitled to all the privileges and immunities of citizens of the several States."

There can be but little question that the purpose of both these provisions is the same, and that the privileges and immunities intended are the same in each. In the article of the Confederation, we have some of these specifically mentioned, and enough perhaps to give some general idea of the class of civil rights meant by the phrase.

Fortunately, we are not without judicial construction of this clause of the Constitution. The first and the leading case on the subject is that of Corfield v. Coryell, decided by Mr. Justice Washington in the Circuit Court for the District of Pennsylvania in 1823.

"The inquiry," he says, "is what are the privileges and immunities of citizens of the several States? We feel no hesitation in confining these expressions to those privileges and immunities which are fundamental; which belong of right to the citizens of all free governments, and which have at all times been enjoyed by citizens of the several States which compose this Union, from the time of their becoming free, independent, and sovereign. What these fundamental principles are it would be more tedious than difficult to enumerate. They may all, however, be comprehended under the following general heads: protection by the government, with the right to acquire and possess property of every kind and to pursue and obtain happiness and safety, subject, nevertheless, to such restraints as the government may prescribe for the general good of the whole." . . .

The constitutional provision there alluded to did not create those rights, which it called privileges and immunities of citizens of the States. It threw around them in that clause no security for the citizen of the State in which they were claimed or exercised. Nor did it profess to control the power of the State governments over the rights of its own citizens.

Its sole purpose was to declare to the several States that, whatever those rights, as you grant or establish them to your own citizens, or as you limit or qualify or impose restrictions on their exercise, the same, neither more nor less, shall be the measure of the rights of citizens of other States within your jurisdiction.[12]

It would be the vainest show of learning to attempt to prove by citations of authority that, up to the adoption of the recent amendments, no claim or pretence was set up that those rights depended on the Federal government for their existence or protection beyond

[12]Rather than interpreting the Fourteenth Amendment as recognizing or creating a set of fundamental privileges or immunities that states had to follow, the Court interprets the law as merely providing that it must treat citizens from other states equal to its own.

the very few express limitations which the Federal Constitution imposed upon the States—such, for instance, as the prohibition against ex post facto laws, bills of attainder, and laws impairing the obligation of contracts. But, with the exception of these and a few other restrictions, the entire domain of the privileges and immunities of citizens of the States, as above defined, lay within the constitutional and legislative power of the States, and without that of the Federal government.[13] Was it the purpose of the fourteenth amendment, by the simple declaration that no State should make or enforce any law which shall abridge the privileges and immunities of citizens of the United States, to transfer the security and protection of all the civil rights which we have mentioned, from the States to the Federal government? And where it is declared that Congress Shall have the power to enforce that article, was it intended to bring within the power of Congress the entire domain of civil rights heretofore belonging exclusively to the States?

All this and more must follow if the proposition of the plaintiffs in error be sound. For not only are these rights subject to the control of Congress whenever, in its discretion, any of them are supposed to be abridged by State legislation, but that body may also pass laws in advance, limiting and restricting the exercise of legislative power by the States, in their most ordinary and usual functions, as in its judgment it may think proper on all such subjects. And still further, such a construction followed by the reversal of the judgments of the Supreme Court of Louisiana in these cases, would constitute this court a perpetual censor upon all legislation of the States, on the civil rights of their own citizens, with authority to nullify such as it did not approve as consistent with those rights, as they existed at the time of the adoption of this amendment. The argument, we admit, is not always the most conclusive which is drawn from the consequences urged against the adoption of a particular construction of an instrument. But when, as in the case before us, these consequences are so serious, so far-reaching and pervading, so great a departure from the structure and spirit of our institutions; when the effect is to fetter and degrade the State governments by subjecting them to the control of Congress in the exercise of powers heretofore universally conceded to them of the most ordinary and fundamental character; when, in fact, it radically changes the whole theory of the relations of the State and Federal governments to each other and of both these governments to the people, the argument has a force that is irresistible in the absence of language which expresses such a purpose too clearly to admit of doubt.[14]

We are convinced that no such results were intended by the Congress which proposed these amendments, nor by the legislatures of the States which ratified them.

Having shown that the privileges and immunities relied on in the argument are those which belong to citizens of the States as such, and that they are left to the State governments for security and protection, and not by this article placed under the special care of the Federal government, we may hold ourselves excused from defining the privileges and immunities of citizens of the United States which no State can abridge until some case involving those privileges may make it necessary to do so.

But lest it should be said that no such privileges and immunities are to be found if those we have been considering are excluded, we venture to suggest some which owe their existence to the Federal government, its national character, its Constitution, or its laws.

One of these is well described in the case of Crandall v. Nevada. It is said to be the right of the citizen of this great country, protected by implied guarantees of its Constitution, "to come to the seat of government to assert any claim he may have upon that government, to transact any business he may have with it, to seek its protection, to share its offices, to engage in administering its functions. He has the right of free access to its seaports, through which operations of foreign commerce are conducted, to the sub-treasuries, land offices, and courts of justice in the several States."

And quoting from the language of Chief Justice Taney in another case, it is said "that, for all the great purposes for which the Federal government was established, we are one people, with one common country, we are all citizens of the United States;" and it is, as such citizens, that their rights are supported in this court in Crandall v. Nevada.

Another privilege of a citizen of the United States is to demand the care and protection of the Federal government over his life, liberty, and property when on the high seas or within the jurisdiction of a foreign government. Of this there can be no doubt, nor that the

[15]None of the rights that Miller identified are necessarily insignificant, and yet most would not collectively provide the kind of substantive protections for either whites or blacks that the most ardent advocates of the Fourteenth Amendment had advocated.

right depends upon his character as a citizen of the United States. The right to peaceably assemble and petition for redress of grievances, the privilege of the writ of habeas corpus, are rights of the citizen guaranteed by the Federal Constitution. The right to use the navigable waters of the United States, however they may penetrate the territory of the several States, all rights secured to our citizens by treaties with foreign nations, are dependent upon citizenship of the United States, and not citizenship of a State.[15] One of these privileges is conferred by the very article under consideration. It is that a citizen of the United States can, of his own volition, become a citizen of any State of the Union by a bona fide residence therein, with the same rights as other citizens of that State. To these may be added the rights secured by the thirteenth and fifteenth articles of amendment, and by the other clause of the fourteenth, next to be considered.

But it is useless to pursue this branch of the inquiry, since we are of opinion that the rights claimed by these plaintiffs in error, if they have any existence, are not privileges and immunities of citizens of the United States within the meaning of the clause of the thirteenth amendment under consideration.

"All persons born or naturalized in the United States, and subject to the jurisdiction thereof, are citizens of the United States and of the State wherein they reside. No State shall make or enforce any law which shall abridge the privileges or immunities of citizens of the United States; nor shall any State deprive any person of life, liberty, or property without due process of law, nor deny to any person within its jurisdiction the equal protection of its laws."

The argument has not been much pressed in these cases that the defendant's charter deprives the plaintiffs of their property without due process of law, or that it denies to them the equal protection of the law. The first of these paragraphs has been in the Constitution since the adoption of the fifth amendment, as a restraint upon the Federal power. It is also to be found in some form of expression in the constitutions of nearly all the States as a restraint upon the power of the States. This law, then, has practically been the same as it now is during the existence of the government, except so far as the present amendment may place the restraining power over the States in this matter in the hands of the Federal government.

We are not without judicial interpretation, therefore, both State and National, of the meaning of this clause. And it is sufficient to say that under no construction of that provision that we have ever seen, or any that we deem admissible, can the restraint imposed by the State of Louisiana upon the exercise of their trade by the butchers of New Orleans be held to be a deprivation of property within the meaning of that provision.

"Nor shall any State deny to any person within its jurisdiction the equal protection of the laws."

In the light of the history of these amendments, and the pervading purpose of them, which we have already discussed, it is not difficult to give a meaning to this clause. The existence of laws in the States where the newly emancipated negroes resided, which discriminated with gross injustice and hardship against them as a class, was the evil to be remedied by this clause, and by it such laws are forbidden.

If, however, the States did not conform their laws to its requirements, then by the fifth section of the article of amendment Congress was authorized to enforce it by suitable legislation. We doubt very much whether any action of a State not directed by way of discrimination against the negroes as a class, or on account of their race, will ever be held to come within the purview of this provision. It is so clearly a provision for that race and that emergency that a strong case would be necessary for its application to any other. But as it is a State that is to be dealt with, and not alone the validity of its laws, we may safely leave that matter until Congress shall have exercised its power, or some case of State oppression, by denial of equal justice in its courts, shall have claimed a decision at our hands. We find no such case in the one before us, and do not deem it necessary to go over the argument again, as it may have relation to this particular clause of the amendment.

In the early history of the organization of the government, its statesmen seem to have divided on the line which should separate the powers of the National government from those of the State governments, and though this line has never been very well defined in public opinion, such a division has continued from that day to this.

The adoption of the first eleven amendments to the Constitution so soon after the original instrument was accepted shows a prevailing sense of danger at that time from the Federal power. And it cannot be denied that such a jealousy continued to exist with many patriotic men until the breaking out of the late civil war. It was then discovered that the true danger to the perpetuity of the Union was in the capacity of the State organizations to combine and concentrate all the powers of the State, and of contiguous States, for a determined resistance to the General Government.

Unquestionably this has given great force to the argument, and added largely to the number of those who believe in the necessity of a strong National government.

But, however pervading this sentiment, and however it may have contributed to the adoption of the amendments we have been considering, we do not see in those amendments any purpose to destroy the main features of the general system. Under the pressure of all the excited feeling growing out of the war, our statesmen have still believed that the existence of the State with powers for domestic and local government, including the regulation of civil rights the rights of person and of property was essential to the perfect working of our complex form of government, though they have thought proper to impose additional limitations on the States, and to confer additional power on that of the Nation.

[16]Once again, the Court explains its opinion as an attempt to preserve the division of powers between the state and national governments (federalism).

But whatever fluctuations may be seen in the history of public opinion on this subject during the period of our national existence, we think it will be found that this court, so far as its functions required, has always held with a steady and an even hand the balance between State and Federal power, and we trust that such may continue to be the history of its relation to that subject so long as it shall have duties to perform which demand of it a construction of the Constitution or of any of its parts.[16]

The judgments of the Supreme Court of Louisiana in these cases are AFFIRMED.

Mr. Justice FIELD, dissenting.

I am unable to agree with the majority of the court in these cases, and will proceed to state the reasons of my dissent from their judgment. . . .

It is not necessary, however, as I have said, to rest my objections to the act in question upon the terms and meaning of the thirteenth amendment. The provisions of the fourteenth amendment, which is properly a supplement to the thirteenth, cover, in my judgment, the case before us, and inhibit any legislation which confers special and exclusive privileges like these under consideration. The amendment was adopted to obviate objections which had been raised and pressed with great force to the validity of the Civil Rights Act, and to place the common rights of American citizens under the protection of the National government. . . .

The amendment does not attempt to confer any new privileges or immunities upon citizens, or to enumerate or define those already existing. It assumes that there are such privileges and immunities which belong of right to citizens as such, and ordains that they shall not be abridged by State legislation.[17] If this inhibition has no reference to privileges and immunities of this character, but only refers, as held by the majority of the court in their opinion, to such privileges and immunities as were before its adoption specially designated in the Constitution or necessarily implied as belonging to citizens of the United States, it was a vain and idle enactment, which accomplished nothing and most unnecessarily excited Congress and the people on its passage. With privileges and immunities thus designated or implied no State could ever have interfered by its laws, and no new constitutional provision was required to inhibit such interference. The supremacy of the Constitution and the laws of the United States always controlled any State legislation of that character. But if the amendment refers to the natural and inalienable rights which belong to all citizens, the inhibition has a profound significance and consequence.

What, then, are the privileges and immunities which are secured against abridgment by State legislation?

In the first section of the Civil Rights Act, Congress has given its interpretation to these terms, or at least has stated some of the rights which, in its judgment, these terms include; it has there declared that they include the right "to make and enforce contracts, to sue, be parties and give evidence, to inherit, purchase, lease, sell, hold, and convey real and personal property, and to full and equal benefit of all laws and proceedings for the security of person and property."[18]

[17]While the majority argued that the Fourteenth Amendment should be interpreted conservatively, Justice Field argued that to do so was to ignore the passionate debate that surrounded the adoption of the amendment and its desire to protect natural rights.

[18]Field observed that Congress had previously given a broad interpretation to the privileges and immunities of U.S. citizens.

That act, it is true, was passed before the fourteenth amendment, but the amendment was adopted, as I have already said, to obviate objections to the act, or, speaking more accurately, I should say, to obviate objections to legislation of a similar character, extending the protection of the National government over the common rights of all citizens of the United States. Accordingly, after its ratification, Congress reenacted the act under the belief that whatever doubts may have previously existed of its validity, they were removed by the amendment.

The terms "privileges" and "immunities" are not new in the amendment; they were in the Constitution before the amendment was adopted. They are found in the second section of the fourth article, which declares that "the citizens of each State shall be entitled to all privileges and immunities of citizens in the several States," and they have been the subject of frequent consideration in judicial decisions. In Corfield v. Coryell, Mr. Justice Washington said he had "no hesitation in confining these expressions to those privileges and immunities which were, in their nature, fundamental, which belong of right to citizens of all free governments, and which have at all times been enjoyed by the citizens of the several States which compose the Union, from the time of their becoming free, independent, and sovereign;" and, in considering what those fundamental privileges were, he said that perhaps it would be more tedious than difficult to enumerate them, but that they might be "all comprehended under the following general heads: protection by the government; the enjoyment of life and liberty, with the right to acquire and possess property of every kind, and to pursue and obtain happiness and safety, subject, nevertheless, to such restraints as the government may justly prescribe for the general good of the whole."[19]

This appears to me to be a sound construction of the clause in question. The privileges and immunities designated are those which of right belong to the citizens of all free governments. Clearly among these must be placed the right to pursue a lawful employment in a lawful manner, without other restraint than such as equally affects all persons. In the discussions in Congress upon the passage of the Civil Rights Act, repeated reference was made to this language of Mr. Justice Washington. It was cited by Senator Trumbull with the observation that it enumerated the very rights belonging to a citizen of the United States set forth in the first section of the act, and

[19]Whereas the majority had attempted to interpret this precedent narrowly, Field interpreted it broadly.

[20]Senator Lyman Trumbull of Illinois had been one of the authors of the Thirteenth Amendment.

with the statement that all persons born in the United States, being declared by the act citizens of the United States, would thenceforth be entitled to the rights of citizens, and that these were the great fundamental rights set forth in the act; and that they were set forth "as appertaining to every freeman."[20]

The privileges and immunities designated in the second section of the fourth article of the Constitution are, then, according to the decision cited, those which of right belong to the citizens of all free governments, and they can be enjoyed under that clause by the citizens of each State in the several States upon the same terms and conditions as they are enjoyed by the citizens of the latter States. No discrimination can be made by one State against the citizens of other States in their enjoyment, nor can any greater imposition be levied than such as is laid upon its own citizens. It is a clause which insures equality in the enjoyment of these rights between citizens of the several States whilst in the same State. . . .

What the clause in question did for the protection of the citizens of one State against hostile and discriminating legislation of other States, the fourteenth amendment does for the protection of every citizen of the United States against hostile and discriminating legislation against him in favor of others, whether they reside in the same or in different States. If, under the fourth article of the Constitution, equality of privileges and immunities is secured between citizens of different States, under the fourteenth amendment, the same equality is secured between citizens of the United States.

It will not be pretended that, under the fourth article of the Constitution, any State could create a monopoly in any known trade or manufacture in favor of her own citizens, or any portion of them, which would exclude an equal participation in the trade or manufacture monopolized by citizens of other States. She could not confer, for example, upon any of her citizens the sole right to manufacture shoes, or boots, or silk, or the sole right to sell those articles in the State so as to exclude nonresident citizens from engaging in a similar manufacture or sale. The nonresident citizens could claim equality of privilege under the provisions of the fourth article with the citizens of the State exercising the monopoly as well as with others, and thus, as respects them, the monopoly would cease. If this were not so, it would be in the power of the State to exclude at any time the citizens of other States from participation in particular branches of commerce or trade, and extend the exclusion from time to time so as effectually to prevent any traffic with them.

Now what the clause in question does for the protection of citizens of one State against the creation of monopolies in favor of citizens of other States, the fourteenth amendment does for the protection of every citizen of the United States against the creation of any monopoly whatever. The privileges and immunities of citizens of the United States, of every one of them, is secured against abridgment in any form by any State. The fourteenth amendment places them under the guardianship of the National authority. All monopolies in any known trade or manufacture are an invasion of these privileges, for they encroach upon the liberty of citizens to acquire property and pursue happiness,[21] and were held void at common law in the great Case of Monopolies, decided during the reign of Queen Elizabeth. . . .

In all these cases, there is a recognition of the equality of right among citizens in the pursuit of the ordinary avocations of life, and a declaration that all grants of exclusive privileges, in contravention of this equality, are against common right, and void.

This equality of right, with exemption from all disparaging and partial enactments, in the lawful pursuits of life, throughout the whole country, is the distinguishing privilege of citizens of the United States. To them, everywhere, all pursuits, all professions, all avocations are open without other restrictions than such as are imposed equally upon all others of the same age, sex, and condition. The State may prescribe such regulations for every pursuit and calling of life as will promote the public health, secure the good order and advance the general prosperity of society, but, when once prescribed, the pursuit or calling must be free to be followed by every citizen who is within the conditions designated, and will conform to the regulations. This is the fundamental idea upon which our institutions rest, and, unless adhered to in the legislation of the country, our government will be a republic only in name. The fourteenth amendment, in my judgment, makes it essential to the validity of the legislation of every State that this equality of right should be respected. How widely this equality has been departed from, how entirely rejected and trampled upon by the act of Louisiana, I have already shown. And it is to me a matter of profound regret that its validity is recognized by a majority of this court, for by it the right of free labor, one of the most sacred and

[21] Justice Field was a champion of free enterprise who viewed the Fourteenth Amendment as providing protections against governmental favoritism (monopolies) and regulation. His laissez-faire economic views would gain increased prominence on the Supreme Court in the following decades.

imprescriptible rights of man, is violated. As stated by the Supreme Court of Connecticut in the case cited, grants of exclusive privileges, such as is made by the act in question, are opposed to the whole theory of free government, and it requires no aid from any bill of rights to render them void. That only is a free government, in the American sense of the term, under which the inalienable right of every citizen to pursue his happiness is unrestrained, except by just, equal, and impartial laws.

Dissenting opinion by Justice Bradley and by Justice Swayne omitted.

CONCLUSION

This restrictive decision, while primarily applying to whites in this case, did not bode well for future federal protection of the freed slaves. In time, the Court would use the due process clause to prohibit what it considered to be unreasonable limits on state and national regulations of industries, but most interpretations involving the rights of African-Americans continued to be quite restrictive until the Supreme Court decision in *Brown v. Board of Education* (1954) declaring the previously-approved system of racial segregation to be unconstitutional.

Source: 83 U.S. 36 (1873).

Civil Rights Act

March 1, 1875

INTRODUCTION

This was the last major act that Congress adopted during Reconstruction to guarantee the rights of freedmen.

[1]Equal political rights may be practically meaningless to those who are denied social equality.

[2]This law was designed to provide equal access in places of public accommodations. In the Civil Rights Cases of 1883, the Supreme Court invalidated this part of the act on the basis that laws could only prohibit unconstitutional state action rather than regulating individual behaviors. When Congress attempted again to guarantee access to public accommodations in the Civil Rights Act of 1964, it therefore relied upon the authority of congressional power to regulate interstate commerce and was subsequently upheld by the Court.

Whereas, it is essential to just government we recognize the equality of all men before the law, and hold that it is the duty of government in its dealings with the people to mete out equal and exact justice to all, of whatever nativity, race, color, or persuasion, religious or political;[1] and it being the appropriate object of legislation to enact great fundamental principles into law: Therefore,

Be it enacted by the Senate and House of Representatives of the United States of America in Congress assembled, That all persons within the jurisdiction of the United States shall be entitled to the full and equal enjoyment of the accommodations, advantages, facilities, and privileges of inns, public conveyances on land or water, theaters, and other places of public amusement; subject only to the conditions and limitations established by law, and applicable alike to citizens of every race and color, regardless of any previous condition of servitude.[2]

SEC. 2. That any person who shall violate the foregoing section by denying to any citizen, except for reasons by law applicable to citizens of every race and color, and regardless of any previous condition of servitude, the full enjoyment of any of the accommodations, advantages, facilities, or privileges in said section enumerated, or by aiding or inciting such denial, shall, for every such offense, forfeit and pay the sum of five hundred dollars to the person aggrieved thereby, to be recovered in an action of debt, with full costs; and shall also, for every such offense, be deemed guilty of a misdemeanor and, upon conviction thereof, shall be fined not less than five hundred nor more than one thousand dollars, or shall be imprisoned not less than thirty days nor more than one year. . . .

SEC. 4. That no citizen possessing all other qualifications which are or may be prescribed by law shall be disqualified for service as a grand or petit juror in any court of the United States, or of any State, on account of race, color, or previous condition of servitude;[3] and any officer or other person charged with any duty in the selection or summoning of jurors who shall exclude or fail to summon any citizen for the cause aforesaid shall, on conviction thereof, be deemed guilty of a misdemeanor and be fined not more than five thousand dollars.

Source: Civil Rights Act of 1875, *U.S. Statutes at Large* 18 (1875), 335.

[3]The Bill of Rights seeks to guarantee rights at trial through jury proceedings. Although this law was evaded by numerous stratagems, it was designed to prevent discrimination in jury selection.

Minor v. Happersett

March 9, 1875

INTRODUCTION

Despite the restrictive decision in the Slaughterhouse Cases, individuals continued to hope that the privileges and immunities clause of the Fourteenth Amendment might protect previously unsecured rights against state interference. This case involved an attempt by a Missouri woman to vote, despite state laws that confined the right to males.

THE CHIEF JUSTICE [Morrison Waite] delivered the opinion of the Court.

. . .

It is contended that the provisions of the constitution and laws of the State of Missouri which confine the right of suffrage and registration therefor to men are in violation of the Constitution of the United States, and therefore void. The argument is that as a woman, born or naturalized in the United States and subject to the jurisdiction thereof, is a citizen of the United States and of the state in which she resides, she has the right of suffrage as one of the privileges and immunities of her citizenship which the state cannot by its laws or constitution abridge.

There is no doubt that women may be citizens. They are persons, and by the Fourteenth Amendment "all persons born or naturalized in the United States and subject to the jurisdiction thereof" are expressly declared to be "citizens of the United States and of the state wherein they reside."[1] But in our opinion it did not need this amendment to give them that position. Before its adoption, the Constitution of the United States did not in terms prescribe who should be citizens of the United States or of the several states, yet there were necessarily such citizens without such provision. There cannot be a nation without a people. The very idea of a political community such as a nation is implies an association of persons for the promotion of their general welfare. Each one of the persons

[1] Although the Court accepted the idea that women, like children, were citizens, it did not believe that citizenship necessarily secured the right to vote.

associated becomes a member of the nation formed by the association. He owes it allegiance and is entitled to its protection. Allegiance and protection are in this connection reciprocal obligations. The one is a compensation for the other; allegiance for protection and protection for allegiance.

For convenience, it has been found necessary to give a name to this membership. The object is to designate by a title the person and the relation he bears to the nation. For this purpose, the words "subject," "inhabitant," and "citizen" have been used, and the choice between them is sometimes made to depend upon the form of the government. Citizen is now more commonly employed, however, and as it has been considered better suited to the description of one living under a republican government, it was adopted by nearly all of the states upon their separation from Great Britain, and was afterwards adopted in the Articles of Confederation and in the Constitution of the United States. When used in this sense, it is understood as conveying the idea of membership of a nation, and nothing more.

To determine, then, who were citizens of the United States before the adoption of the amendment, it is necessary to ascertain what persons originally associated themselves together to form the nation and what were afterwards admitted to membership.

Looking at the Constitution itself, we find that it was ordained and established by "the people of the United States," and then going further back, we find that these were the people of the several states that had before dissolved the political bands which connected them with Great Britain and assumed a separate and equal station among the powers of the earth, and that had by Articles of Confederation and Perpetual Union, in which they took the name of "the United States of America," entered into a firm league of friendship with each other for their common defense, the security of their liberties, and their mutual and general welfare, binding themselves to assist each other against all force offered to or attack made upon them, or any of them, on account of religion, sovereignty, trade, or any other pretense whatever.

Whoever, then, was one of the people of either of these states when the Constitution of the United States was adopted became *ipso facto* a citizen—a member of the nation created by its adoption. He was one of the persons associating together to form the nation, and was consequently one of its original citizens. As to this there has never been a doubt. Disputes have arisen as to whether or not certain persons or certain classes of persons were part of the people at the time, but never as to their citizenship if they were.

Additions might always be made to the citizenship of the United States in two ways: first, by birth, and second, by naturalization. This is apparent from the Constitution itself, for it provides that "No person except a natural-born citizen or a citizen of the United States at the time of the adoption of the Constitution shall be eligible to the office of President," and that Congress shall have power "to establish a uniform rule of naturalization." Thus, new citizens may be born or they may be created by naturalization.[2]

The Constitution does not in words say who shall be natural-born citizens. Resort must be had elsewhere to ascertain that. At common law, with the nomenclature of which the framers of the Constitution were familiar, it was never doubted that all children born in a country of parents who were its citizens became themselves, upon their birth, citizens also. These were natives or natural-born citizens, as distinguished from aliens or foreigners. Some authorities go further and include as citizens children born within the jurisdiction without reference to the citizenship of their parents.[3] As to this class there have been doubts, but never as to the first. For the purposes of this case, it is not necessary to solve these doubts. It is sufficient for everything we have now to consider that all children born of citizen parents within the jurisdiction are themselves citizens. The words "all children" are certainly as comprehensive, when used in this connection, as "all persons," and if females are included in the last, they must be in the first. That they are included in the last is not denied. In fact, the whole argument of the plaintiffs proceeds upon that idea.

Under the power to adopt a uniform system of naturalization, Congress, as early as 1790, provided "that any alien, being a free white person," might be admitted as a citizen of the United States, and that the children of such persons so naturalized, dwelling within the United States, being under twenty-one years of age at the time of such naturalization, should also be considered citizens of the United States, and that the children of citizens of the United States that might be born beyond the sea, or out of the limits of the United

[2] The Court is citing provisions in the Constitution that preceded the adoption of the Fourteenth Amendment.

[3] Although Article II of the Constitution requires a presidential candidate to be a "natural born citizen," which might leave some room for ambiguity, the Fourteenth Amendment confers the rights of citizenship on "all persons born or naturalized in the United States and subject to the jurisdiction thereof." Under current interpretations of this amendment, persons born in the United States, other than those born to diplomatic personnel (who are not fully under U.S. jurisdiction) are considered to be U.S. citizens regardless of their parents' citizenship.

States, should be considered as natural-born citizens. These provisions thus enacted have in substance been retained in all the naturalization laws adopted since. In 1855, however, the last provision was somewhat extended, and all persons theretofore born or thereafter to be born out of the limits of the jurisdiction of the United States, whose fathers were or should be at the time of their birth citizens of the United States were declared to be citizens also.

As early as 1804 it was enacted by Congress that when any alien who had declared his intention to become a citizen in the manner provided by law died before he was actually naturalized, his widow and children should be considered as citizens of the United States and entitled to all rights and privileges as such upon taking the necessary oath; and in 1855 it was further provided that any woman who might lawfully be naturalized under the existing laws, married, or who should be married to a citizen of the United States should be deemed and taken to be a citizen.

From this it is apparent that from the commencement of the legislation upon this subject, alien women and alien minors could be made citizens by naturalization, and we think it will not be contended that this would have been done if it had not been supposed that native women and native minors were already citizens by birth.

But if more is necessary to show that women have always been considered as citizens the same as men, abundant proof is to be found in the legislative and judicial history of the country. . . .

If the right of suffrage is one of the necessary privileges of a citizen of the United States, then the Constitution and laws of Missouri confining it to men are in violation of the Constitution of the United States, as amended, and consequently void. The direct question is therefore presented whether all citizens are necessarily voters.[4]

The Constitution does not define the privileges and immunities of citizens. For that definition we must look elsewhere. In this case, we need not determine what they are, but only whether suffrage is necessarily one of them.[5]

It certainly is nowhere made so in express terms. The United States has no voters in the states of its own creation. The elective officers of the United States are all elected directly or indirectly by state voters.

The members of the House of Representatives are to be chosen by the people of the states, and the electors in each state must have the qualifications requisite for electors of the most numerous branch of the state legislature. Senators are to be chosen by the legislatures of the states, and necessarily the members of the legislature required to make the choice are elected by the voters of the state. Each state must appoint in such manner, as the legislature thereof may direct, the electors to elect the President and Vice-President. The times, places, and manner of holding elections for Senators and Representatives are to be prescribed in each state by the legislature thereof, but Congress may at any time, by law, make or alter such regulations, except as to the place of choosing Senators. It is not necessary to inquire whether this power of supervision thus given to Congress is sufficient to authorize any interference with the state laws prescribing the qualifications of voters, for no such interference has ever been attempted. The power of the state in this particular is certainly supreme until Congress acts.

[6]The Court is interpreting the privileges and immunities of U.S. citizenship according to past usage, which did not include suffrage, but left its determination to the states.

The amendment did not add to the privileges and immunities of a citizen. It simply furnished an additional guaranty for the protection of such as he already had. No new voters were necessarily made by it. Indirectly it may have had that effect because it may have increased the number of citizens entitled to suffrage under the constitution and laws of the states, but it operates for this purpose, if at all, through the states and the state laws, and not directly upon the citizen.[6]

It is clear, therefore, we think, that the Constitution has not added the right of suffrage to the privileges and immunities of citizenship as they existed at the time it was adopted. This makes it proper to inquire whether suffrage was coextensive with the citizenship of the states at the time of its adoption. If it was, then it may with force be argued that suffrage was one of the rights which belonged to citizenship, and in the enjoyment of which every citizen must be protected.

But if it was not, the contrary may with propriety be assumed.

When the federal Constitution was adopted, all the states with the exception of Rhode Island and Connecticut had constitutions of their own. [The Court proceeds to show that only one state, New Jersey, which later rescinded it, extended suffrage to women.] . . .

In this condition of the law in respect to suffrage in the several states, it cannot for a moment be doubted that if it had been intended to make all citizens of the United States voters, the framers of the Constitution would not have left it to implication. So important a change in the condition of citizenship as it actually existed, if intended, would have been expressly declared.[7]

But if further proof is necessary to show that no such change was intended, it can easily be found both in and out of the Constitution. By Article IV, Section 2, it is provided that "The citizens of each state shall be entitled to all the privileges and immunities of citizens in the several states." If suffrage is necessarily a part of citizenship, then the citizens of each state must be entitled to vote in the several states precisely as their citizens are. This is more than asserting that they may change their residence and become citizens of the state and thus be voters. It goes to the extent of insisting that, while retaining their original citizenship, they may vote in any state. This, we think, has never been claimed. And again, by the very terms of the amendment we have been considering (the fourteenth), "Representatives shall be apportioned among the several states according to their respective numbers, counting the whole number of persons in each state, excluding Indians not taxed. But when the right to vote at any election for the choice of electors for President and Vice-President of the United States, representatives in Congress, the executive and judicial officers of a state, or the members of the legislature thereof, is denied to any of the male inhabitants of such state, being twenty-one years of age and citizens of the United States,[8] or in any way abridged, except for participation in the rebellion, or other crimes, the basis of representation therein shall be reduced in the proportion which the number of such male citizens shall bear to the whole number of male citizens twenty-one years of age in such state."

Why this if it was not in the power of the legislature to deny the right of suffrage to some male inhabitants? And if suffrage was necessarily one of the absolute rights of citizenship, why confine the operation of the limitation to male inhabitants? Women and children are, as we have seen, "persons." They are counted in the enumeration upon which the apportionment is to be made, but if they were necessarily voters because of their citizenship unless clearly excluded, why inflict the penalty for the exclusion of males alone? Clearly no such form of words would have been selected to express the idea here indicated if suffrage was the absolute right of all citizens.

[7] As in the Slaughterhouse Cases, the Court was convinced that the Constitution would not have granted such an important right by mere implication.

[8] The Court notes that Section 2 of the Fourteenth Amendment specifically threatened to penalize only those states that withheld the suffrage from males.

And still again, after the adoption of the Fourteenth Amendment, it was deemed necessary to adopt a fifteenth, as follows: "The right of citizens of the United States to vote shall not be denied or abridged by the United States or by any state on account of race, color, or previous condition of servitude."[9]

The Fourteenth Amendment had already provided that no state should make or enforce any law which should abridge the privileges or immunities of citizens of the United States. If suffrage was one of these privileges or immunities, why amend the Constitution to prevent its being denied on account of race &c.? Nothing is more evident than that the greater must include the less, and if all were already protected, why go through with the form of amending the Constitution to protect a part?

It is true that the United States guarantees to every state a republican form of government. It is also true that no state can pass a bill of attainder, and that no person can be deprived of life, liberty, or property without due process of law. All these several provisions of the Constitution must be construed in connection with the other parts of the instrument and in the light of the surrounding circumstances.

The guaranty is of a republican form of government. No particular government is designated as republican; neither is the exact form to be guaranteed in any manner especially designated. Here, as in other parts of the instrument, we are compelled to resort elsewhere to ascertain what was intended.

10Although Section IV of the Constitution guaranteed states "a republican form of government," the Constitution had long accepted state governments that had not included female suffrage.

The guaranty necessarily implies a duty on the part of the states themselves to provide such a government. All the states had governments when the Constitution was adopted. In all, the people participated to some extent, through their representatives elected in the manner specially provided.[10]

These governments the Constitution did not change. They were accepted precisely as they were, and it is therefore to be presumed that they were such as it was the duty of the states to provide. Thus we have unmistakable evidence of what was republican in form, within the meaning of that term as employed in the Constitution. As has been seen, all the citizens of the states were not invested with the right of suffrage. In all save perhaps New Jersey, this right was only bestowed upon men, and not upon all of them. Under these circumstances, it is certainly now too late to contend that a government is not republican, within the meaning of this guaranty in the Constitution, because women are not made voters.

The same may be said of the other provisions just quoted. Women were excluded from suffrage in nearly all the states by the express provision of their constitutions and laws. If that had been equivalent to a bill of attainder, certainly its abrogation would not have been left to implication. Nothing less than express language would have been employed to effect so radical a change. So also of the amendment which declares that no person shall be deprived of life, liberty, or property without due process of law, adopted as it was as early as 1791. If suffrage was intended to be included within its obligations, language better adapted to express that intent would most certainly have been employed. The right of suffrage, when granted, will be protected. He who has it can only be deprived of it by due process of law, but in order to claim protection, he must first show that he has the right.

But we have already sufficiently considered the proof found upon the inside of the Constitution. That upon the outside is equally effective.

The Constitution was submitted to the states for adoption in 1787, and was ratified by nine states in 1788, and finally by the thirteen original states in 1790. *[Again, the Court demonstrates that states had not extended the suffrage to women.]*

Certainly if the courts can consider any question settled, this is one. For nearly ninety years, the people have acted upon the idea that the Constitution, when it conferred citizenship, did not necessarily confer the right of suffrage. If uniform practice long continued can settle the construction of so important an instrument as the Constitution of the United States confessedly is, most certainly it has been done here. Our province is to decide what the law is, not to declare what it should be.

We have given this case the careful consideration its importance demands. If the law is wrong, it ought to be changed; but the power for that is not with us.[11] The arguments addressed to us bearing upon such a view of the subject may perhaps be sufficient to induce those having the power to make the alteration, but they ought not to be permitted to influence our judgment in determining the present

[11]The Court indicates that it is neither making a policy judgment about the wisdom of woman suffrage nor is it denying the right of the people to extend voting rights to women through constitutional amendment.

[12]The Court is simply declaring that it does not believe the Fourteenth Amendment, the Guarantee Clause, or other provisions of the existing Constitution, guarantee such a right.

rights of the parties now litigating before us. No argument as to woman's need of suffrage can be considered. We can only act upon her rights as they exist. It is not for us to look at the hardship of withholding. Our duty is at an end if we find it is within the power of a state to withhold.[12]

Being unanimously of the opinion that the Constitution of the United States does not confer the right of suffrage upon anyone, and that the constitutions and laws of the several states which commit that important trust to men alone are not necessarily void, we

Affirm the judgment.

CONCLUSION

Women had been seeking the right to vote since the Seneca Falls Convention of 1848, but they would not have a national guarantee against sexual discrimination in voting until the ratification of the Nineteenth Amendment in 1920.

Source: 88 U.S. (21 Wall), 162.

The Page Act
March 1875

This law dealing with immigration is sometimes designated as the Act to Prohibit the Importation of Lewd Women and sometimes called the Page Act, after Congressman Horace F. Page of California, who sponsored it. It is notable as being the first law that sought to restrict immigration into the United States. Although their numbers were far smaller, immigrants from China and Japan had come to America (they would later be joined by immigrants from the Philippines), especially the West, where they worked on the transcontinental railroad and set us businesses, especially laundries, to serve individuals who had come to California during the Gold Rush of 1848.

Western states often treated Chinese and Japanese much as Southern states had treated African Americans. Most such individuals arrived in the United States as single men who planned to return to their homelands, and the thought that they might marry and have children in America (who would be citizens under the Fourteenth Amendment) seemed threatening. It seemed easier to assume that women coming to America from China were coming for immoral purposes. Although Chinese won some court victories, twentieth-century laws, which we largely predicated on the need to preserve the nation's existing racial composition, imposed strict quotas on immigrants from this area of the world.

CHAP. 141.—An act supplementary to the acts in relation to immigration.

Be it enacted by the Senate and House of Representatives of the United States of America in Congress assembled, That in determining whether the immigration of any subject of China, Japan, or any Oriental country, to the United States, is free and voluntary, as provided by section two thousand one hundred and sixty-two of the Revised Code, title "Immigration," it shall be the duty of the consul-general or consul of the United States residing at the port from which it is proposed to convey such subjects, in any vessels enrolled or licensed in the United States, or any port within the same, before delivering to the masters of any such vessels the permit or certificate provided for in such section, to ascertain whether such immigrant bas entered into a contract or agreement for a term of service within the United States, for lewd and immoral purposes; and if there be such contract or agreement, the said consul-general or consul shall not deliver the required permit or certificate.

SEC. 2. That if any citizen of the United States, or other person amenable to the laws of the United States shall take, or cause to be taken or transported, to or from the United States any subject of China, Japan, or any Oriental country, without their free and voluntary consent, for the purpose of holding them to a term of service, such citizen or other person shall be liable to be indicted therefore, and, on conviction of such offense, shall be punished by a fine not exceeding two thousand dollars[1] and be imprisoned not exceeding one year; and all contracts and agreements for a term of service of such persons in the United States, whether made in advance or in pursuance of such illegal importation, and whether such importation shall have been in American or other vessels, are hereby declared void.

SEC. 3. That the importation into the United States of women for the purposes of prostitution is hereby forbidden; and all contracts and agreements in relation thereto, made in advance or in pursuance of such illegal importation and purposes, are hereby declared void;[2] and whoever shall knowingly and willfully import, or cause any importation of, women into the United States for the purposes of prostitution, or shall knowingly or willfully hold, or attempt to hold, any woman to such purposes, in pursuance of such illegal importation and contract or agreement, shall be deemed guilty of a felony, and, on conviction thereof, shall be imprisoned not exceeding five years and pay a fine not exceeding five thousand dollars.

SEC. 4. That if any person shall knowingly and willfully contract, or attempt to contract, in advance or in pursuance of such illegal importation, to supply to another the labor of any cooly or other person brought into the United States[3] in violation of section two thousand one hundred and fifty-eight of the Revised Statutes, or of any other section of the laws prohibiting the cooly-trade or of this act, such person shall be deemed guilty of a felony, and, upon conviction thereof, in any United States court, shall be fined in a sum not exceeding five hundred dollars and imprisoned for a term not exceeding one year.

[1]This sentiment is not unlike modern concerns about human trafficking.

[2]Although American concern with prostitution was genuine, there is little evidence indicating that Chinese women who sought to come to America planned to support themselves by prostitution.

[3]Chinese, like earlier indentured servants, often came to the United States under fixed contracts that would pay for their voyage. Such laborers were often derogatorily called "coolies."

SEC. 5. That it shall be unlawful for aliens of the following classes to immigrate into the United States, namely, persons who are undergoing a sentence for conviction in their own country of felonious crimes other than political or growing out of or the result of such political offenses, or whose sentence has been remitted on condition of their emigration, and women "imported for the purposes of prostitution." Every vessel arriving in the United States may be inspected under the direction of the collector of the port at which it arrives,[4] if he shall have reason to believe that any such obnoxious persons are on board; and the officer making such inspection shall certify the result thereof to the master or other person in charge of such vessel, designating in such certificate the person or persons, if any there be, ascertained by him to be of either of the classes whose importation is hereby forbidden. When such inspection is required by the collector as aforesaid, it shall be unlawful without his permission, for any alien to leave any such vessel arriving in the United States from a foreign country until the inspection shall have been had and the result certified as herein provided; and at no time thereafter shall any alien certified to by the inspecting officer as being of either of the classes whose immigration is forbidden by this section, be allowed to land in the United States, except in obedience to a judicial process issued pursuant to law. If any person shall feel aggrieved by the certificate of such inspecting officer stating him or her to be within either of the classes whose immigration is forbidden by this section, and shall apply for release or other remedy to any proper court or judge, then it shall be the duty of the collector at said port of entry to detain said vessel until a hearing and determination of the matter are had, to the end that if the said inspector shall be found to be in accordance with this section and sustained, the obnoxious person or persons shall be returned on board of said vessel, and shall not thereafter be permitted to land, unless the master, owner or consignee of the vessel shall give bond and security, to be approved by the court or judge hearing the cause, in the sum of five hundred dollars for each such person permitted to land, conditioned for the return of such person, within six months from the date thereof, to the country whence his or her emigration shall have taken place, or unless the vessel bringing such obnoxious person or persons shall be forfeited, in which event the proceeds of such forfeiture shall be paid over to the collector of the port of arrival, and applied by him, as far as necessary, to the return of such person or persons to his or her own country within the said period of six months. And for all violations of this act, the

[4] Although Ellis Island was a common point of entry, especially for European immigrants, it was not the only one. Angel Island, in the San Francisco Bay, served as the entry point for about one million immigrants, most of whom were from Asian nations.

vessel, by the acts, omissions, or connivance of the owners, master, or other custodian, or the consignees of which the same are committed, shall be liable to forfeiture, and may be proceeded against as in cases of frauds against the revenue laws, for which forfeiture is prescribed by existing law.

Approved March 3, 1875.

Source: Sect. 141, 18 Stat. 477, 1873–March 1875.

United States v. Cruikshank

March 27, 1876

INTRODUCTION

This case arose from the bloody Colfax Massacre in Louisiana in which more than 100 black men were killed by armed whites in an electoral dispute. The case is a near "bookend" to the Reconstruction Era and marks a time when the Supreme Court continued to limit the application of federal civil rights legislation under the postbellum amendments.

MR. CHIEF JUSTICE WAITE delivered the opinion of the court.

This case comes here with a certificate by the judges of the Circuit Court for the District of Louisiana that they were divided in opinion upon a question which occurred at the hearing. It presents for our consideration an indictment containing sixteen counts, divided into two series of eight counts each, based upon sect. 6 of the Enforcement Act of May 31, 1870. That section is as follows:—

"That if two or more persons shall band or conspire together, or go in disguise upon the public highway, or upon the premises of another, with intent to violate any provision of this act, or to injure, oppress, threaten, or intimidate any citizen, with intent to prevent or hinder his free exercise and enjoyment of any right or privilege granted or secured to him by the Constitution or laws of the United States, or because of his having exercised the same, such persons shall be held guilty of felony, and, on conviction thereof, shall be fined or imprisoned, or both, at the discretion of the court—the fine not to exceed $5,000, and the imprisonment not to exceed ten years—and shall, moreover, be thereafter ineligible to, and disabled from holding, any office or place of honor, profit, or trust created by the Constitution or laws of the United States." 16 Stat. 141.

The question certified arose upon a motion in arrest of judgment after a verdict of guilty generally upon the whole sixteen counts, and is stated to be whether "the said sixteen counts of said indictment are severally good and sufficient in law, and contain charges of criminal matter indictable under the laws of the United States."

The general charge in the first eight counts is that of "banding," and in the second eight that of "conspiring" together to injure, oppress, threaten, and intimidate Levi Nelson and Alexander Tillman, citizens of the United States, of African descent and persons of color, with the intent thereby to hinder and prevent them in their free exercise and enjoyment of rights and privileges "granted and secured" to them "in common with all other good citizens of the United States by the Constitution and laws of the United States."

The offences provided for by the statute in question do not consist in the mere "banding" or "conspiring" of two or more persons together, but in their banding or conspiring with the intent, or for any of the purposes, specified. To bring this case under the operation of the statute, therefore, it must appear that the right, the enjoyment of which the conspirators intended to hinder or prevent, was one granted or secured by the Constitution or laws of the United States. If it does not so appear, the criminal matter charged has not been made indictable by any act of Congress.

We have in our political system a government of the United States and a government of each of the several States. Each one of these governments is distinct from the others, and each has citizens of its own who owe it allegiance and whose rights, within its jurisdiction, it must protect.[1] The same person may be at the same time a citizen of the United States and a citizen of a State, but his rights of citizenship under one of these governments will be different from those he has under the other. *Slaughter-House Cases*, 16 Wall. 74.

Citizens are the members of the political community to which they belong. They are the people who compose the community, and who, in their associated capacity, have established or submitted themselves to the dominion of a government for the promotion of their general welfare and the protection of their individual as well as their collective rights. In the formation of a government, the people may confer upon it such powers as they choose. The government, when so formed, may, and when called upon should, exercise all the powers it has for the protection of the rights of its citizens and the people within its jurisdiction, but it can exercise no other. The duty of a

[1] As in its first interpretation of the Fourteenth Amendment in the Slaughterhouse Cases, the Court continues to distinguish state and national citizenship.

government to afford protection is limited always by the power it possesses for that purpose.

Experience made the fact known to the people of the United States that they required a national government for national purposes. The separate governments of the separate States, bound together by the articles of confederation alone, were not sufficient for the promotion of the general welfare of the people in respect to foreign nations, or for their complete protection as citizens of the confederated States. For this reason, the people of the United States, "in order to form a more perfect union, establish justice, insure domestic tranquillity, provide for the common defence, promote the general welfare, and secure the blessings of liberty" to themselves and their posterity (Const. Preamble), ordained and established the government of the United States, and defined its powers by a Constitution, which they adopted as its fundamental law, and made its rule of action.

The government thus established and defined is to some extent a government of the States in their political capacity. It is also, for certain purposes, a government of the people. Its powers are limited in number, but not in degree. Within the scope of its powers, as enumerated and defined, it is supreme, and above the States; but beyond, it has no existence. It was erected for special purposes, and endowed with all the powers necessary for its own preservation and the accomplishment of the ends its people had in view. It can neither grant nor secure to its citizens any right or privilege not expressly or by implication placed under its jurisdiction.

The people of the United States resident within any State are subject to two governments—one State and the other National—but there need be no conflict between the two. The powers which one possesses the other does not. They are established for different purposes, and have separate jurisdictions. Together, they make one whole, and furnish the people of the United States with a complete government, ample for the protection of all their rights at home and abroad. True, it may sometimes happen that a person is amenable to both jurisdictions for one and the same act. Thus, if a marshal of the United States is unlawfully resisted while executing the process of the courts within a State, and the resistance is accompanied by an assault on the officer, the sovereignty of the United States is violated by the resistance, and that of the State by the breach of peace in the assault. So, too, if one passes counterfeited coin of the United States within a State, it may be an offence against the United States and the State: the United States because it discredits the coin, and the State because of the fraud upon him to whom it is passed. This does not, however, necessarily imply that the two governments possess powers in common, or bring them into conflict with each other. It is the natural consequence of a citizenship which owes allegiance to two sovereignties and claims protection from both. The citizen cannot complain, because he has voluntarily submitted himself to such a form of government. He owes allegiance to the two departments, so to speak, and, within their respective spheres, must pay the penalties which each exacts for disobedience to its laws. In return, he can demand protection from each within its own jurisdiction.

The Government of the United States is one of delegated powers alone. Its authority is defined and limited by the Constitution. All powers not granted to it by that instrument are reserved to the States or the people. No rights can be acquired under the Constitution or laws of the United States, except such as the Government of the United States has the authority to grant or secure. All that cannot be so granted or secured are left under the protection of the States.[2]

We now proceed to an examination of the indictment, to ascertain whether the several rights, which it is alleged the defendants intended to interfere with, are such as had been in law and in fact granted or secured by the Constitution or laws of the United States.

The first and ninth counts state the intent of the defendants to have been to hinder and prevent the citizens named in the free exercise and enjoyment of their "lawful right and privilege to peaceably assemble together with each other and with other citizens of the United States for a peaceful and lawful purpose."

The right of the people peaceably to assemble for lawful purposes existed long before the adoption of the Constitution of the United States. In fact, it is, and always has been, one of the attributes of citizenship under a free government. It "derives its source," to use the language of Chief Justice Marshall in Gibbons v. Ogden, 9 Wheat. 1, 22 U.S. 211, "from those laws whose authority is acknowledged by civilized man throughout the world." It is found wherever civilization

[2]The Court is reiterating the doctrine that branches of the national government can only exercise powers delegated by the Constitution.

exists. It was not, therefore, a right granted to the people by the Constitution. The Government of the United States, when established, found it in existence, with the obligation on the part of the States to afford it protection. As no direct power over it was granted to Congress, it remains, according to the ruling in *Gibbons v. Ogden, id.,* 22 U.S. 203, subject to State jurisdiction.

Only such existing rights were committed by the people to the protection of Congress as came within the general scope of the authority granted to the national government.

The first amendment to the Constitution prohibits Congress from abridging "the right of the people to assemble and to petition the government for a redress of grievances." This, like the other amendments proposed and adopted at the same time, was not intended to limit the powers of the State governments in respect to their own citizens, but to operate upon the National Government alone.[3] *Barron v. The City of Baltimore,* 7 Pet. 250. . . .

The particular amendment now under consideration assumes the existence of the right of the people to assemble for lawful purposes, and protects it against encroachment by Congress. The right was not created by the amendment; neither was its continuance guaranteed, except as against congressional interference. For their protection in its enjoyment, therefore, the people must look to the States. The power for that purpose was originally placed there, and it has never been surrendered to the United States.[4]

The right of the people peaceably to assemble for the purpose of petitioning Congress for a redress of grievances, or for any thing else connected with the powers or the duties of the national government, is an attribute of national citizenship, and, as such, under the protection of, and guaranteed by, the United States. The very idea of a government republican in form implies a right on the part of its citizens to meet peaceably for consultation in respect to public affairs and to petition for a redress of grievances. If it had been alleged in these counts that the object of the defendants was to prevent a meeting for such a purpose, the case would have been within the statute, and within the scope of the sovereignty of the United States. Such, however, is not the case. The offence, as stated in the indictment, will be made out, if it be shown that the object of the conspiracy was to prevent a meeting for any lawful purpose whatever.

[3]The chief justice is reiterating prior decisions that indicated that the provisions of the Bill of Rights applied only to the states and could therefore be protected only by them. In the twentieth century, the Court would eventually decide that most such rights were also protected by the due process clause of the Fourteenth Amendment, but it had not yet come to this conclusion.

[4]Consigning African Americans in the South to seek constitutional protection from their white-dominated states essentially meant that they would not receive such help.

The second and tenth counts are equally defective. The right there specified is that of "bearing arms for a lawful purpose." This is not a right granted by the Constitution. Neither is it in any manner dependent upon that instrument for its existence. The second amendment declares that it shall not be infringed, but this, as has been seen, means no more than that it shall not be infringed by Congress. This is one of the amendments that has no other effect than to restrict the powers of the national government, leaving the people to look for their protection against any violation by their fellow citizens of the rights it recognizes, to what is called, in *The City of New York v. Miln*, 11 Pet. 139, the "powers which relate to merely municipal legislation, or what was, perhaps, more properly called internal police," "not surrendered or restrained" by the Constitution of the United States.

The third and eleventh counts are even more objectionable. They charge the intent to have been to deprive the citizens named, they being in Louisiana, "of their respective several lives and liberty of person without due process of law." This is nothing else than alleging a conspiracy to falsely imprison or murder citizens of the United States, being within the territorial jurisdiction of the State of Louisiana. The rights of life and personal liberty are natural rights of man. "To secure these rights," says the Declaration of Independence, "governments are instituted among men, deriving their just powers from the consent of the governed." The very highest duty of the States, when they entered into the Union under the Constitution, was to protect all persons within their boundaries in the enjoyment of these "unalienable rights with which they were endowed by their Creator." Sovereignty, for this purpose, rests alone with the States. It is no more the duty or within the power of the United States to punish for a conspiracy to falsely imprison or murder within a State, than it would be to punish for false imprisonment or murder itself.

[5]The Court is articulating the "state action" doctrine, which would blossom more fully in the Civil Rights Cases of 1883, by which it interpreted the Fourteenth Amendment to limit state discriminatory actions but left violations of rights by individual citizens to state laws.

The Fourteenth Amendment prohibits a State from depriving any person of life, liberty, or property without due process of law, but this adds nothing to the rights of one citizen as against another. It simply furnishes an additional guaranty against any encroachment by the States upon the fundamental rights which belong to every citizen as a member of society. . . .[5]

These counts in the indictment do not call for the exercise of any of the powers conferred by this provision in the amendment.

The fourth and twelfth counts charge the intent to have been to prevent and hinder the citizens named, who were of African descent and persons of color, in "the free exercise and enjoyment of their several right and privilege to the full and equal benefit of all laws and proceedings, then and there, before that time, enacted or ordained by the said State of Louisiana and by the United States, and then and there, at that time, being in force in the said State and District of Louisiana aforesaid, for the security of their respective persons and property, then and there, at that time enjoyed at and within said State and District of Louisiana by white persons, being citizens of said State of Louisiana and the United States, for the protection of the persons and property of said white citizens."

There is no allegation that this was done because of the race or color of the persons conspired against.[6] When stripped of its verbiage, the case as presented amounts to nothing more than that the defendants conspired to prevent certain citizens of the United States, being within the State of Louisiana, from enjoying the equal protection of the laws of the State and of the United States.

[6]The Court says that the prosecution has been unable to show that the violent actions at issue were specifically done on account of the race of those who were killed.

The Fourteenth Amendment prohibits a State from denying to any person within its jurisdiction the equal protection of the laws; but this provision does not, any more than the one which precedes it, and which we have just considered, add anything to the rights which one citizen has under the Constitution against another. The equality of the rights of citizens is a principle of republicanism. Every republican government is in duty bound to protect all its citizens in the enjoyment of this principle, if within its power. That duty was originally assumed by the States, and it still remains there. The only obligation resting upon the United States is to see that the States do not deny the right.[7] This the amendment guarantees, but no more. The power of the national government is limited to the enforcement of this guaranty.

[7]Again, the Court is distinguishing between unconstitutional state action and private action, against which it does not believe the Fourteenth Amendment provided protection.

No question arises under the Civil Rights Act of April 9, 1866 (14 Stat. 27), which is intended for the protection of citizens of the United States in the enjoyment of certain rights, without discrimination on account of race, color, or previous condition of servitude, because, as has already been stated, it is nowhere alleged in these counts that the wrong contemplated against the rights of these citizens was on account of their race or color.

Another objection is made to these counts that they are too vague and uncertain. This will be considered hereafter, in connection with the same objection to other counts.

The sixth and fourteenth counts state the intent of the defendants to have been to hinder and prevent the citizens named, being of African descent, and colored, "in the free exercise and enjoyment of their several and respective right and privilege to vote at any election to be thereafter by law had and held by the people in and of the said State of Louisiana, or by the people of and in the parish of Grant aforesaid."

In *Minor v. Happersett*, 21 Wall. 178, we decided that the Constitution of the United States has not conferred the right of suffrage upon anyone, and that the United States have no voters of their own creation in the States. In *United States v. Reese et al., supra*, p. 92 U.S. 214, we hold that the Fifteenth Amendment has invested the citizens of the United States with a new constitutional right, which is, exemption from discrimination in the exercise of the elective franchise on account of race, color, or previous condition of servitude. From this, it appears that the right of suffrage is not a necessary attribute of national citizenship, but that exemption from discrimination in the exercise of that right on account of race, &c., is. The right to vote in the States comes from the States, but the right of exemption from the prohibited discrimination comes from the United States. The first has not been granted or secured by the Constitution of the United States, but the last has been.[8]

Inasmuch, therefore, as it does not appear in these counts that the intent of the defendants was to prevent these parties from exercising their right to vote on account of their race, &c., it does not appear that it was their intent to interfere with any right granted or secured by the Constitution or laws of the United States. We may suspect that race was the cause of the hostility, but it is not so averred. This is material to a description of the substance of the offence, and cannot be supplied by implication. Everything essential must be charged positively, and not inferentially. The defect here is not in form, but in substance.

The seventh and fifteenth counts are no better than the sixth and fourteenth. The intent here charged is to put the parties named in great fear of bodily harm, and to injure and oppress them, because,

[8]The Court is arguing, as it had in *Minor v. Happersett*, that the Constitution does not positively confer the right to vote on anyone but merely prevents interference with such a right on the basis of race or color, which it does not believe the prosecution has established in this case.

being and having been in all things qualified, they had voted "at an election before that time had and held according to law by the people of the said State of Louisiana, in said State, to-wit, on the fourth day of November, A.D. 1872, and at divers other elections by the people of the State, also before that time had and held according to law."

There is nothing to show that the elections voted at were any other than State elections, or that the conspiracy was formed on account of the race of the parties against whom the conspirators were to act. The charge as made is really of nothing more than a conspiracy to commit a breach of the peace within a State. Certainly it will not be claimed that the United States have the power or are required to do mere police duly in the States. If a State cannot protect itself against domestic violence, the United States may, upon the call of the executive, when the legislature cannot be convened, lend their assistance for that purpose. This is a guaranty of the Constitution (art. 4, sect. 4), but it applies to no case like this.

We are therefore of the opinion that the first, second, third, fourth, sixth, seventh, ninth, tenth, eleventh, twelfth, fourteenth, and fifteenth counts do not contain charges of a criminal nature made indictable under the laws of the United States, and that consequently they are not good and sufficient in law. They do not show that it was the intent of the defendants, by their conspiracy, to hinder or prevent the enjoyment of any right granted or secured by the Constitution.

We come now to consider the fifth and thirteenth and the eighth and sixteenth counts, which may be brought together for that purpose. The intent charged in the fifth and thirteenth is "to hinder and prevent the parties in their respective free exercise and enjoyment of the rights, privileges, immunities, and protection granted and secured to them respectively as citizens of the United States, and as citizens of said State of Louisiana . . . for the reason that they, . . . being then and there citizens of said State and of the United States, were persons of African descent and race, and persons of color, and not white citizens thereof"; and in the eighth and sixteenth, to hinder and prevent them "in their several and respective free exercise and enjoyment of every, each, all, and singular the several rights and privileges granted and secured to them by the Constitution and laws of the United States."

The same general statement of the rights to be interfered with is found in the fifth and thirteenth counts.

According to the view we take of these counts, the question is not whether it is enough, in general, to describe a statutory offence in the language of the statute, but whether the offence has here been described at all. The statute provides for the punishment of those who conspire "to injure, oppress, threaten, or intimidate any citizen, with intent to prevent or hinder his free exercise and enjoyment of any right or privilege granted or secured to him by the Constitution or laws of the United States."

These counts in the indictment charge, in substance that the intent in this case was to hinder and prevent these citizens in the free exercise and enjoyment of "every, each, all, and singular" the rights granted them by the Constitution, &c. There is no specification of any particular right. The language is broad enough to cover all.

[9] In order to protect the innocent, courts demand special specificity when it comes to criminal indictments. The Court does not believe the prosecution has met this burden in this case.

The conclusion is irresistible that these counts are too vague and general. They lack the certainty and precision required by the established rules of criminal pleading. It follows that they are not good and sufficient in law. They are so defective that no judgment of conviction should be pronounced upon them.[9]

The order of the Circuit Court arresting the judgment upon the verdict is, therefore, affirmed; and the cause remanded, with instructions to discharge the defendants.

Source: *United States v. Cruikshank*, 92 U.S. 542.

Ulysses S. Grant's Speech to the Centennial Exhibition in Philadelphia

May 10, 1876

INTRODUCTION

The Civil War years brought into question the continuing existence of the United States, and yet it survived this conflict and sponsored an exhibition in Philadelphia, the nation's birthplace, on the centennial of the year the nation had celebrated the Declaration of Independence. Then President Ulysses S. Grant, who was finishing his second term in office, delivered the following speech at the exhibition's opening.

My Countrymen,—It has been thought appropriate, upon this centennial occasion, to bring together in Philadelphia, for popular inspection, specimens of our attainments in the industrial and fine arts, and in literature, science, and philosophy, as well as in the great business of agriculture and of commerce.

That we may the more thoroughly appreciate the excellences and deficiencies of our achievements, and also give emphatic expression to our earnest desire to cultivate the friendship of our fellow-members of this great family of nations, the enlightened agricultural, commercial, and manufacturing people of the world have been invited to send hither corresponding specimens of their skill to exhibit on equal terms in friendly competition with our own. To this invitation they have generously responded; for so doing we tender them our hearty thanks.

The beauty and utility of the contributions will this day be submitted to your inspection by the managers of this exhibition. We are glad to know that a view of specimens of the skill of all nations will afford you unalloyed pleasure, as well as yield to you a valuable practical knowledge of so many of the remarkable results of the wonderful skill existing in enlightened communities.

One hundred years ago our country was new and but partially settled. Our necessities have compelled us to chiefly expend our means and time in felling forests, subduing prairies, building dwellings, factories, ships, docks, warehouses, roads, canals, machinery, etc., etc. Most of our schools, churches, libraries, and asylums have been established within a hundred years. Burdened by these great primal works of necessity, which could not be delayed, we yet have done what this exhibition will show, in the direction of rivalling older and more advanced nations in law, medicine, and theology; in science, literature, philosophy and the fine arts.[1] While proud of what we have done, we regret that we have not done more. Our achievements have been great enough however, to make it easy for our people to acknowledge superior merit wherever found.

And now, fellow-citizens, I hope a careful examination of what is about to be exhibited to you will not only inspire you with a profound respect for the skill and taste of our friends from other nations, but also satisfy you with the attainments made by our own people during the past 100 years. I invoke your generous cooperation with the worthy commissioners to secure a brilliant success to this international exhibition, and to make the stay of our foreign visitors—to whom we extend a hearty welcome—both profitable and pleasant to them.

I declare the international exhibition now open.

[1] Grant stresses that the nation is still in its infancy and that much of its attention has been spent on taming the wilderness than on devotion to arts and letter.

CONCLUSION

The speech might be most remarkable for its failure to speak directly of the principles of equality and individual rights that the Second Continental Congress had articulated in 1776, which Lincoln had so closely relied upon during the Civil War and which had recently been incorporated into the Fourteenth Amendment. Grant chose instead to focus on the nation's rapid progress and on its rapid agricultural and industrial advances. Many of the prints that celebrated the centennial focused on industrial progress.

One hundred years later, the nation celebrated its bicentennial, with far greater attention to the nation's ideological origins (the Philadelphia exhibit of that year featured a copy of the English Magna Carta).

Source: James D. McCabe, *The Illustrated History of the Centennial Exhibition*. Philadelphia: National Publishing Company, 1876, 290–292.

An Act Creating an Electoral Commission

January 29, 1877

INTRODUCTION

Most presidential elections prove relatively unproblematic. Electoral votes are tallied, and the winning candidate is the one who captures a majority of the electoral vote. Because most states use a winner-take-all system in which all votes go to a single candidate, however, it is possible for an individual to win without getting a majority of popular votes. Moreover, the vote in a single state, where election results are disputed, can tip the election in one way or another.

It is generally conceded that in the presidential election of 1876, Samuel Tilton, the Democratic candidate, received a popular vote majority in which he captured 184 electoral votes. However, voting was highly irregular, especially in some of the Southern states, and 20 electoral votes in the states of Florida, Louisiana, Oregon, and South Carolina were disputed. Congress created a commission to resolve the election, and the commission ultimately gave the disputed electoral votes to Rutherford B. Hayes, the Republican candidate, who had previously secured 165 votes, thus giving him a one-vote margin of victory. Democrats were generally reconciled to this decision, with the understanding that Hayes would support the withdrawal of Northern troops from Southern states.

Notably, the disputed presidential election of 2000, which was otherwise somewhat similar, was ultimately resolved by a Supreme Court decision rather than by such a commission.

AN ACT to provide for and regulate the counting of votes for President and Vice President, and the decision of questions arising thereon, for the term commencing March fourth, anno Domini eighteen hundred and seventy-seven.

Be it enacted by the Senate and House of Representatives of the United States of America in Congress assembled, That the Senate and House of Representatives shall meet in the hall of the House of Representatives, at the hour of one o'clock post meridian, on the first Thursday in February, anno Domini eighteen hundred and seventy-seven; and the President of the Senate shall be their presiding officer. Two tellers shall be previously appointed on the part of the Senate, and two on the part of the House of Representatives, to whom shall be handed, as they are opened by the President of the Senate, all the certificates, and papers purporting to be certificates, of the electoral votes, which certificates and papers shall be opened, presented, and acted upon in the alphabetical order of the States . . .

SECTION 2. That if more than one return, or paper purporting to be a return from a State, shall have been received by the President of the Senate, purporting to be the certificates of electoral votes given at the last preceding election for President and Vice President in such State (unless they shall be duplicates of the same return,) all such returns and papers shall be opened by him in the presence of the two houses when met as aforesaid, and read by the tellers, and all such returns and papers shall thereupon be submitted to the judgment and decision as to which is the true and lawful electoral vote of such State, of a commission constituted as follows, namely: During the session of each house on the Tuesday next preceding the first Thursday in February, eighteen hundred and seventy-seven each house shall, by viva voce vote, appoint five of its members who with the five associate justices of the Supreme Court of the United States, to be ascertained as hereinafter provided, shall constitute a commission for the decision of all questions upon or in respect of such double returns named in this section.[1] On the Tuesday next preceding the first Thursday in February, anno Domini eighteen hundred and seventy-seven, or as soon thereafter as may, be, the associate justices of the Supreme Court of the United States now assigned to the first, third, eighth, and ninth circuits shall select, in such manner as a majority of them shall deem fit, another of the associate justices of said court, which five persons shall be members of said commission, and the person longest in commission of said five justices shall be the president of said commission. The members of said commission shall respectively take and subscribe the following oath: "I, _____ _____, do solemnly swear (or affirm, as the case may be) that I will impartially examine and consider all questions submitted to the commission of which I am a member, and a true judgment give thereon, agreeably to the Constitution and the laws: so help me God," which oath shall be filed with the Secretary of the Senate. When the commission shall have been thus organized, it shall not be in the power of either house to dissolve the same, or to withdraw any of its members. . . .

[1]Although they did so as commissioners, members of the Supreme Court ultimately resolved this election in favor of Hayes.

SEC. 3. That while the two houses shall be in meeting, as provided in this act, no debate shall be allowed and no question shall be put by the presiding officer, except to either house on a motion to withdraw, and he shall have power to preserve order.

SEC. 4. That when the two houses separate to decide upon an objection that may have been made to the counting of any electoral vote or votes from any State, or upon objection to a report of said commission, or other question arising under this act, each Senator and Representative may speak to such objection or question ten minutes, and not oftener than once; but after such debate shall have lasted two hours, it shall be the duty of each house to put the main question without further debate.

SEC. 6. That nothing in this act shall be held to impair or affect any right now existing under the Constitution and laws to question by proceeding in the judicial courts of the United States, the right or title of the person who shall be declared elected or who shall claim to be President or Vice President of the United States, if any such right exists.

SEC. 7. That said commission shall make its own rules, keen a record of its proceedings, and shall have power to employ such persons as may be necessary for the transaction of its business and the execution of its powers.

Approved, January 29, 1877.

Source: *U.S. Statutes at Large*, 44th Cong., 2d Sess., 37, 1877.

Rutherford B. Hayes's Inaugural Address

March 5, 1877

INTRODUCTION

The 1876 election was one of the most controversial in U.S. history, but an electoral commission ultimately decided the contest on behalf of Republican Rutherford B. Hayes, and Republicans assured Democrats that they would remove federal troops from the South. In his inaugural address, Hayes had the task of assuring the nation that the electoral crisis had passed.

Fellow-Citizens:

We have assembled to repeat the public ceremonial, begun by Washington, observed by all my predecessors, and now a time-honored custom, which marks the commencement of a new term of the Presidential office. Called to the duties of this great trust, I proceed, in compliance with usage, to announce some of the leading principles, on the subjects that now chiefly engage the public attention, by which it is my desire to be guided in the discharge of those duties. I shall not undertake to lay down irrevocably principles or measures of administration, but rather to speak of the motives which should animate us, and to suggest certain important ends to be attained in accordance with our institutions and essential to the welfare of our country.

At the outset of the discussions which preceded the recent Presidential election it seemed to me fitting that I should fully make known my sentiments in regard to several of the important questions which then appeared to demand the consideration of the country. Following the example, and in part adopting the language, of one of my predecessors, I wish now, when every motive for misrepresentation has passed away, to repeat what was said before the election, trusting that my countrymen will candidly weigh and understand it, and that they will feel assured that the sentiments declared in accepting the nomination for the Presidency will be the standard of my conduct in the path before me, charged, as I now am, with the grave and difficult task of carrying them out in the practical administration of the Government so far as depends, under the Constitution and laws on the Chief Executive of the nation.

The permanent pacification of the country upon such principles and by such measures as will secure the complete protection of all its citizens in the free enjoyment of all their constitutional rights is now the one subject in our public affairs which all thoughtful and patriotic citizens regard as of supreme importance.

Many of the calamitous efforts of the tremendous revolution which has passed over the Southern States still remain. The immeasurable benefits which will surely follow, sooner or later, the hearty and generous acceptance of the legitimate results of that revolution have not yet been realized. Difficult and embarrassing questions meet us at the threshold of this subject. The people of those States are still impoverished, and the inestimable blessing of wise, honest, and peaceful local self-government is not fully enjoyed. Whatever difference of opinion may exist as to the cause of this condition of things, the fact is clear that in the progress of events the time has come when such government is the imperative necessity required by all the varied interests, public and private, of those States. But it must not be forgotten that only a local government which recognizes and maintains inviolate the rights of all is a true self-government.[1]

With respect to the two distinct races whose peculiar relations to each other have brought upon us the deplorable complications and perplexities which exist in those States, it must be a government which guards the interests of both races carefully and equally. It must be a government which submits loyally and heartily to the Constitution and the laws—the laws of the nation and the laws of the States themselves—accepting and obeying faithfully the whole Constitution as it is.

Resting upon this sure and substantial foundation, the superstructure of beneficent local governments can be built up, and not otherwise. In furtherance of such obedience to the letter and the spirit of the Constitution, and in behalf of all that its attainment implies, all so-called party interests lose their apparent importance, and party lines may well be permitted to fade into insignificance. The question we have to consider for the immediate welfare of those

[1]Hayes is indicating that it is time to restore self-government to the Southern states by removing federal troops.

States of the Union is the question of government or no government; of social order and all the peaceful industries and the happiness that belongs to it, or a return to barbarism. It is a question in which every citizen of the nation is deeply interested, and with respect to which we ought not to be, in a partisan sense, either Republicans or Democrats, but fellow-citizens and fellowmen, to whom the interests of a common country and a common humanity are dear.

[2]Hayes reminds the American people of the massive changes brought about by emancipation.

The sweeping revolution of the entire labor system of a large portion of our country and the advance of 4,000,000 people from a condition of servitude to that of citizenship, upon an equal footing with their former masters, could not occur without presenting problems of the gravest moment, to be dealt with by the emancipated race, by their former masters, and by the General Government, the author of the act of emancipation.[2] That it was a wise, just, and providential act, fraught with good for all concerned, is not generally conceded throughout the country. That a moral obligation rests upon the National Government to employ its constitutional power and influence to establish the rights of the people it has emancipated, and to protect them in the enjoyment of those rights when they are infringed or assailed, is also generally admitted.

The evils which afflict the Southern States can only be removed or remedied by the united and harmonious efforts of both races, actuated by motives of mutual sympathy and regard; and while in duty bound and fully determined to protect the rights of all by every constitutional means at the disposal of my Administration, I am sincerely anxious to use every legitimate influence in favor of honest and efficient local self-government as the true resource of those States for the promotion of the contentment and prosperity of their citizens. In the effort I shall make to accomplish this purpose I ask the cordial cooperation of all who cherish an interest in the welfare of the country, trusting that party ties and the prejudice of race will be freely surrendered in behalf of the great purpose to be accomplished. In the important work of restoring the South it is not the political situation alone that merits attention. The material development of that section of the country has been arrested by the social and political revolution through which it has passed, and now needs and deserves the considerate care of the National Government within the just limits prescribed by the Constitution and wise public economy.

But at the basis of all prosperity, for that as well as for every other part of the country, lies the improvement of the intellectual and moral condition of the people. Universal suffrage should rest upon universal education. To this end, liberal and permanent provision should be made for the support of free schools by the State governments, and, if need be, supplemented by legitimate aid from national authority.[3]

Let me assure my countrymen of the Southern States that it is my earnest desire to regard and promote their truest interest—the interests of the white and of the colored people both and equally—and to put forth my best efforts in behalf of a civil policy which will forever wipe out in our political affairs the color line and the distinction between North and South, to the end that we may have not merely a united North or a united South, but a united country.

I ask the attention of the public to the paramount necessity of reform in our civil service—a reform not merely as to certain abuses and practices of so-called official patronage which have come to have the sanction of usage in the several Departments of our Government,[4] but a change in the system of appointment itself; a reform that shall be thorough, radical, and complete; a return to the principles and practices of the founders of the Government.[5] They neither expected nor desired from public officers any partisan service. They meant that public officers should owe their whole service to the Government and to the people. They meant that the officer should be secure in his tenure as long as his personal character remained untarnished and the performance of his duties satisfactory. They held that appointments to office were not to be made nor expected merely as rewards for partisan services, nor merely on the nomination of members of Congress, as being entitled in any respect to the control of such appointments.

The fact that both the great political parties of the country, in declaring their principles prior to the election, gave a prominent place to the subject of reform of our civil service, recognizing and strongly urging its necessity, in terms almost identical in their specific import with those I have here employed, must be accepted as a conclusive argument in behalf of these measures. It must be regarded as the expression of the united voice and will of the whole country upon this subject, and both political parties are virtually pledged to give it their unreserved support.

[3]Through early American history, most education was the responsibility of state and local governments. The Morrell Act of 1862 and the Freedman's Bureau Act were examples of the kinds of federal support that Hayes probably anticipated continuing.

[4]The so-called spoils system (from the expression "to the victor, go the spoils"), which permitted winners to appoint friends and members of the party to public offices, was a constant irritant to proponents of good government who thought that it corrupted the political system.

[5]The central impetus for such reform would come with the assassination of President James E. Garfield in 1881 and the subsequent adoption of the Pendleton Act (1883).

The President of the United States of necessity owes his election to office to the suffrage and zealous labors of a political party, the members of which cherish with ardor and regard as of essential importance the principles of their party organization; but he should strive to be always mindful of the fact that he serves his party best who serves the country best.[6]

In furtherance of the reform we seek, and in other important respects a change of great importance, I recommend an amendment to the Constitution prescribing a term of six years for the Presidential office and forbidding a reelection. . . .[7]

Fellow-citizens, we have reached the close of a political contest marked by the excitement which usually attends the contests between great political parties whose members espouse and advocate with earnest faith their respective creeds. The circumstances were, perhaps, in no respect extraordinary save in the closeness and the consequent uncertainty of the result.

For the first time in the history of the country it has been deemed best, in view of the peculiar circumstances of the case, that the objections and questions in dispute with reference to the counting of the electoral votes should be referred to the decision of a tribunal appointed for this purpose.

That tribunal—established by law for this sole purpose; its members, all of them, men of long-established reputation for integrity and intelligence, and, with the exception of those who are also members of the supreme judiciary, chosen equally from both political parties; its deliberations enlightened by the research and the arguments of able counsel—was entitled to the fullest confidence of the American people.[8] Its decisions have been patiently waited for, and accepted as legally conclusive by the general judgment of the public. For the present, opinion will widely vary as to the wisdom of the several conclusions announced by that tribunal. This is to be anticipated in every instance where matters of dispute are made the subject of arbitration under the forms of law. Human judgment is never unerring, and is rarely regarded as otherwise than wrong by the unsuccessful party in the contest.

The fact that two great political parties have in this way settled a dispute in regard to which good men differ as to the facts and the law no less than as to the proper course to be pursued in solving the question in controversy is an occasion for general rejoicing.

Upon one point there is entire unanimity in public sentiment—that conflicting claims to the Presidency must be amicably and peaceably adjusted, and that when so adjusted the general acquiescence of the nation ought surely to follow.[9]

It has been reserved for a government of the people, where the right of suffrage is universal, to give to the world the first example in history of a great nation, in the midst of the struggle of opposing parties for power, hushing its party tumults to yield the issue of the contest to adjustment according to the forms of law.

Looking for the guidance of that Divine Hand by which the destinies of nations and individuals are shaped, I call upon you, Senators, Representatives, judges, fellow-citizens, here and everywhere, to unite with me in an earnest effort to secure to our country the blessings, not only of material prosperity, but of justice, peace, and union—a union depending not upon the constraint of force, but upon the loving devotion of a free people; "and that all things may be so ordered and settled upon the best and surest foundations that peace and happiness, truth and justice, religion and piety, may be established among us for all generations."

Source: James D. Richardson, *A Compilation of the Messages and Papers of the Presidents*, vol. 7. New York: Bureau of National Literature, 1896.

[9] In both the 2000 and 2016 presidential elections, the winner of the Electoral College did not win the popular vote.

Chief Sitting Bull's Speech

1877

INTRODUCTION

North America remained divided into former European immigrants and their descendants, African Americans once held in slavery, immigrants from China and Japan, and Native American Indians, who were continually pushed to the West. In 1876, at the Battle of Little Big Horn, Lakota tribes led by Sitting Bull and Red Cloud wiped out an army of about 700 men led by General George Custer. In a speech he delivered to fellow natives the next year, Chief Sitting Bull presented his perspective on what he believed to be the acquisitiveness and the hypocrisy of the whites.

Behold, my friends, the spring is come; the earth has gladly received the embraces of the sun, and we shall soon see the results of their love! Every seed is awakened, and all animal life. It is through this mysterious power that we too have our being, and we therefore yield to our neighbors, even to our animal neighbors, the same right as ourselves to inhabit this vast land.

Yet hear me, friends! we have now to deal with another people, small and feeble when our forefathers first met with them, but now great and overbearing. Strangely enough, they have a mind to till the soil, and the love of possessions is a disease in them. These people have made many rules that the rich may break, but the poor may not! They have a religion in which the poor worship, but the rich will not! They even take tithes of the poor and weak to support the rich and those who rule. They claim this mother of ours, the Earth, for their own use, and fence their neighbors away from her, and deface her with their buildings and their refuse. They compel her to produce out of season, and when sterile she is made to take medicine in order to produce again. All this is sacrilege.[1]

This nation is like a spring freshet; it overruns its banks and destroys all who are in its path.

[1] Although white Americans believed that they were a people upon whom God's destiny had smiled, Chief Sitting Bull sees them as an acquisitive race that do not pay adequate homage to the earth.

We cannot dwell side by side. Only seven years ago we made a treaty by which we were assured that the buffalo country should be left to us forever. Now they threaten to take that from us also. My brothers, shall we submit? or shall we say to them: "First kill me, before you can take possession of my fatherland!"[2]

[2]Sitting Bull was further convinced that only resistance could stop white expansion, but as his previous words indicated, the whites had already grown "great and overbearing," and they had both the power of numbers and technology on their side in such conflicts. The last major Indian battle was the Battle of Sugar Point, which occurred in 1898.

Source: Charles A. Eastman (Ohiyesa), *Indian Heroes and Great Chieftains.* Boston: Little Brown, 1918, 119–121.

Timeline of Events

1776

Thirteen North American colonies declare their independence from Great Britain and assert that "all men are created equal."

1787

A convention of 55 men proposes a Constitution to replace the Articles of Confederation. The document leaves slavery in place without specifically mentioning it by name.

1789

The Constitution goes into effect, and George Washington is selected as the first president.

1820

The Missouri Compromise admits Missouri as a slave state and Missouri as a free one and shows the widening division between Northern and Southern states.

1828

The so-called tariff of abominations ignites Southern calls for state nullification.

1850

Kentucky senator Henry Clay cobbles together another compromise designed to avert disunion.

1854

The Kansas-Nebraska Act, the brainchild of Stephen A. Douglas, applies the doctrine of popular sovereignty to U.S. territories.

1857

The Supreme Court declares in *Dred Scott v. Sandford* that blacks are not and cannot become U.S. citizens, and Congress has no power to exclude slavery from the territories.

1860

President Abraham Lincoln wins the presidency in a four-man race and becomes the first Republican to occupy the office.

Southern states, beginning with South Carolina, adopt ordinances of secession.

1861

A Peace Convention of 132 delegates from 21 states meets in Washington, DC, to propose a multifaceted amendment attempting to save the Union.

Jefferson Davis is inaugurated as president of a confederacy, which then consisted of seven states.

Congress adopts the Corwin Amendment, proposing to guarantee slavery in states where it already existed.

Lincoln is inaugurated as president of the United States.

The Confederate states adopt a new Constitution.

In his "Cornerstone Speech," Confederate vice president Alexander Stevens says the Confederacy is built on the principle of white superiority to blacks.

Southerners fire on Fort Sumter off the coast of South Carolina as Lincoln tries to reinforce it.

Additional Southern states secede, bringing the total number to 11.

John C. Freemont issues a military order, which Lincoln revokes, freeing the slaves of Southern supporters in Missouri.

1862

Julia Ward Howe pens the words to "The Battle Hymn of the Republic".

Congress sets aside land for the creation of Yellowstone National Park.

Congress commits land to firms, seeking to connect East and West through railroad construction.

Congress adopts the Morrill Act, creating land-grant colleges and universities.

1863

Abraham Lincoln uses his power as commander in chief to issue the Emancipation Proclamation, freeing slaves behind enemy lines.

Congress adopts a Conscription Act.

The Supreme Court upholds seizures under Lincoln's blockade of southern ports in *The Prize Cases*.

The Union admits West Virginia, which had broken with Virginia over the issue of slavery, as the 35th state.

Union troops halt the advance of Robert E. Lee's army in Gettysburg, Pennsylvania.

Northern troops capture Vicksburg, Mississippi.

Abraham Lincoln delivers his Gettysburg Address.

1864

Congress adopts a law equalizing the pay for African-American soldiers.

Congress authorizes the use of the motto "In God We Trust" on U.S. coins.

Congress proposes the Wade-Davis Bill to Reconstruction of the South, which Lincoln will pocket veto.

General Sherman burns Atlanta on his march to the coast.

Lincoln is reelected as president.

Congress creates the Freedmen's Bureau.

1865

Lincoln delivers his Second Inaugural Address.

The Southern states adopt a law allowing for the enlistment of slaves to fight for the Confederacy.

General Lee surrenders his forces to General Grant at Appomattox Courthouse in Virginia.

John Wilkes Booth assassinates President Lincoln, and Vice President Andrew Johnson becomes president.

The states ratify the Thirteenth Amendment abolishing slavery.

The Ku Klux Klan is founded in Tennessee.

Southern states begin enacting restrictive codes that seek to return slaves to a virtual state or peonage.

1866

In *Ex Parte Milligan*, the Supreme Court overturns the conviction of a civilian in a military court.

Congress adopts an expansive civil rights bill.

1867

Congress divides Southern states into military districts for the purpose of reconstructing the governments and protecting the rights of freedmen. The law passes over Johnson's veto.

The United States acquires Alaska from Russia.

1868

The House of Representatives impeaches President Johnson, but the Senate falls a single vote short of the necessary two-thirds to convict him.

The requisite number of states adopts the Fourteenth Amendment, defining citizenship and seeking to guarantee equal rights to all.

The people elect Ulysses S. Grant as president over Horatio Seymour.

1869

Texas v. White declares that the Union is "an indestructible union . . . of indestructible states."

The first transcontinental railroad line is completed.

1870

The states ratify the Fifteenth Amendment prohibiting discrimination on the basis of race.

Faced with Southern violence against African Americans, Congress adopts the Enforcement Act.

1871

Congress adopts an additional enforcement act.

1872

Ulysses S. Grant wins a second term over Horace Greeley.

1873

The Slaughterhouse Cases give a restrictive reading to the privileges and immunities clause of the Fourteenth Amendment.

1875

Congress adopts a Civil Rights Act that guarantees equal public accommodations to members of all races.

The Court rejects an argument that the privileges and immunities clause of the Fourteenth Amendment intended to give women the right to vote.

The Page Act seeks to restrict the immigration of Chinese women.

1876

In *United States v. Cruikshank*, the Court again interprets the Fourteenth Amendment narrowly.

Alexander Graham Bell invents the telephone.

The United States opens an international exhibition in Philadelphia to celebrate its centennial.

The electoral outcome in the presidential contest is disputed.

Native American Indians win a victory over General Custer at the Battle of Little Big Horn.

1877

Republican Rutherford B. Hayes is selected president with the understanding that he will withdraw troops from the South.

1883

The Civil Rights cases invalidate the Civil Rights Act of 1875 on the basis that it improperly sought to control private actions.

1896

Plessy v. Ferguson accepts the "separate but equal" doctrine to justify racial segregation.

1920

The Nineteenth Amendment forbids discrimination in voting on the basis of sex.

Further Reading

Ackerman, Bruce. 1998. *We the People: Transformations.* Cambridge, MA: Harvard University Press.

Araiza, William D. 2015. *Enforcing the Equal Protection Clause: Congressional Power, Judicial Doctrine, and Constitutional Law.* New York: New York University Press.

Boritt, Gabor. 2006. *The Gettysburg Gospel: The Lincoln Speech That Nobody Knows.* New York: Simon & Schuster.

Bowers, Claude. 1920. *The Tragic Era: The Revolution after Lincoln.* New York: Blue Ribbon Books.

Brands, H.W. 2013. *The Man Who Saved the Union: Ulysses Grant in War and Peace.* New York: Anchor.

Brandwein, Pamela. 2011. *Rethinking the Judicial Settlement of Reconstruction.* New York: Cambridge University Press.

Carleton, David. 2002. *Landmark Congressional Laws on Education.* Westport, CT: Greenwood Press.

Chaffin, Tom. 2014. *Pathfinder: John Charles Freemont and the Course of American Empire.* Norman: University of Oklahoma Press.

Conlin, Michael F. 2015. *One Nation Divided by Slavery: Remembering the American Revolution While Marching toward the Civil War.* Kent, OH: Kent State University Press.

Cooper, William J., Jr. 2001. *Jefferson Davis, American.* New York: Vintage.

Davis, William C. 1994. *"A Government of Our Own": The Making of the Confederacy.* New York: Free Press.

DeRosa, Marshall L. 1991. *The Confederate Constitution of 1861: An Inquiry into American Constitutionalism.* Columbia: University of Missouri Press.

Donald, David Herbert. 1995. *Lincoln.* New York: Simon & Schuster.

Dumond, Dwight L. 1973. *The Secession Movement, 1860–1861.* New York: Octagon Books.

Epps, Garrett. 2006. *Democracy Reborn: The Fourteenth Amendment and the Fight for Equal Rights in Post-Civil War America.* New York: Henry Holt.

Flack, Horace Edgar. 1908. *The Adoption of the Fourteenth Amendment.* Baltimore, MD: Johns Hopkins Press.

Foner, Eric. 1988. *Reconstruction: America's Unfinished Revolution, 1863–1877.* New York: Harper & Row.

Foote, Shelby. 1986. *The Civil War: A Narrative.* 3 vols. New York: Vintage.

Gienapp, William E. 2001. *The Civil War and Reconstruction: A Documentary Collection.* New York: W.W. Norton.

Goodwin, Doris Kearns. 2005. *Team of Rivals: The Political Genius of Abraham Lincoln.* New York: Simon & Schuster.

Guelzo, Allen C. 1999. *Abraham Lincoln: Redeemer President.* Grand Rapids, MI: William B. Eerdmans.

Guelzo, Allen C. 2004. *Lincoln's Emancipation Proclamation: The End of Slavery in America.* New York: Simon & Schuster.

Gunderson, Robert Gray. 1961. *Old Gentleman's Convention: The Washington Peace Conference of 1862.* Madison: University of Wisconsin Press.

Hall, Kermit L., ed. 2005. *The Oxford Companion to the Supreme Court of the United States.* 2nd ed. New York: Oxford University Press.

Holt, Michael F. 2008. *By One Vote: The Disputed Presidential Election of 1876.* Lawrence: University Press of Kansas.

Horn, Jonathan. 2015. *The Man Who Would Not Be Washington: Robert E. Lee's Civil War and His Decision That Changed American History.* New York: Scribner.

Huebner, Timothy S. 2016. *Liberty and Union: The Civil War Era and American Constitutionalism.* Lawrence: University Press of Kansas.

Hyman, Harold M. 1975. *A More Perfect Union: The Impact of the Civil War and Reconstruction on the Constitution.* Boston: Houghton Mifflin.

James, Joseph B. 1956. *The Framing of the Fourteenth Amendment.* Urbana: University of Illinois Press.

James, Joseph B. 1984. *The Ratification of the Fourteenth Amendment.* Macon, GA: Mercer University Press.

Labbe, Donald M., and Jonathan Lurie. 2005. *The Slaughterhouse Cases: Regulation, Reconstruction, and the Fourteenth Amendment.* Lawrence: University Press of Kansas.

Langguth, A.J. 2015. *After Lincoln: How the North Won the Civil War and Lost the Peace.* New York: Simon & Schuster.

Lash, Kurt T. 2014. *The Fourteenth Amendment and the Privileges and Immunities of American Citizenship.* New York: Cambridge University Press.

Lee, Charles Robert, Jr. 1963. *The Confederate Constitutions.* Chapel Hill: University of North Carolina Press.

Lemann, Nicholas. 2006. *Redemption: The Last Battle of the Civil War.* New York: Farrar, Straus and Giroux.

Litwack, Leon F. 1980. *Been in the Storm So Long: The Aftermath of Slavery.* New York: Vintage.

Magliocca, Gerald N. 2013. *America's Founding Son: John Bingham and the Invention of the Fourteenth Amendment.* New York: New York University Press.

Maltz, Earl M. 1990. *Civil Rights, the Constitution, and Congress, 1863–1869.* Lawrence: University Press of Kansas.

Matthews, John M. 1909. *Legislative and Judicial History of the Fifteenth Amendment.* Reprint. New York: Da Capo Press, 1971.

McDougall, Walter A. 2008. *Throes of Democracy. The American Civil War Era, 1829–1877.* New York: Harper.

McGinty, Brian. 2008. *Lincoln & the Court.* Cambridge, MA: Harvard University Press.

McPherson, James M. 1990. *Abraham Lincoln and the Second American Revolution.* New York: Oxford University Press.

Miller, William Lee. 2002. *Lincoln's Virtues: An Ethical Biography.* New York: Alfred A. Knopf.

Neely, Mark E., Jr. 1991. *The Fate of Liberty: Abraham Lincoln and Civil Liberties.* New York: Oxford University Press.

Nelson, William E. 1988. *The Fourteenth Amendment: From Political Principle to Judicial Doctrine.* Cambridge, MA: Harvard University Press.

Paludin, Phillip Shaw. 1994. *The Presidency of Abraham Lincoln.* Lawrence: University Press of Kansas.

Pohlmann, Marcus D. and Linda Vallar Whisenhunt. 2002. *Student's Guide to Landmark Congressional Laws on Civil Rights.* Westport, CT: Greenwood Press.

The Reconstruction Amendments' Debates: The Legislative History and Contemporary Debates in Congress on the 13th, 14th, and 15th Amendments. 1967. Richmond: Virginia Commission on Constitutional Government.

Richards, David A.J. 1993. *Conscience and the Constitution: History, Theory, and Law of the Reconstruction Amendments.* Princeton, NJ: Princeton University Press.

Richards, Leonard L. 2015. *Who Fred the Slaves?: The Fight over the Thirteenth Amendment.* Chicago: University of Chicago Press.

Samito, Christian G., ed. 2009. *Changes in Law and Society during the Civil War and Reconstruction.* Carbondale: Southern Illinois University Press.

Samito, Christian G., ed. 2015. *Lincoln and the Thirteenth Amendment.* Carbondale: Southern Illinois University Press.

Simon, James F. 2006. *Lincoln and Chief Justice Taney: Slavery, Secession, and the President's War Power.* New York: Simon & Schuster.

Smith, Gene. 1977. *High Crimes and Misdemeanors: The Impeachment and Trial of Andrew Johnson.* New York: William Morrow.

Smith, Jean Edward. 2002. *Grant.* New York: Simon & Schuster.

Stewart, David O. 2009. *Impeached: The Trial of President Andrew Johnson and the Fight for Lincoln's Legacy.* New York: Simon & Schuster.

Tsesis, Alexander. 2004. *The Thirteenth Amendment and American Freedom: A Legal History.* New York: New York University Press.

Urofsky, Melvin I. 1989. *Documents of American Constitutional & Legal History: Vol. 1: From Settlement through Reconstruction.* New York: Alfred A. Knopf.

Vile, John R. 2016. *The Antebellum Period: Documents Decoded.* Santa Barbara, CA: ABC-CLIO.

Vile, John R. 2015. *A Companion to the United States Constitution and Its Amendments,* 6th ed. Santa Barbara, CA: Praeger.

Vile, John R. 2015. *Encyclopedia of Constitutional Amendments, Proposed Amendments, and Amending Issues, 1789–2015,* 4th ed. 2 vols. Santa Barbara, CA: ABC-CLIO.

Vile, John R. 2016. *The Early Republic: Documents Decoded.* Santa Barbara, CA: ABC-CLIO.

Vile, John R. 2014. *Essential Supreme Court Decisions: Summaries of Leading Cases in U.S. Constitutional Law,* 16th ed. Lanham, MD: Rowman & Littlefield.

Vile, John R. 2015. *Founding Documents of America: Documents Decoded.* Santa Barbara, CA: ABC-CLIO.

Vile, John R. 2002. *Presidential Winners and Losers: Words of Victory and Concession.* Washington, DC: CQ Press.

Vorenberg, Michael. 2001. *Final Freedom: The Civil, the Abolition of Slavery, and the Thirteenth Amendment.* New York: Cambridge University Press.

Waugh, John C. 1997. *Reelecting Lincoln: The Battle for the 1864 Presidency.* New York: Crown Publishing, Inc.

White, Ronald C., Jr. 2009. *A. Lincoln: A Biography.* New York: Random House.

White, Ronald C., Jr. 2002. *Lincoln's Greatest Speech: The Second Inaugural.* New York: Simon & Schuster.

Wills, Garry. 2006. *Lincoln at Gettysburg: The Words That Remade America.* New York: Simon & Schuster.

Winik, Jay. 2001. *April 1865: The Month That Saved America.* New York: HarperCollins.

Index

About the Author

John R. Vile, PhD, is professor of political science and dean of the University Honors College at Middle Tennessee State University. He has previously published three books in this *Documents Decoded* series: *Founding Documents of America* (2015), *The Early Republic* (2016), and *The Jacksonian and Antebellum Eras* (2016).

He has written and edited a variety of other books on legal issues, the U.S. Constitution, and the American Founding period, including *American Immigration and Citizenship: A Documentary History* (2016); *The Constitutional Convention of 1787: A Comprehensive Encyclopedia of America's Founding*, rev. 2nd ed. (2016); *Conventional Wisdom: The Alternative Article V Mechanism for Proposing Amendments to the U.S. Constitution* (2016); *A Companion to the United States Constitution and Its Amendments*, 6th ed. (2015); *The United States Constitution: One Document, Many Choices* (2015); *The Wisest Council in the World: Restoring the Character Sketches by William Pierce of Georgia of the Delegates to the Constitutional Convention of 1787* (2015); *Encyclopedia of Constitutional Amendments, Proposed Amendments, and Amending Issues, 1789–2015*, 4th ed. (2015); *Re-Framers: 170 Eccentric, Visionary, and Patriotic Proposals to Rewrite the U.S. Constitution* (2014); *The United States Constitution: Questions and Answers*, 2nd ed. (2014); *Essential Supreme Court Decisions: Summaries of Leading Cases in U.S. Constitutional Law*, 16th ed. (2014); *The Men Who Made the Constitution: Lives of the Delegates to the Constitutional Convention* (2013); *Encyclopedia of the Fourth Amendment* (2013); *The Writing and Ratification of the U.S. Constitution: Practical Virtue in Action* (2012); *Encyclopedia of the First Amendment* (2009); *James Madison: Founder, Philosopher, Founder and Statesman* (2008); *The Encyclopedia of Civil Liberties in America* (2005); *Great American Judges: An Encyclopedia* (2003); *Great American Lawyers: An Encyclopedia* (2001); and *History of the American Legal System: Interactive Encyclopedia* (CD-ROM, 2000).